C000112919

THE
SECOND JEZEBEL

by

Peter Mowbray

◆

**Grosvenor House
Publishing Limited**

The right of Peter Mowbray to be identified as the author of this
work has been asserted in accordance with Section 78
of the Copyright, Designs and Patents Act 1988

The book cover picture is copyright to Catherine de Medicis/
Bridgeman Images

This book is published by
Grosvenor House Publishing Ltd
Link House
140 The Broadway, Tolworth, Surrey, Kt6 7Ht.
www.grosvenorhousepublishing.co.uk

A CIP record for this book
is available from the British Library

ISBN 978-1-78623-046-1

◆

The Serpent of the Valois

◆

◆

For

Oliver & Ross

No father could be more proud of his sons

◆

Cast of Characters

CATHERINE DE MEDICI, QUEEN MOTHER OF FRANCE

THE HOUSE OF VALOIS:
Claude, Duchesse of Lorraine
Charles IX
Henri III
Marguerite, (Margot) Queen of Navarre
Hercule, (rechristened François) Duke of Alençon

Three other children died in infancy.
Catherine's two eldest children François II and Elizabeth, Queen of Spain had died by the year in which this story begins.

THE HOUSE OF CHÂTILLON
Gaspard de Coligny (Admiral of France)
Charles de Teligny (the Admiral's son in law)

THE HOUSE OF BOURBON:
Henri, King of Navarre (son of Antoine and Jeanne) *
Charles, Cardinal d'Bourbon (Navarre's uncle)

THE HOUSE OF GUISE:
Henri, Duke of Guise (son of François) *
Charles, Cardinal of Lorraine (his uncle)

Some other players:

Cosimo & Lorenzo Ruggieri (Astrologers to the Queen Mother)

Charlotte de Suave, (a member of the Queen Mother's *"escardon"*)

Jean Louis de la Valette, Duke of Épernon (one of Henri III's mignons)

Anne d'Arques, Duke of Joyeuse (one of Henri III's mignons)

Elizabeth, Queen of England

William Cecil, (later Lord Burghley) Elizabeth's chief minister

Philip, King of Spain

PLUS

Assorted other Royalty, courtiers and officials,
with a generous helping of innocent victims
and a sprinkling of spies and assassins.

♦

In order not to confuse the reader (or, indeed, the author!) I have decided that as the story here has three principal characters all with the christian name of Henri, I will adopt the rule of reverting to family name rather than a forename in order to distinguish who is who! Therefore, Henri of Navarre will become simply Navarre; Henri de Guise will similarly be identified as Guise. It seems both protocol and good manners dictate that King Henri Trois be titled either the King or Henri.

Author's Note

The events in this story follow, in chronological sequence, those described and related in my previous book – The Serpent of the Valois.

At the end of the book I have noted some of the excellent reference books used as the basis for the story, all of them are scholarly works from master historians, and I thank them for such valuable information.

Naturally some artistic licence has been taken in some aspects of the book, and will no doubt horrify serious academics, but remember – this humble tale is only an interpretation!

Peter Mowbray 2016

Foreword

France by the summer of 1572 was a country on the brink of complete collapse. The civil wars, fought between the Catholics and the French Protestants, (known as the Huguenots) had almost torn the country apart.

The great families of Catholic nobility, the Guises and the leaders of the Huguenots, the Bourbons, and Châtillon, had raged war on one another for almost 12 years, ostensibly in the name of religion, but with an enmity between personalities that transcended all theological reasoning, and was becoming cruelly exposed as blind, murderous hatred.

Ruling this war-torn nation was the House of Valois whose King, Charles the ninth, leads an unhappy existence, torn between friends and family, duty and dishonour. His remaining siblings were his younger brothers, Henri and François and sisters, Marguerite (Margot) and Claude.

It is however, the King's mother that commands the greatest power. A woman that in the annals of French history embody all that is wicked and deceptive. A woman who the French, be they Catholic or Huguenot, revile more than any other – the Queen Mother of France, Catherine de Medici.

Charles's younger brother, François had died in December 1560, and his young wife, (a Guise) the infamous Mary, Queen of Scots, had left her beloved France for a trouble-filled life that would end in the cold, damp hall of Fotheringay Castle in 1587. By the time of his ascension Charles had not yet come of age, his formidable mother therefore claimed the regency.

A country that was controlled by a regent was, at best, a vulnerable state in 16th Century Europe. That its regent was a woman, rendered it, in this *"Anciem Regime"* on a fast track to destruction!

Catherine de Medici was certainly a formidable force. She was neither liked nor respected by the vast majority of the French people. She trusted no one, and was considered to be without scruples, morals, compassion or kindness.

Those who stood in her way paid a heavy price for doing so. What had for her begun as a regency to protect the interests of her young family became a personal thirst for ultimate power and control. Whatever needed to be done to ensure that power was in no way threatened was done. All were expendable in the eyes of "Madame Serpent."

Poisoner, mistress of the occult, murderess, the great dissembler. All these terms were used to describe her. Both main religious parties hated the Queen Mother of France. A rather "lukewarm" Catholic herself, she was seen as too tolerant of the Huguenots, who in turn distrusted her motives because of her faith.

Catherine's main fear was her former son-in-law, the mighty King Philip of Spain. His power and his obsession with a Catholic League throughout Europe caused him to question Catherine's policy and her own commitment to such a great cause.

The Admiral of France, Gaspard de Coligny, head of the Châtillon family, was the Huguenot's main figurehead, and he was reported to have much influence with the increasingly unstable King.

A message of clear intent, evidence that she was as good a Catholic and would stem the flow of Huguenots in France, needed to be made and, during private talks with one of Philip's senior ministers, Catherine divulged a plan to rid the realm once and for all of heresy, when the opportunity arose to carry it out.

The chance for the instigation of the Queen Mother's *"remedy for all ills in the realm"* came on the occasion of the wedding of her daughter, the Princess Margot to Henri, King of Navarre. The union of a Catholic Princess to a Bourbon King drew hundreds of Huguenots to Paris, unknowingly walking straight into the trap that history would title, "the Massacre of Saint Bartholomew."

An assassination attempt was made on the Huguenot hero Coligny, and whilst the bungled attempt resulted in severe injury rather than death, such a crime was bound to create a dangerous mood throughout the Huguenot followers.

The Queen Mother held council with Guise and other Catholic intimates, and informed them of her plans. She then convinced the mentally fragile King that a plot to avenge the attempt on the Admiral's life by storming the palace and killing all the Royal family was imminent, and that striking first was the only way to prevent the Huguenots from committing regicide.

Coligny had narrowly escaped the attempt to kill him, only for Henri of Guise to command his men to break into the victim's house and see the job properly carried out. The Admiral's body was then thrown from the window for his enemy to confirm himself satisfied and thereafter, leaving the remains to be decapitated with a knife and the head taken to the Louvre as a gift for the Queen Mother.

Catherine had held her nerve and resolve right up until the ringing of the bells in the south tower of the church of St. Germain l'Auxerrois, the pre-arranged signal for the slaughter to begin. At this point one can imagine that the cold rush of fear coursed through her blood like ice, and she was about to cancel the commands she had given earlier that day.

Such indecision (rare as it was for the Queen Mother) and her uncertainty could not call a halt to the events she had set in motion. The reality however was evident once the head of the Admiral was laid at her feet!

Less than seventeen years later, Catherine de Medici lies dying at the Palace of Blois, and while she hovers close to death, her moments of lucidity are spent in recollection of these and many other events that have brought her long, eventful life to its climax.

Looked on only by her physician, her confessor, and at various times, ladies in waiting, the Queen Mother drifts from the haze of death to the clarity of her memories...

♦

It did not take many hands to hold her down, as the woman was old and frail, her muscles weak against the strong arms of her assailants.

Someone pulled roughly at the black skullcap on her head, exposing the thinning auburn streaks. Someone spat at her, the warm phlegm trickled towards her eye, but she had no free hand to wipe it away. All around her noise, shouting and screaming and a red haze of fire. She looked through the smoke and her eyes focussed on the frightful images in front of her.

People everywhere were running around, their swords and daggers seemed to appear from nowhere, but their swift work created so much blood; it was splattered onto cobbled streets, streams of it clung to her shabby gown, her hands dripped with it as though it was pouring from her own body.

All around her, corpses began to pile up, slowly at first and then so many that they fell closer and closer to her but she could not move to pull away. All manner of severed limbs and headless cadavers reeked of the foul stench of death and seemed ready to swallow her up.

Then, suddenly she was staring at a figure clad in a long dark cowl, without image save for bony, white hands that gripped a dagger, the tip of which was pressed lightly against her throat, its point just piercing her skin. The figure spoke in a deep, hateful snarl "Welcome lady to your own Saint Bartholomew's night"

The last thing she heard was the crackling noise as the dagger was pushed straight into her throat...

The sudden loud gasp from the dying Queen Mother startled the three other people in her chamber. She had tried to sit up in her obvious anguish, her fevered brow now soaked in a cold sweat. Strands of her once full head of hair stuck to her skin like the harsh raindrops that ran down the outside of the windows of her chamber.

Her physician, Dr Cavriani, nearly upset the tincture that he was carefully preparing. The Queen Mother's confessor who had been sat with her for so many hours, dropped his prayer book in alarm, and the two of Catherine's ladies of her bedchamber who had kept close by their mistress should they be needed, noticeably jumped.

Catherine de Medici was trembling, in fear as much as anything else; the dreams were vivid enough, her life playing out before her, she could close her eyes and it would all be there, as though it were a mummers play of which she had been so fond. It was the violence of this latest nightmare that had a realism she feared even when she had been woken from its terrifying clutches. Those events of Saint Bartholomew's Eve, the nightmares of it had been more vivid as she slipped closer towards her death.

Cavriani, with the attendants, helped the Queen Mother to settle again, wiping the beads of perspiration from her face and down her chin and around her neck with a cloth bathed in cool rosewater. The physician was not optimistic about a miracle recovery, but his patient had at least regained the use of her limbs, and could manage some movement, limited though it was.

The chamber was stifling; the fireplace was stoked with pine logs the scent of which wafted around the room, whilst its fierce heat seemed to devour all the air. Now and again, one of the attending ladies would be handed a cordial or other concoction to give her mistress, and she would carefully support the Queen Mother's head as it was trickled into her dry mouth.

The chamber was gloomy and dull, its once luxurious décor was old and fading, threadbare tapestries hung on grey walls, and dust had settled into the folds of the heavy cumbersome bedclothes. Catherine had in recent times felt no desire to update the ornate, dated façade of the room. Her son, the King, had remonstrated with her time and again to have the chamber redecorated, and refurnished he would specify the colours and designs himself. Catherine had always smiled, she who had taken such great delight in building, said she had no mind to have anything changed, she was happier with it as it was.

Even as she looked to every corner of the room, figures seemed to step out of the shadows and a scene would play out in front of her. It was as though faces in some of the costly paintings looked away from her. The firelight would throw gross figures across the ornate ceiling of the chamber like ghosts; although it was often painful to move her neck, her eyes followed the shapes as they grew ever larger, and she would close her eyes tightly and shut them out.

Now as she began to calm after the nightmare, everyone in the room seemed to drift away until they had all gone. She peered over to one of the corners of the chamber, and there she could see figures running around, there was shouting and screaming, and there…yes, she was there! She could see herself standing watching everything. She was talking to someone, a familiar face, that of her good Italian friend Petrucci. He had laid something at her feet, and she was now telling him to take it away, her face aghast with horror. The images began to take form more clearly, and she felt she was floating closer and closer to the scene before her…

♦

PART ONE

♦

"This Kingdom is still so weak that I fear even the slightest relapse may cause it to fade and die."
—Catherine de Medici

♦

Paris was a city growing more and more dense and filthy with each passing year. The streets of the capital were dark and polluted with all manner of filth. In its very depths, beggars scratched around for food and especially anything of value that may have been dropped by the melee of the hundreds that had arrived so recently. Wine had flowed from every fountain, and those who barely ate from day to day, filled their gnawing stomachs with the rich liquid; so much so, that the very streets that had so recently watched the passing cortege of exalted figures with an unsettling silence, now lay amongst the debris, unconscious in their intoxication.

The sewers that did exist in the city were hopelessly inadequate, and the gutters ran slowly, carrying along the putrid, rotten matter that congested in almost every evil smelling street and its maze of dark back alleys. All that had been cleared away and cleaned to impress the visiting dignitaries and the French nobility, was now again awash with human waste and the careless litter from the visiting hordes who had followed their leaders into the city for the recent Royal wedding.

Across the capital however, the eerie silence that had seemed to settle over the city, began to turn to an alarming sound that would soon awake even the most inebriated of its citizens.

The Royal palace of the Louvre by contrast, was ablaze with colour and light from almost every window. Richly coloured drapes adorned the large windows, vast sconces held ornate candles, and almost seemed to set the rooms alight with their dazzling flicker. A visitor to this noble building would swear that one of the famous masques or balls that the Louvre had become famous for would soon take place.

Yet its atmosphere was very different from the gaiety and colour that were the hallmark of such festivities. One could ascend the sweeping staircases, passing rich tapestries and hangings in sumptuous red and gold that covered the walls, and step on the ornate patterned floors and feel a very different atmosphere than one of laughter and music.

Soldiers seemed to be everywhere. Captains shouted their instructions as the Royal guards were sent in all directions. Their usual plain expressions now gave way to concerned glances to one another, their normal fearlessness underlined by a feeling of great uncertainty. Their number had been doubled in and around the Royal apartments.

The Queen Mother of France, Catherine de Medici presented a sinister figure dressed in a gown of black, a colour she had adopted after the accident that had killed her husband, Henri Deux. The only other colours to show were a short white trimmed collar at her neck, and the slightest wisp of auburn hair, just visible at the edges of her black skull-cap. Her large hooded eyes, they too almost black in colour, could strike fear in any who crossed her. Her demeanour was generally one of calm, and few could read from her placid appearance what went on inside the cautious, quick mind.

She had at first been horrified by the sight of the severed head of the Admiral of France, Gaspard de Coligny. Now as she looked into the lifeless face of the man who she had come to regard as her deadliest enemy, she was unusually calmed by it. Strange, she thought, that as she cast her gaze from the staring horrified eyes to the grey neck with its fringe of roughly cut strands of skin, she felt almost empowered, lucid again after a brief unfamiliar feeling of dread.

When she looked once more at the bringer of this gift, her faithful countryman, Petrucci, she at last, smiled. "Guard this prize well my friend," she said and, after taking a deep breath, she returned her attention once more to the scene she was witnessing beyond the very gates of the Louvre.

Some hours before she had given instructions that the city gates were to be closed, and that there was to be no traffic on the Seine. At first her orders had caused some consternation. Those who had been given commands knew better than to disobey her, and all precautions had been made. Almost at once, she could hear cries from within the very palace itself.

She started, alarmed again that maybe she had made a miscalculation, and that the Huguenots would be mounting a counter attack. No, she was certain that the she and the rest of the Royal family were well guarded. Some shouts outside her very chamber did cause her to jump violently, she strode to the door and flung it open, uncertain of what to expect. The figure standing in the doorway was a Huguenot assistant of the great surgeon Pare. He stood staring wide-eyed at her for a second and then fell at her feet; his tunic soaked in blood. Immediately behind him, sword in hand was one of the Duke of Guise's henchmen. He bowed curtly, and with indecent haste, dragged the victim away from the doorway. One of Catherine's ladies who with several others had witnessed the scene screamed, clutching at her mouth in horror.

The Queen Mother turned to her and those with her "Return to your chambers at once. Lock the doors and admit no one that you are uncertain about. Go at once!" The terrified women, and other servants who had watched the scene and were now aware of the violence that was taking place, ran to the sanctuary of their chambers and offices.

It seemed that the noise from outside grew with each passing moment. Catherine had by now completely overcome her earlier anxiety, and privately cursed herself for her weakness. Had she not lived in fear for herself and her children daily, never knowing when a traitorous mob would descend on her and butcher them all?

She and her brood had to survive. For Catherine, this was the only way, to safeguard both her very life and the commanding position she had. Power could not be shared with the Admiral Coligny. She had needed his death to eliminate a potential rival for control of her son, the King, as well as a sign to the mighty Philip of Spain that she earnestly desired to rid France of the Huguenot heretics. How convenient that such drastic measures as this intended butchery could be concealed by the enmity that existed between the Catholic Guise family and the Huguenot Admiral.

From her vantage point, Catherine could now watch the unfolding massacre; the lights from flares lit up the night sky like a shower of sparks. Screams from both adults and children hung in the air that was beginning to smell of death.

It had been agreed that all Catholics could be identified by a white cross on the back of their tunics or white handkerchiefs attached to their sleeves, and the

Queen Mother could pick out many such emblems, as they darted around in a frenzy of murderous activity.

At first there had been only a trickle of people running from their homes. The streets were now a deluge of men women and children who dashed forth from the buildings like a burst dam. Despite the veil of secrecy to ensure that the imminent massacre was not known to the populace, Guise had obviously let some details be known to his own generals, and by process, many of the leading Catholic citizens had been afforded some measure of forewarning.

As a result, many of the houses belonging to these leading citizens had been decorated on their doors by a white cross identifying their households as the faithful rather than the heretic.

All around the city Huguenots were dragged from their beds and slaughtered. Those who attempted escape were seldom fortunate and once caught, could expect no pity. On the bridge of Pont Notre-Dame lived many Huguenots who were butchered before being thrown from their upstairs windows into the river below. One such victim was the wife of the King's *plumassier* whose head struck a column of the bridge and was caught by her long, much admired hair. It became entangled, and her weakening body could not wrestle it free. The woman had by now been noticed and some Catholics took to hurling stones at her until she no longer struggled.

People were dragged from their homes and beaten to death with any weapon available. Throats were cut, limbs severed and bodies defiled as the frenzy of killing grew. This slaughter was not reserved for the Huguenot leaders alone. Indeed, no sooner had the Duke of Guise's men heard the rallying cry of "To arms! Kill! Kill!" than they were urging all good honest citizens of Paris to do the Lord's work and rid France of the Huguenot scourge and defend their God and King.

Soldiers under the Duke of Guise as well as the palace soldiers tore around the city, invading all known Huguenot areas, and dragging their hapless victims into the street, dispatching them with ferocity and by many garish methods. Men, women and children were killed with equal fervour. Those who were not Catholic were soon trying to paint the symbolic white cross on their doors and on the back of their clothing, but few escaped with such a ruse. Those who ran from their attackers would only receive a more brutal assassination. Flight merely inflamed a growing frenzy, and those who were caught could expect no mercy. The stifling city seemed to be erupting in fresh violence as the hours went by, and the air hung with the putrid smell of death and burning, as Huguenot owned houses and shops were set ablaze.

To the victims, there seemed to be no escape. The night sky was gradually giving way to dawn, but still the massacre continued.

In the basement of his house in the rue de Seine, Nicholas L'Mercier hugged his wife and two children as the noise of people trampling about upstairs set them shivering in terror. He was in no doubt that his premises were being looted by the insane mob that he had a short time ago witnessed murdering before his very eyes. The merchant desperately prayed that they would not be uncovered, and yet he could almost sense the danger that approached, his heart sank as the trap door to the basement creaked as it was opened from the room above, and the sound of footsteps could be heard. His daughter and small son began to whimper, his wife clasped her hands together in prayer. Seeking to conceal them all behind him as though they would not be seen, the Huguenot merchant raised an arm to deflect the first thrust of a sword from the two figures that stood over them.

Not far away, in the rue Saint-Germain-l'Auxerrois, Madame Baillet, the wife of Lussant the Queen Mother's goldsmith had heard the approaching assailants, and could see no means of escape other than out of an upstairs window. In her desperation she therefore climbed upon her stool and eased herself through the small opening. She had intended to leap to the safest area down below, which appeared to be the pile of dead meat and rotting vegetables from the eating-house next door. She retched at the thought, but there was no other choice. Unfortunately, in her haste she had mistimed her jump, and as a result caught her foot on the iron window fastener and landed with a crash on the stone ground. All she could feel was the most excruciating pain in her legs, and she gathered up her skirts to find to her horror that both her legs lay in distorted angles, a bone protruded from one like a bloody spear. She tried to stifle her screams, but could not control the cries of agony. Her Catholic killers found her thus and merely laughed at her injury, well deserved for being a filthy Huguenot. Before running her through with their swords however, they noticed her expensive bangles and sliced off both her hands in their eagerness to have these unexpected treasures. Moments later as the cruelly disfigured body of Françoise Baillet lay dead and mutilated a stray dog picked up one of the severed hands, and slunk away into a back alley. The Catholic owner next door had always hated his neighbours, and delighted therefore in finally running the woman's corpse through with his spit.

The dark alley off the rue aux Ours had no means of escape, and even a man as large as Jacques d'Mazier could not pass through the thick chains that had been set across the end of the alley from where he had sought liberty. He stopped momentarily, the perspiration streaming down his fleshy face, his body heaved as he drew in great breaths of the foul stench of Parisian air. Suddenly a face appeared at his side. He jumped in alarm, and the blade sliced swiftly across his cheek, and then to his neck, and finally his chest and stomach. He fell onto the heavy chains, where his assailants robbed him of his purse, and his fine clothing. The pair of killers were not Catholics, but having ensured that their white handkerchiefs were still placed accordingly, they spat on the bulky body of their Huguenot neighbour. A man they had detested during a long business feud. After all, who would ever know? What would one more Huguenot body matter? In a night of such brutality, none could trace this crime back to their door.

Nor was it just adults who gloried in the slaughter of so many. Young children were openly encouraged by their parents and elders to kill the scourge of France that was the Huguenots.

At the Pont aux Meuniers, Madeleine Briconnet struggled to dress herself in the disguise of a Catholic nun, and after assuring herself that she could pass unnoticed, she set out from the back yard of her house and began to move as swiftly as she could, her heart beating so loudly she felt sure it could be heard. Several men carrying flares and bloodied swords and daggers watched her as she went by, but must have been convinced by her attire, as they did not hinder her. Almost as she began to feel she might make her escape from the madness that seemed to be all around, she noticed two soldiers had stopped before her. She tried to speak, and held up her crucifix as evidence of her sacred position.

One of the soldiers stared at her and she followed his eyes as they studied her apparel until coming to rest at her feet. He glanced up at her and smiled, exposing the yellow stumps of his rotten teeth. Only after a moment did she look down and see to her horror that she had misjudged the length of the false habit, which cruelly exposed her rich velvet dress beneath. The men cut her down brutally and left her bloodied body to the dogs.

The slaughter and mayhem raged throughout the long night. Many old scores were settled that night as neighbours turned on each other, husbands gave up wives to the mobs, children forced to watch as their parents were slain before them, before even they were not spared. Many who could afford it, tried to buy their lives from their assailants. Pregnant women were slain, even one who went into early labour from the shock of the massacre.

The Seine was now running red from the blood of so many of the victims thrown into it which were almost bringing the water to a standstill before men were instructed to keep it flowing by untangling the mess of bodies that threatened to cause a dam.

The English Ambassador in Paris, Francis Walsingham paced his apartments, deep in anxious thought. It had been several hours since the Catholic Duke of Nevers had been instructed to set guards on the embassy in order to ensure his personal safety. Since the middle of the night, several English Protestants had hurried to the building in the Faubourg Saint-Germain begging for sanctuary from the mob. The tall, dark figure of the ambassador went over to the window of his main chamber that looked out onto the bloody scene, wondering if he would even get out of Paris alive.

As dawn finally broke, the smoke filled air lay heavily over Paris and its Catholic citizens emerged from their frenzied activity of the past few hours, their thirst for Huguenot blood now sated. The slaughter had not ceased entirely, but the majority stared around them as though in a daze. Dead bodies seemed to be everywhere; severed limbs raw from the ravenous appetite of the stray dogs that roamed the city. Many victims were beyond recognition. All had seemed as one during the fanatical violence that had raged.

Salvation had only existed for those who wore the white cross, and although some Huguenots had survived the terror, none of them had ventured out to the streets, not daring to abandon their hiding places. It would be a brave soul that would raise a fist in defiance. All remained tense as citizens gradually began to take in the full horror of what had happened since midnight when the bells of Saint-Germain l'Auxerrois had rung out their chilling alarm.

♦

Whilst the massacre had been at its zenith in the streets of Paris, inside the Louvre, the tensions were just as palpable, and France's King was becoming consumed with a rage to kill without mercy. Charles had wreaked havoc by tearing through the palace screaming at his guards to kill any Huguenots in the vicinity of the Louvre. "None shall live!" he had shouted, "None shall survive to reproach me when this night's work is done!" Soldiers were despatched in all directions as the mayhem spread.

The King cut a pitiful sight. At nearly six foot tall, he should have cut a majestic figure; instead his face was drawn and haggard, grey in pallor, his bloodshot eyes were sunken and streaming. He looked more than double his age of twenty three, an old man almost, and one that was quite clearly bordering on the very edge of reason. He tore at his clothes, ripping at his white laced shirt that was now drenched in sweat. "I am the King!" he screamed. "None shall live to plunge a dagger into my heart! Take them! Take them all! Every heretic in Paris...!"

He stopped abruptly, as though suddenly realising something of great importance. He turned to speak to members of the court who would normally be in attendance at this time. Almost all the courtiers had taken refuge either in their own apartments if they resided in the palace, or had risked the streets, before the general mayhem and sickening bloodshed were really underway. The few attendants that had hurried to keep pace with him were now startled by his abruptness.

"No!" the King announced to any who cared to listen. "My dear friend Rochefoucauld shall not go; he must not be taken! Nor Pare, my doctor Pare shall not die this night! Marie, my beloved mistress...ah, but no," he smiled suddenly, and pulling one of his valets to one side, spoke in a low, conspiratorial manner, that the terrified servant could barely hear.

"No, my beloved Marie is safe...but we shall tell no-one where I have hidden her and my nurse, my sweet darlings...they are safe, safe from..." He turned around quickly to check he was not being overheard. "Safe... from *her*!"

He giggled suddenly and then with a deep resigned sigh, as though his fury was spent, he at once again began to scream and tore after one of his guards who was dragging a body down a passageway, leaving a bloody trail in its wake. The sight of the red coloured smear seemed to inflame his madness still more and he raced to where the corpse was unceremoniously pushed over a balcony to the floor below.

Charles ran to see where the victim had been thrown, and saw a mound of dead bodies, there seemed to be chaos everywhere. The King stared open-mouthed, down at the pile of cadavers. Soon tears welled in his eyes and slowly dripped on to the bloody scene below. Then, almost as though he had woken from a sleep, he shouted for his guards again, and raced up another flight of steps with his hounds in excited pursuit.

♦

The Queen Mother was now receiving regular reports about the carnage that was taking place throughout Paris and indeed, the Louvre itself. There was, she had been informed, indiscriminate butchery being carried out with many taking the opportunity to rid themselves of an enemy or a business rival, even an unwanted spouse. It was as though the city had gone completely mad.

All around her, Catherine could hear the cries and screams from the courtyards below as well as from the apartments and chambers throughout the palace. She could now ignore the violence with a dispassionate mind. With each passing hour she became more and more convinced that there had been no alternative to this night's work. There was still however, one final guarantee that the power of the Huguenots was now severely checked, and she went in search of the Charles.

Upon the orders of the King, Navarre and his cousin Henri, Prince de Condé, had been held under close guard. Condé paced up and down his chamber where he had been confined with only a few servants. He too had heard the cries and screams from outside the gates of the Louvre. A scuffle had broken out earlier when the Swiss Guards had arrived to ensure he did not escape. His own men had naturally objected to their Prince being treated thus, and after a brief but bloody skirmish, at least eight of his soldiers had been cut down in front of his eyes. It seemed that the guards had neither pity nor concern for their actions, and one or two had even been seen to smile at their deeds.

The young Prince had been informed that the King and the Queen Mother had deemed it safer this night for him to be closely confined. Thus it was that he could do nothing until he was summoned.

The King of Navarre was better informed than his cousin, and ensured that his own spies were diligent and reported to him any goings on outside the palace. All he had been able to ascertain was that a Huguenot plot to kill the King, the Queen Mother and the rest of the Royal family had been uncovered, and it had been necessary to strike first before they were attacked.

Navarre did not need to be cleverer than he was to realise that this must be a great deal more than merely rounding up the instigators of a plot and having them examined under torture. Moreover, any proposed attack worth considering would never have been attempted without either himself or the Admiral Coligny being aware of it, and the old soldier and friend had implied nothing of the sort when they had last spoken.

He knew the brave Coligny would even now be remonstrating with the King and his mother. Navarre would certainly be glad to see the Admiral, who he felt still had some influence with the impressionable Charles.

As for himself he had always felt distinctly uneasy about being in Paris more so now that he was ever closer affiliated to the tainted Valois dynasty.

♦

Throughout the Louvre, the Swiss Guard were now carrying out the Queen Mother's orders that the palace should be secured, and all apartments thoroughly searched to seek out any remaining Huguenots that may be hiding. All along the palace galleries, dead bodies lay, some with throats slit, others with stab wounds that bloodied the ornate flooring, Women as well as men lay piled on either side of the walkways, heaped together in a tangle of butchered limbs.

As for the King, Catherine had sought him out and found him at the window in one of the chambers that looked out directly on to the Seine. He was taking careful aim with a harquebus and shooting at the bodies that were slowly moving down the river. A frightened attendant stood close by, recharging a second pistol to be exchanged once the first had been fired.

Charles was in a hysterical state; he was laughing with joy at hitting his target one moment and yet the next, he would begin whimpering pathetically, shouting how sorry he was. After some moments he leant against a wall and began to weep bitterly.

Catherine immediately snapped her fingers ordering that the attendants leave at once and take both the fire-arms and the ever-present hounds out of the chamber. Once they had gone, she turned on her son, grabbing him by his shirt, and shaking him violently "Charles, Charles-" she began.

However, the son that she had always been able to control, suddenly turned on his mother as he had never done before, and in one quick movement, he had his bloodied hand up at her throat, pressing his thumb and finger against the fleshy neck and gripping her tightly. Catherine's eyes widened with horror, and she tried in vain to pull his hand away as he came close to her face, spitting the words with a frightening edge of menace.

"Now my mother," he rasped, "I am master of this realm, and I will shoot you or my brothers or any I wish, yet it is your foul dealings that has led to this! See how I shoot at my own people? It is you who have brought me to this! You who have drenched France in blood...perhaps it is *you* who should perish this night, eh? You who should feel the close hand of death at your throat. Ah, yes I can do it...quite easily, I can kill you."

Catherine felt terrified and her son's grip was tightening with every word. He was becoming more and more unpredictable. With this madness upon him he was capable of anything and now, having dismissed all his attendants, she found herself totally at his mercy. Then suddenly, she could breathe again as something caused the King's hand to drop away. The Duke d'Anjou had sought out his mother, and had grabbed his brother, pulling his grip from their mother's throat. At once the Queen Mother gasped for air and fell to her knees, coughing. Anjou wrestled the King away, but then found himself under threat, as the maniacal Charles now leaned over him with a raised dagger.

Catherine dared to watch, although she was helpless to do anything, but strangely, Charles stopped breathing so heavily, and gradually it seemed that the madness had left him; his grip on the dagger loosened, and he rolled away from a relieved Anjou and lay on the floor, curled up into as tight a shape as he could, and began to wail uncontrollably. The Queen Mother allowed Anjou to quickly help her from the chamber as the King of France lay rocking from side to side, his loud sobs echoing down the deserted passageway.

Catherine gently rubbed a salve from her own cabinet of ointments on her bruised throat, and almost at once began to feel its powerful properties working to soothe her discomfort. She had dismissed her dwarf attendant once she had allowed Anjou to help her to her chamber, and he paced the room like a caged lion. The young Prince, the current heir to the throne was flushed after the incident with his older brother. Henri was as tall as the King, with striking good looks, high cheekbones and a flawless olive coloured skin, with large eyes like his mother's, black and glittering.

"My dearest," Catherine said quietly, in a voice strained and croaky as she motioned for him to sit, "I'm afraid we have to consider that your brother is beyond our help. God only knows what would have become of me if you had not bravely intervened, my darling."

Anjou sighed, and picked at a thread from his doublet as he watched his mother, now quite calm after the vicious episode with the King. "He is a monster maman!" he exclaimed "He cannot carry on in this way." Catherine held a delicate finger to his lips. "Hush, my son, you must not talk so rashly. Even as his madness comes upon him, he is still the King. He will quieten and then he will be calm again, he will need his mother. He will be full of remorse, and will beg forgiveness."

Anjou made a dismissing motion with his hand, and stood up to begin pacing again. Catherine talked as he did so. "I have news that this evening has been more successful than we could have hoped." Her eyes almost lit up at what had been a few hours filled with anxiety and fear. "Now we must check the Guise, it is no time for our valiant murderer to become the hero of the hour. If he is allowed that, then we have merely exchanged one threat for another." Mother and son sat in companionable silence as they considered such implications.

♦

Despite having shaken off her earlier anxiety, Catherine could not entirely dismiss her fears that a revenge attack could well be planned. It was only when she had been assured that the majority of Huguenots had indeed been virtually wiped out in Paris, that she then sought out Charles to insist that he should now issue a Royal proclamation that all arms must be laid down, and the citizens must return to their homes while the streets of the capital were again brought to order – the killing must stop. She advised Anjou to lie low for a further few hours while she dealt with his older brother.

Charles was now becoming too unpredictable, and would certainly not thank the younger brother he detested for being a witness to his earlier assault against their mother.

She took up her cane, and walked purposefully along the corridor towards the apartments of the King. The palace was still eerily quiet, with only muffled voices from the distance that could be heard along with the now familiar tapping of her walking cane on the hard flooring.

Catherine noticed smears of blood on the walls, where hands had desperately clung on before being dragged to their death; she tried to ignore the groans that she could still hear. Cries that rose from outside assailed her, and she moved quickly on.

Despite the stench of so much slaughter, she felt calmer than she had for many weeks. Nevertheless, there were still some important issues to deal with. She stopped and turned slightly, snapping her fingers. One of her faithful dwarves that followed in attendance, bowed low to her and nodded as she leant down and whispered her instruction to him. He bowed again and left her, running along the corridor.

As she mounted the two steps that led up to the King's suite, she caught sight of the city from an open window where one of the ornate panes had been broken. She stopped for a moment and looked out over the houses, churches and streets. There was still noise, and she could clearly see men still attacking one another in the streets. Dogs barked and she noticed several carts that appeared to be piled high with corpses as they ambled their way to the Seine, where the cadavers would be thrown into the water. They would travel down to Le Havre and finally out into the English

Channel. She carried on, allowing her fingers to flutter around her throat nervously as she entered the apartments of her son.

The King now lay on a couch, while his mistress, Marie was applying a soothing cool compress to his forehead as she whispered soothing words that had almost helped him drift off to sleep. He started as his mother approached. Marie rose and curtsied, before leaving the chamber. The Queen Mother smiled at the girl as she left, before turning to face her son as soon as the door had shut.

Charles looked sheepishly at his mother as she wiped away the thinning hair from his eyes where it had stuck to his perspiring skin. Charles was beginning to calm from all his exertions during the last few hours, and exhaustion was finally setting in. He was of a heavy heart, and his ghost-like pallor had shocked even his mother. Although he could not help but feel some suspicion, as she tended to him maternally as she had always done; the Queen Mother said nothing of his earlier assault against her, indeed acting as though nothing untoward had taken place between them.

Instead, she fussed at the state of his clothes, his white shirt covered in blood, his fine blue doublet torn and missing several of its pearl buttons. Instructions were given to his valets, who were only now beginning to emerge from cupboards, and underneath beds where they had concealed themselves during the last few hours, and soon several of them were scurrying about following her orders

At length the Queen Mother sank onto a chair beside her son, and leant onto her silver handled cane with one of her delicate hands over the other.

"My son," she said quietly. "It is time to put an end to the violence that has taken grip of all Paris. Your generals have reported to me that we are safe, and they believe the threat of an uprising against ourselves and the leading Catholic nobles has been averted by our orders to rid the city of the traitors."

Charles felt a wave of emotion coming over him, and he went to sink to his knees at her feet, but she put a hand up to stay him. "No my son, now we are more secure, you must not weep so, your court expects you to lead the way in our celebration of our victory. Yet," she paused, ensuring they were not being overheard, "there is work still to do, and we must be firm in our resolution."

Catherine paused as valets arrived with fresh clothes for the King, and while he allowed his servants to undress him and put on clean garments, she rose from her seat, and quickly scrutinised some of the letters that lay scattered on her son's desk.

How foolish that letters like this should be carelessly left where anyone could see them. She recognised the small mark that she herself wrote onto the documents to indicate that she had already seen them. Nevertheless, this was typical of Charles to almost invite attention to his correspondence. She looked around as his valets put the finishing touches to his fresh outfit, and for some moments, felt strangely sad as she watched him.

Try as she might to ignore the situation, it was becoming apparent to her that something was different between herself and this eldest son. She had been despairing of him for some time; he was now becoming something of a liability to her and his family. Where once she had felt a natural instinct to care and protect him, she now felt pity for the pathetic state he presented. He was clearly sick in mind as well as in body and, moreover, he had failed to keep control of events, allowing his own persona to dominate his behaviour.

A strong King would have been in charge and not allowed the mob to take control as they clearly had done. More worrying was the little or no confidence in the King by the populace. Why else would they dismiss any concern about any Royal retribution for what had taken place that night?

What more could she do for this son who was becoming so detached from reality, and could thwart her plans at any moment? Did she still even love him as a mother should? Was her pity a strong enough replacement for that love? In that moment it came to her that he was becoming a weight that she could no longer bear. Charles, her son was, she realised – no longer of any use to her. The future was surely her dearest darling Henri. For a brief moment she felt a welling of emotion, but she swallowed hard and suppressed the weakness.

Having dismissed his servants, Catherine now seated herself again and spoke seriously to her son. "Charles, as I said, we must be resolute in how we act. What has occurred has been necessary to repel the traitorous Huguenots who plotted a complete destruction of us all; but now they must cease their butchery, there must be no further bloodshed."

Charles nodded in agreement at her words. He was so tired, exhausted emotionally as well as physically. "What do you advise we do?" he asked wearily.

Catherine had noticed her dwarf standing at the doorway carrying a silver tray – on it an object covered in a black velvet cloth which as instructed, he placed on a nearby table. She had no qualms about the discretion of her closest servants, especially her dwarves. They were her creatures and devoted to their powerful mistress. Once he had carefully put down the tray she instructed him further.

"Go and notify the King of Navarre and the Prince of Condé that they are to attend His Majesty the King at once." She then sat back and leaning her cane against the chair, she thoughtfully fingered her talisman bracelet, touching each of the different stones design delicately as she considered the forthcoming meeting.

Charles tore his gaze from the covered object and more than once hesitantly opened his mouth to ask about it, but his mother silenced him with a wave of her hand.

"We must deal with this matter of our dear Navarre and his cousin. They are dangerous if we let them have their liberty, and yet to have them in prison, or put to death, would invite rebellion throughout the Kingdom. There are those who would not miss them, but we cannot afford any further bloodshed. Remember, Navarre is wed to Margot, and she will be an adept spy in her husband's court, I have no doubt. She knows her loyalty to her family is absolute."

Privately, Catherine was uncertain about Margot's loyalties, her daughter was certainly mischievous but that must be dealt with later. Firstly, she must force a wedge between Navarre, Condé and their followers, and then do something to check the growing arrogance of the Duke of Guise.

A short time later, the chamber door opened, and the King of Navarre strode in, followed closely by his cousin, the Prince de Condé. Navarre ran his rough hands through his mass of hair before bowing. As usual, his hair was unkempt and his overall appearance was one of a scruffy country youth. While a slight carefree smile was usual on his face, he seemed more anxious now. His small dark eyes glittered as he looked from one to the other. Charles seemed to have aged in just a day, he thought, while the Queen Mother looked composed, but one could never know what this disciple of Machiavelli was thinking behind those pale expressionless features.

Condé bowed stiffly. Unlike his cousin, the Prince was one who wore his concerns on his face, which was plain, but drawn. Neither guest was invited to sit. Even as they stood before the King and his mother, noises outside the chamber indicated that the palace was again returning to some normality, and the usual watch could be heard taking up positions outside the King's chambers, even though his personal guards had never been far behind him throughout the terrible night. Catherine was pleased to hear the guard, at such a propitious moment.

Navarre was first to speak. "Your Majesties," he said, "I welcome the chance to speak with you both, since I have until now been held prisoner in my chambers."

Catherine chuckled "My son, surely a young bridegroom like yourself would not want to be elsewhere when just married to the sister of your King?"

Navarre inclined his head. "No, messieurs," the Queen Mother continued, "you are merely held for your own protection. You know of course what has taken place this last night. Your King my son, has uncovered a deadly conspiracy too horrible to contemplate, and we have had to take decisive action."

Condé interrupted, feeling a brief surge of anger at what the Queen Mother had casually called 'action.' "The streets of this capital run red with Huguenot blood," he stated; "My own followers are cut down, my soldiers butchered in the palace itself. You would slaughter us all. Has the Admiral not been asked about this conspiracy, for I declare I know nothing of it!"

Navarre spoke sternly. "A conspiracy you say? Have its instigators been caught? Were there so many who planned this that all need to pay the price?"

Catherine sighed as though trying to explain a situation to a small child. "A plot was discovered, and the instigators had to be punished, or would you have your King slain in the middle of the night? God knows we also have the interminable feud between the Admiral and the House of Guise, which we are alas powerless to control. There have as a result, been…victims."

She took up her cane and slowly walked behind both men. Her very movement seemed to make them uneasy, and Condé played with the rings on his fingers nervously. The very word "victims" certainly felt more chilling when spoken by the Queen Mother.

"You see, my sons," Catherine eventually spoke, "you are, as has already been said, here for your protection. Alas, neither myself, nor the King are able to guarantee your safety. You say that your followers have been struck down. God knows we have tried to shield them from all harm, but their allegiance to you identifies them as merely more Huguenots to add to the other traitorous souls. My concern for you could not be greater than if I was indeed a mother to both of you, but I have to abide by the wishes of the King and our close advisers. The Huguenot cause is lost my sons. Your only hope of salvation, in this world as well as the next, is to agree to accept the mass and embrace the Catholic Church."

To her annoyance, Condé laughed aloud, a bitter, hollow sound that was completely bereft of joy or amusement. "Never!" he almost shouted, "I believe that you, Madame, have quite lost your wits. I have been brought up another way from you, and my faith determines my life. Whilst I would gladly die for it, I would rather be left to practice my faith freely. If not then I should choose to be slain like the poor souls in the streets yonder, than suffer the fate of abandoning my soul for the sake of my skin."

Catherine felt a sudden rush of anger, but before she had time to speak, Charles has leapt to his feet and held his dagger up to Condé's throat, his features distorted with anger. "Then you will die a traitor as have the rest of the Huguenots. You will abandon your faith or you will suffer for it."

Catherine stood at her son's side, and calmly placed her hand on his arm gently pushing it downwards; she kept her sharp, gimlet eyes on Condé the whole time until he felt a chill run throughout his body. He could hold her gaze no longer and directed his eyes downwards.

Navarre was acutely aware that he had to think fast. As he stood next to his cousin he knew that there was little choice in this matter. Catherine had surely killed his mother, and she, or indeed the King, would not hesitate to eliminate him and Condé if it suited their plans to do so. He had to get away from Paris and its stench of death. He was sick at heart.

The issue was an important one for his cousin; but changing religion had never seemed such a momentous decision for him. Henri of Navarre had certainly not inherited his mother's fanatical adherence to the faith. Ironically, his attitude to religion was more like Catherine's.

He believed in life, and the pleasure he gained from it. No, he had too much to live for. He had his beliefs but he was not sure he would die for them. In any case, he reasoned, the Almighty God would soon see through the ruse, and regret saving this particular soul.

Nevertheless, some show of defiance seemed the right thing to do, and whilst Condé had argued most forcefully against such a catastrophe as becoming Catholic, Navarre was certain they would never leave the Louvre alive unless they did so. At length, his cousin buried his face in his hands in desperation, and Navarre spoke up.

"We must have time to consult with our advisors, Madame. We must find the Admiral and take advice on this issue, we cannot decide here and now. Allow us some time, we beg you."

Catherine smiled sweetly at him, and walked slowly to the covered object on the silver tray that had been delivered earlier.

"Ah yes, and so we come to the Admiral." she said with a cold voice, bereft of all emotion. "Your mentor will not however be joining you in council. As you will see, he has already paid the price for his treachery." At that moment she lifted the velvet cloth and there on the tray was the severed head of Gaspard de Coligny, its skin now thin and grey, his face still covered in blood, now cracking and peeling. His previously full beard had been savagely cut so that little remained. His eyes were cast over and sinking back into his skull and the crude cut of his throat had set the head at an angle. Charles stared as though transfixed, but said nothing.

Catherine did not take her eyes off either of the young men, both of whom she heard audibly gasp at the horror before them. "The result of ambition and treachery, my sons. Look well at it and question whether the beliefs you cling to are worth this."

Condé held up a hand up to his mouth and felt the bile rise in his throat, which he could only just contain. Navarre looked from the horrific sight to the Queen Mother – and he understood.

Catherine could easily conceal her desire for the massacre behind the enmity between the Guises and Coligny. How dangerous she was, he thought, how much she must hate.

Navarre swallowed hard. He fought back the stinging in his eyes, suppressed the roar of grief that threatened to burst from him. The horror of their predicament was all too clear to him. If the Admiral could be slain without mercy, then surely his only course must be to live on and fight to avenge the Huguenots that remained.

For all his foolish bluster, Navarre was blessed with an acute mind, and had inherited his mother's good sense. What could happen to both he and his cousin if they refused the ultimatum with which the Queen Mother presented them? He knew that neither of them would ever leave Paris again – certainly not alive.

He eventually averted his eyes from the grim spectacle and in one swift movement knelt to the King. "Your Majesty," he said soberly "If you would have me be your brother in faith, as well as in truth, then I will embrace the sacrament."

Condé stared at his cousin in horror for a moment, but Navarre had turned to meet his gaze, and he saw in his eyes a pleading look, and knew he had no choice but to agree. He also knelt at the King's feet.

Catherine stood looking down at these potentially dangerous young men and permitted herself a smile of triumph. She watched them being escorted away, and turned from the chamber door to see Charles stretch out a trembling hand and gently touch the grey decaying skin of the Admiral.

A tear ran down his cheek and he closed his eyes tightly as though committing the grim sight to his mind forever. He opened them again and, taking up the black velvet cloth, draped it carefully back over the head. He rose without looking at his mother, and Catherine watched him as he walked slowly to his bedchamber, and quietly closed the door behind him.

The Queen Mother, accompanied by the King as well as Navarre, Condé and several members of the court, had left the palace of the Louvre for the first time in two days. The air in the city was still oppressive and tensions were still obvious, yet for the King there was a fascination about the piles of bodies that littered the courtyard and reached the very steps of the palace itself. Charles seemed wild-eyed at the sight of so much blood, and many of the courtiers privately wondered about the wisdom in encouraging him to see such sights.

Catherine watched the King closely. Ah, yes his eyes had widened in horror and awe at the spectacle before him. For herself, she along with some of the ladies of her *escardon* found great amusement in some of the bodies that had been stripped naked after death and lay uncovered and exposed. Several of the women giggled and whispered to one another, pointing out and comparing some of their physical attributes.

Catherine smiled at such behaviour, not just for itself; mockery of dead people did not matter once they no longer breathed, but also the scandalous looks from some of the older members of the court, horrified at such lewd behaviour as much as they were sickened by the killing of so many people. Catherine knew they detested her, but they also feared her, and that was more important. The Queen Mother would even occasionally ask that a particular body be presented to her so that she might identify members of the court that had been slain.

After some time, the smell of the bodies became too much to bear, and Catherine retired back inside the palace. Charles was noticeably reluctant to leave the sight of such carnage, and it was observed that for once, his mother made no attempts to drag him from a scene that would almost certainly unnerve him. Some even believed that his mother had deliberately encouraged him to see the work of the Catholic mobs.

Later, Catherine watched from an upstairs window as her son the King was seen pathetically looking at each victim. He had his guards bring him each body in turn, and he wept afresh if there were any he knew personally.

His dearest Rochefoucauld had been slain in his own bedchamber, and the King had insisted on washing the blood from his dear friend's face, crying as he cradled the dead man. Why did he not warn the nobleman to take refuge as he had with Ambrose Parre. Marie

Touchet, and his dearest Nanon his nurse, as well as the few other precious people he could not bear to live without? He would never forgive himself.

It was becoming clear to many that the events of the past few days, and the role he had played in the massacre would torture the King to death as certainly as if he had been a Huguenot merchant. He feared, as did his mother, that a counter attack on the palace could occur at any moment.

The Queen Mother looked on at the scene with contempt, the very sight of her son was starting to sicken her.

◆

In a tiny corridor of the Louvre, was a small chamber, dimly lit and sparsely furnished. In a large ornate bed lay an old woman, almost shrunken into the heavy bedclothes that covered her.

Here lay the King's aged former nurse, Madeleine, or as the King insisted on calling her still-Nanon. She was all but bedridden now in these recent weeks, her delicate frame was covered in a paper thin skin, her cheekbones prominent, her eyes sunken and rheumy, with a grey dull colour that held no joy. The Kings own physician had told her that the swelling in her breast had grown larger and that the end was near. She had insisted that the news must be kept from the King, he must believe she had merely an ague, that though severe, would pass. Apart from a niece, she would leave no family, and perhaps that was for the best.

She had lived long at court, firstly as a nursemaid to the King's grandfather, François, the first. She had held sway over almost all the Royal children since, indeed being well tolerated by the present Queen Mother, even though all the nurses or governesses had been instructed to receive all their orders from the infamous mistress of Henri Deux – Diane de Poitiers.

Madeleine had often wondered how Catherine de Medici was able to accept this indignity as well as she did. Ah, but that was all past now, Diane had been dead for some years, and all those days seemed a lifetime ago to the old nurse. She would lie awake so often now, and it was the state of the King that saddened her so much. Charles, "little Charlot" had been the gentlest of her charges when still an infant, but time however, had changed him greatly; he had found the burden of Kingship too heavy a weight to bear, and so few believed him capable of ruling without his mother.

So often, even before the massacre in Paris, had the King sought refuge with his old nurse. She would soothe his worries, and read to him or even sing one of the old lullabies he used to love so much. The King was by now a sad and forlorn figure, barely eating or sleeping. He raged at all his servants, barely spoke to his ministers, and hated his mother with a vengeance, but lived in terrible fear of her, and completely unable to free himself from her hold over him.

Madeleine had wept so often after the King had left her, her heart breaking for the pitiful creature Charles had become. The massacre in Paris had all but pushed the young King to the very edge of madness; the images that were as vivid to him now as they had been on that very night. His words and, his gestures, both erratic and violent. He had certainly saved her life and that of his mistress, the gentle Marie Touchet on that fateful night.

The danger to them lay in the fact that they were Huguenots, a great many of whom he had a few hours before, agreed to annihilate. He had come to her that evening, when they had both sat in the nurse's chamber together, and had almost dragged them from the room, and back in to his own apartments where he opened the door of a small outer room and virtually pushed them both inside. His eyes had been wide and blazing, spittle forming at the corners of his mouth. "Only here," he had told them, "only here will you be safe, but you must be silent, shhh! I will come later, when this night is over, but my mother must not know! He had put his finger to his mouth "Shhh.... none must hear you, I will come back, I promise you, I will come for you!"

He had returned for them many hours later, but still the madness was upon him. His mistress and his nurse had wept together at at the sight of him. Dishevelled, and dirty, his blood-stained doublet had alarmed them greatly, then he was gone again, followed by his pages and his hounds.

Both women had retired, exhausted and frightened from the ordeal. They had fled quickly to the nurse's apartments, and remained there waiting for some semblance of order to return to the palace. The nurse cried, not only for those who had been slaughtered, but for the King who she was sure would never regain his complete faculties. She prayed for him constantly; he who she doted on as though he were her own.

At last however, God had spoken to her, guiding her to the only remedy would end the King's suffering. Could she carry out such a task? Before the recent massacre, she would have been horrified at such thoughts, but she could no longer watch an innocent, and gentle spirit like the King be used and dominated so much that he did not now even know his own mind.

So, the old nurse wept and prayed, and tried to form a way in which she could give her dearest Charlot the peace he so badly needed. Assistance would be necessary, and she thanked God every day that he had brought her beloved niece to court. The girl had married well, and now held a position at court in serving the Queen Mother. She was bold, daring and impetuous; and whilst she had converted to Catholicism when she had married, she too had been as appalled as her aunt at the atrocities.

Madeleine had thought long and hard about involving the girl, but if she was to carry out her plan, she needed another's hand to assist, and the vehemence that her niece had shown at the massacre convinced her that her purpose was clear.

All that remained now was to wait until the right moment, and Charles, King of France would suffer no longer.

♦

Explanations, recriminations and argument continued throughout Europe in the weeks following the massacre. Word reached Catherine and Charles that the killings had not remained exclusively to Paris. Indeed, although Catherine had advised Charles to write to provincial governors outside of the capital fearing as much. Violent outbreaks began in many of the large cities, Lyon, Provence and Rouen in particular, and for many weeks it seemed as though the killing would never cease.

Although these and other cities had been warned to keep the peace, Charles did not hesitate to lay the blame for the massacre in Paris on the Duke of Guise. The Protestant states began receiving estimates of the number of people slain, and it was generally accepted that several thousand Huguenots had met their tragic end during those terrifying days in August 1572, whilst a Parisian butcher later boasted to have killed at least four hundred of them himself.

An eerie silence fell over the Palace of the Louvre in the weeks following the massacre. The outer provinces were still reporting killings despite the King's orders that all attacks on Huguenots must stop. Even in Paris itself, those Huguenots that had managed to survive those awful days, barely left their barricaded homes.

It was however, a strange occurrence at the Louvre palace itself that had created the most unrest. The day after the massacre, a number of black ravens had been seen landing on the roofs of the palace. As the hours passed more and more of the birds began to settle, until the sky was almost dark with their continuous shadow. When Catherine overheard one of her ladies mention the birds, she insisted on leaving the building to observe them for herself. The palace was indeed covered by ravens, as though a thick black veil had been draped across the top of the building. And so they would remain for many days.

The Queen Mother was a keen follower of the supernatural – the black arts. She had consulted with the eminent minds of the age, and the sight of these evil looking birds had a visible effect on her. This was surely as sign, a dark omen that portended a warning, a message. Her thoughts immediately turned to the events of the past few days; she had been unable to think of little else. She must speak to her advisers and learn the significance of this extraordinary, unsettling phenomenon.

Meanwhile, the King had become extremely distressed about the birds and had firstly ordered shots to be fired into the air that would frighten the ravens away, but only a few would be scared off, and even those few would merely circle around and land back on the roof. It was, he announced in hysteria, the souls of those who had been slaughtered, it represented a warning that these birds would attack him in his bed, pecking out his eyes and digging into his flesh with their sharp beaks.

As the days went by the King became obsessed with the image of so many dead returning to haunt him. His sleep had now become fitful and troubled. He would stay awake all through the night, forcing his pages and some of his closest courtiers to do likewise. All this Catherine watched with growing concern, as well as extreme displeasure.

For a nature as superstitious as Catherine's the ravens were, nevertheless, a cause for concern, and their presence needed explanation. With this in mind, she hastened to her chambers and once again changed into the worn gown and shawl that she kept in one of her secret closets; and exchanging her elaborate silver handled cane for a plain walking stick.

She drew back the heavy velvet hangings to reveal a small door that she unlocked with one of the many keys on a large ring attached to her belt. Then picking up a lantern that she lit from a sconce on the wall, she passed through the low doorway and descended the narrow passage towards a secret exit at back of the palace.

The air was heavy and fetid along the route, and several rats scampered out of small gaps between the dirt floor and the base of the damp stone walls. Catherine had used this route on many occasions enabling her to leave the Louvre without anyone being aware of it. She had first been shown this by her father in law – Francis I who had often found it a most useful means of exit. It had served her well in the past to know what was being said by ordinary citizens rather than the fawning courtiers.

Finally emerging into an unused yard, and checking she was unobserved, she locked the small door behind her, and pulling the shawl further over her face, ventured out onto the street.

The city was relatively quiet with a morose, almost haunting atmosphere. Evidence of the massacre could be clearly seen; blood stained a great deal of the cobbled stone as well as walls and indeed, the smell of death pervaded the heavy air.

A number of dead bodies could still be found in the darkness of the narrow streets, the charred remains of some of the shops, wet now from the water used to extinguish them, gave evidence of the fury unleashed only a few nights before. As she neared one of the large markets, the crowds were thicker where people queued for the offerings of fruit wine, bread and vegetables.

Carts rumbled along with their usual loads of slaughtered pigs and geese; only some hours previously their load had been high with corpses transporting the slaughtered cadavers to the Seine where they had been thrown in to the blood-red water.

Catherine could not help but be amused as she watched a shocked, and still fearful, crowd of Catholic

Parisians that huddled in groups, discussing the massacre and their own part in it. Horrified as they doubtless were, life would go on as before; the shops must open for business as usual. The taverns would do well, as men and women met to exchange stories and shocking details of the carnage that had erupted around them.

Of course, it would be the Queen Mother who would be blamed for the terrors of the past few days of that she was certain. How much simpler it was to ease their conscience by blaming her for all of the ills that beset the capital, cursing her for virtually holding the knives, swords and heavy wooden clubs that had stabbed, or beaten to death so many. Any mothers in the crowd would surely understand the need to act when their children were in potential danger. No, they would blame her to assuage their own guilt. Better to heap the burden of their sins on the shoulders of the Catherine de Medici than admit their own crimes. She permitted herself a smile, but it was merely one of contempt. The people of France had never cared for her; whatever she did, they would never trust her – nor she them.

She shuffled along, leaning on her sturdy walking stick. The streets were infested with all manner of filth. Mice and other vermin scurried from one building to another, and many of the stray dogs that regularly roamed the streets, now lay under the sun, exhausted and sated from their recent banquet.

The very atmosphere was heavy and oppressive. Even as Catherine held her herb infused pomander to her nose she shuddered; here in the streets of Paris where the butchery had taken place, was an unnerving experience, even for one who had lived their life so close to danger.

As she ventured nearer to her destination, the streets narrowed, and the upper floors of the houses almost seemed to touch overhead, the smells from the trapped sewage made the stench almost unbearable, especially as the ferocious drying, rendered the putrid air heavy and oppressive.

She was relieved when some moments later, she emerged into a small market square where a group of minstrels attracted her attention. A small audience had gathered, and she was soon to learn why. The small band of musicians, were singing a song about – *herself.* She drew nearer, ensuring she was well disguised as the words rang out –

*"The vengeance of God made the dogs eat Jezebel,
But when Catherine dies – not even the dogs will
touch her carrion.*

When the minstrels had finished there was warm applause, and the song was repeated. Far from being enraged and offended at the insult aimed at her, Catherine laughed with the small crowd, and applauded as enthusiastically.

So, proof, if it had been needed, that Paris did indeed look upon her as the instigator of all ills. Well, it did not hurt for them to realise it. Was she not perhaps pleased that at least they were not indifferent to her?

Few noticed the small insignificant old woman that applauded with them before she passed on towards the sheltered area of the market, and again into a dark warren of streets, her walking stick tapping against the cobbled ground.

The Queen Mother stopped at a dirty crooked building where she rapped sharply on the wooden door with the end of her stick. The windows of the hovel were covered in dirt and grime, too green and moulded to see through the paint-work on the outside was dry and had flaked off. A single rusted holder with no hanging, dangled dangerously from just above the doorway.

A shuffle of feet could be heard on the other side of the door, and a bolt was drawn back before it was opened. Catherine had already sent word to the Ruggieri brothers that she would be calling on them, and they bowed low as she swept past them.

The interior of the first room she entered was far more furnished than one would have expected, at odds with the humble, run down exterior. A fire blazed in a small grate, its acrid smoke occasionally billowing out into the chamber. Though dark, the walls were partly covered by some large and very worn tapestries. The room had few other furnishings.

Two elaborately carved armchairs dominated the centre of the room where piles of books and scrolls lay scattered on the stone flooring. Of course, Catherine surmised, it would not be wise to draw any attention to the building, by appearing run down it was safer from prying eyes as well as the reputation these two had as sorcerers, feared for their magic as well as their association with their Italian benefactress. The brothers Lorenzo and Cosimo Ruggieri had long been in favour with the Queen Mother. As well as being Italian, they were masters of the dark arts, and possessed the gift of black magic, in which she had always taken such a keen interest.

They had held her favour, and as she had needed to consult them more often, she had moved them from their previous laboratory high up in a tower of the hated Castle of Chaumont, and installed them here in Paris, where they could enjoy the Queen Mother's patronage and protection.

Catherine cast a slightly disgusted eye over the two brothers, both of who wore long shabby robes and stained leather sandals.

Lorenzo, tall and gaunt with a sallow complexion, long greasy hair, a large nose and thin lips. His hands were gnarled and bony with long fingernails that were chipped and dirty. Cosimo was by comparison a much healthier figure although just as unattractive, with a wider face and full lips that seemed too big, and which he wiped frequently to remove the spittle that collected around its corners. A scar ran from his forehead and down his cheek. Like his brother, his hands were dirty and unkempt, two of his fingers were now merely stumps, a result of crime or punishment, Catherine did not know or care. It was their gift of foresight and the occult was important.

The brothers led the Queen Mother through to a further chamber that was used to carry out their work. The small windows offered very little light, and indeed, even that was extinguished when Lorenzo drew a wooden blind across it.

A worktable in the centre of the room was covered with all manner of jars and caskets, as well as a quill and some parchment. A small candle heated a glass jar of brown liquid. Beside it were a small pile of human remains a hand, a foot, and a small dish of eyeballs. Catherine smiled, the brothers had clearly made good use of the carrion available from the recent massacre. Bottles empty and full cluttered the shelves around the room a sickly sweet odour the product of the large cauldron that hung over a fire was slightly nauseating.

Large graphs with all manner of symbols and diagrams on them lined one wall, and a further stack of books and papers spilled over the edges of the table beneath, weighted down with a small skull. Beside that was a large wooden cupboard with an intricate grill inserted on one side.

Catherine seated herself at the table in a large ornate chair with threadbare upholstery, which she reluctantly accepted, and cast her eyes over the strange drawings.

Lorenzo began to extinguish the light of the many candles in the room while Cosimo pulled up two further seats onto which they sat, before unfolding a selection of the papers and scrolls and consigning the remaining sheets and books to the stone floor. The subdued lighting lent eeriness to the chamber with its many bottles and instruments casting large dramatic shapes against the covered walls.

The Queen Mother listened intently while the brothers explained their charts, Lorenzo running a long bony finger across some of the drawings and incantations, his overgrown fingernail occasionally tapping the paper at certain points as though to re-emphasise a particular item of importance.

"You see, here Madame my Queen?" Lorenzo indicated a deeply drawn line that ran over the width of one of the sheets that they poured over. "Here is the line of Valois, your sons and daughters; the line is strong until we reach the point at where the constellation of the stars crosses that line, and here the line becomes weaker, much weaker." Catherine stared at the sheet, these charts never failed to alarm or delight her. "But what does this prophesise Lorenzo?" The brothers looked from one to the other before Cosimo answered, "Death Madame" he stated soberly.

Catherine gasped slightly, "but whose death does your chart foresee? A King perhaps...."

".... Or a Queen" Lorenzo cut in "We must all be ready to die Madame. You will see here again that the stars cross this line here again, the line is weakening, your Majesty, and it must be made strong again." Catherine felt as though her fear and nerve would desert her, but she forced herself to be strong and looked up sharply at the brothers. "What you imply my friends strikes fear into me. You say that death will come to my family, or indeed myself. What must I do? What of a child? Do you see a child? A child born to my family that will be strong and healthy? The child my daughter-in-law now carries; it will be a boy I am certain of it."

The brothers shook their heads in unison. "The charts suggest there is a child, but it is of the female line and will not bear the crown of Kings." The Queen Mother stared at them for several moments as she realised what the charts signified. There must be a new King, one that was bold and brave and could bring about the change and strong governance that France needed.

Now more than ever, she realised how weak Charles was. Indeed, had he not tried to kill *her* in the throws of his madness? Charles and his Queen, the timid Elizabeth were expecting their first child within the next couple of months, but the young Queen's physicians who were instructed to report to Catherine regularly, confirmed that the Queen was often ill for days and that they did not foresee her giving birth to a healthy child. Alas, it seemed that fate would again play her a cruel lesson.

After some time when the brothers had relayed more of their charts and the messages they contained, attention was turned to the presence of the mass of ravens that had settled menacingly on the roof of the Louvre. As arranged some days before, one of the birds had been shot and its dead body delivered to the brothers.

Cosimo rose and picked up that same raven, its claws shrivelled and tight. One wing hung down, which Cosimo snapped off, and after deftly ripping the feathers out, he put the smallest ones on a small metal dish and taking a small bottle picked from one of the many on the surrounding shelves, he dribbled some of its dark mixture over the feathers into the dish.

After throwing the remainder of the dead creature to one side, he carefully carried the dish back to the table where the Queen Mother sat nervously anticipating the experiment. Cosimo then handed the dish towards his brother. Lorenzo muttered some incoherent whispers over it, before using one of his fingers and making stirrings and movements across the liquid, his fingernail scratching across the pewter.

All three of them stared into the dish, where the mixture bubbled slightly for a second or two before turning black as soot "What can you see?" the Queen Mother asked. Lorenzo nodded sagely, and Cosimo wiped the spittle foaming from the corner of his mouth, as he made small nods of comprehension. "The birds are the devil himself Majesty," Lorenzo said in his deep, Italian voice. "The devil lives in these birds. He comes to you as the spirit of those who have perished. But the images are unclear. The dead raven will offer few of its secrets. The great enemy is slain, but there will come another. Alas, the images dim and the face of this second danger will not reveal itself. It is too soon..."

Lorenzo appeared to slump as though exhausted by the revelation. Cosimo rose and fetched a pitcher of water and poured some into a goblet, which he held for his brother who drank deeply, revived by the refreshment.

Catherine was further alarmed at such news; she had believed Coligny her most mortal enemy, and that his death would have rid her of any threat to herself or her brood. She sat thoughtfully for some time before Lorenzo's voice again warned her. "The Royal palace will repel all evil, but there is another that must be avoided...the great Tuileries must never be your host my Queen" Catherine was puzzled by the warning; the Tuileries had been an enjoyable building project that she had begun back in 1564, and she had delighted in adding to its splendour over the past few years. To hear now that she must abandon it seemed odd. "Should you stay there only a single night, Madame, it will be your last."

The Queen Mother sighed again. Whilst insignificant compared to the proposed unknown threat, the warning to abandon her building projects had an unsettling effect. Obviously these were all warning signs. Dangers were everywhere – she must never forget it.

Although by now feeling sick at heart, she asked several more questions of the two Italians only stopping when a knock was heard. The brothers looked to each other with slight frowns on their faces. The knock was heard again. "You have a customer my friends," Catherine stated and she rose to leave. "I do not need to remind you that our dealings this day must remain confidential" Both brothers bowed low, and Cosimo wiped his mouth once again as he moved the table for her.

At that moment, the knock was heard again and this time a voice-a woman's voice could be clearly heard. "Monsieur Ruggieri, are you there?"

Catherine at once recognised the voice, surely that of Mademoiselle Clarice de Moulette, a young lady of Catherine's *"escardon volant."* The ladies of this small, but carefully chosen band were ladies who served the Queen Mother, her *"flying squadron"* as they were known. These ladies were a similar band of those once served Catherine's own late father-in-law, King Francis. He had the most beautiful ladies of his court work for him in a number of ways, befriending enemies or ambassadors for their secrets using their own feminine powers of seduction.

Of course many found their morals questionable, but they were treated respectfully, such was their close-ness to the Queen Mother. The women were Catherine's creatures, and she watched them carefully. All of them knew that the wealth and luxurious lifestyle they enjoyed were in jeopardy should they ever cross their mistress. So, it was puzzling to Catherine that the young woman should visit the Italian brothers; what reason had she to visit such a place as this?

Curiosity forced her to tell Lorenzo to answer the door and admit his visitor, whilst she instructed Cosimo to conceal her somewhere that she might hear all that was said but remain hidden. A small alcove would suit the purpose, and seating Catherine on a small stool, he moved a wooden panelled screen across in front of her. The small gaps between the panels also allowed her to see as well as hear all that was to transpire.

Clarice de Moulette felt nervous as she stood in the dark narrow street waiting for the door to be answered. All manner of atrocities had visited this city in the past few days, and she felt vulnerable, she was glad she had been able to persuade one of the palace guard to accompany her. He stood dutifully to one side as she knocked again.

Lorenzo opened the door and ushered his client into the back room. She was plainly dressed in a blue woollen gown with a cape and hood, which was almost certainly part of a disguise. The weather was still too humid to warrant such a heavy cloak. Her face wore no rouge nor was there paint on her lips, and yet she was most startlingly beautiful. Her eyes were of the brightest blue, and her small nose and high cheekbones completed her perfect olive coloured complexion; some strands of dark hair hung lightly on her forehead, which she nervously brushed away. The rest of her hair was pulled back severely and tied at the back. covered by a lace net.

The lady had visited the brothers once previously, and enquired about a particular remedy. The details were unimportant and indeed, most personal, and she would say no more than that.

Lorenzo regarded the young woman with interest, and wiped his mouth before smiling at her, revealing yellowing stumps of teeth. Clarice shivered, but straightened up in as dignified a pose as she could. She must show no nervousness. She knew of the Italian brothers, and had even seen them at court on one occasion. This was her second visit to their workshop, but she nevertheless felt even more nervous than she had previously. They in turn knew of her connection to the Queen Mother.

The reason for this type of potion was of no concern to the Italians, their remedies were procured from all manner of people for all manner of purposes. Cosimo felt certain however that the woman currently concealed behind the wooden panelled screen would surely love to hear more.

"This matter is of a most delicate kind – no?" he asked as Clarice watched the taller man concoct the mixture from a tiny flask, and taking a small purse from a pocket in his threadbare gown, carefully adding a brightly coloured powder. The mixture made a slight but audible hiss upon this addition and Clarice was distracted for a moment. "Why yes...oh, yes, most delicate." she eventually stammered, unable to take her eyes off the small bottle.

Lorenzo completed the mixture but looked at the woman sternly. "Madame, this potion is indeed, most efficacious, it will suit your purpose." He chuckled causing a rasping cough that sprung up and rattled in his throat. He hawked, and Clarice was almost overcome with a wave of nausea as he turned to one side and spat out a quantity of phlegm. "All secrets are safe with us Madame; we have a reputation for the utmost discretion."

Clarice gasped as Lorenzo leant closer to her. His foul breath and leering features made her feel ill as though she would faint and she could barely suppress a shudder. She went to take the small bottle, but Lorenzo gripped it tightly, his wild eyes remained fixed on her own. "Madame," he spoke with a stern tone, "you must be wary of the strength of this liquid. It need only to be given in a small quantity; two drops in a goblet of wine will easily suffice. Beware of its power Madame. We naturally take no responsibility for any careless misuse.... you have not yet told us why you should want such a potion as this?"

So smoothly did the man change from warning her to asking for the victim's name that she was again taken aback. Finally, she summoned up as much dignity and confidence as she could. "You are well paid so need no explanation."

The tall man released the bottle, arching one of his bushy eyebrows, without taking his piercing stare from the woman's face. He stroked the soft skin of her hand with his gnarled fingers as it slipped from his hand to hers. "Your custom is always welcome Madame."

Clarice quickly took a heavy purse of coins from inside her cloak, and handed it to the grasping, gnarled hand, and giving the brothers one final look of disgust, she threw open the small door and hurried out, the fragrance of lavender she wore hung in the air before blending into the prominent stifling aromas of the laboratory.

Once their customer had gone, both brothers looked at one another and chuckled, it was so often amusing to enjoy the effect they had on some of their clients. The brothers cast a glance of understanding at one another; it was not always necessary to tell their benefactress of every customer they had. Their reputation, evil or otherwise had brought them some considerable wealth, despite appearances. Certainly, they could not survive with just the Queen Mother's patronage.

It was Cosimo who, some moments later drew back the wooden screen that had concealed the Queen Mother who had seen and heard everything. "How very interesting my friends, your remedies are indeed sought after by many. The potion, it will do as the lady wishes?

"Madame," Lorenzo assured her, "the particular tincture I have prepared is indeed a most powerful love potion, as soon as we knew the recommendation came from yourself, we ensured that the remedy would not fail." Both brothers bowed low to her again.

The Queen Mother smiled, her eyes narrowing with a sinister look. "That would indeed be well, my friends, except that I did not send Mademoiselle Moulette to you. The lady, it would appear has acted alone – quite alone." She paused a moment, "Ah, let her enjoy her flirtations where she may, the girl is a timid thing, how some are emboldened by love."

After a moments pause, the Queen Mother, requested several potions and powders for her own personal closet, and covering her head again, dismissed the brothers with a wave of her hand, and stepped out into the warm, airless street.

◆

News of the massacre had soon reached the courts of Europe, and Catherine insisted on knowing from her ambassadors exactly how the news had been received, and the reaction it had provoked.

Philip of Spain finished reading the report from his own agent Diego de Zuniga and amazed his sombre, pious court by roaring with laughter, the first time that most of them could remember him ever doing so. He at

once summoned the French ambassador, and congratulated him as though he himself had slain the
heretics in Paris. Furthermore, the Spanish King
congratulated the French nation on their good fortune
in having such a bold King, who is so wisely advised by
his mother.

"Happy the mother who has such a son, happy the
son who has such a mother." Later, he wrote personally
to Catherine. *"The punishment of the Admiral and his
sect was indeed of such service, glory and honour to
God and universal benefit to all Christendom, that
to hear of it was the best and most cheerful news which
at present could come to me."*

♦

In the palace of Woodstock, Elizabeth Tudor finally
granted an audience to the French Ambassador La
Motte-Fénelon after having kept him waiting for more
than four days. When he entered the audience chamber,
he was to find the courtiers all attired in black clothes
for the deepest mourning. As he passed each person,
they turned their backs towards him – a grave insult.

Fénelon braced himself before the Queen. His sharp
green eyes looked quickly in every direction, his pointed
features tightened in his nervousness. The Queen did
not speak, and he therefore knelt before her for some
time before she uttered in a harsh voice, "Get up
Monsieur!"

The ambassador stretched out a hand that held
letters from the King and Queen Mother. Elizabeth
nodded to her secretary who leant over and took
them.

For some time after, Fénelon explained the situation that had pre-empted the massacre, justifying and reasoning that it had been inevitable.

"Do you tell me," the Queen eventually addressed him, her voice betraying the rising emotion she felt "that Catherine de Medici and her son cannot control a mob of fanatics? You suggest this was as a result of an exposed plot to kill the King, his mother and indeed all of the Royal family, and yet the retribution was visited on *all* the Huguenots in Paris, even the aged, women and babies?"

The Queen's normally pale features looked flushed, and her eyes flashed an icy glare that the Frenchman could not meet.

"Little man," she spoke with such disgust that the ambassador almost welcomed the dismissal. "When you write to your master the King, tell him that you found this court in mourning for the many Huguenots slaughtered during those evil hours. Remind him that he, and indeed the rest of his family will answer to a higher judge for this abuse."

Elizabeth rose, and swept straight past him without any further comment. The audience for this humiliation once again afforded the Frenchman the insult of turning their backs to him as he left the chamber as quickly as he could.

◆

An eerie silence fell over the Palace of the Louvre in the days following the massacre, as though the capital had had its feast of violence, and was only now taking in the reality of what had occurred.

Word reached Catherine and the King that the killings had not been confined to Paris; indeed, whilst the Queen Mother had advised her son to write to provincial governors outside the capital, it was to no avail. There had been violent outbreaks in many of the larger cities.

♦

Whilst the courts of Germany and England condemned the massacre in Paris, in the Vatican palace, Pope Gregory gathered his Cardinals together and imparted the good news from France before instructing a special medal to be struck to commemorate such an event. He invited them all to a mass in celebration, to give thanks to God for such divine deliverance.

The Venetian ambassador wrote after an audience with the Queen Mother, that Catherine had the appearance and bearing of someone who had just overcome a serious illness, and was indeed, looking at least ten years younger than before the massacre.

Catherine glowed in the praise from the Catholic courts, and sought to justify herself to the Protestant ones. She had been, she stated, horrified by the bloodshed and had blamed the enmity between the Guise and the Admiral for sparking off the killings that had from there got completely out of hand.

She had laughed heartily when her confidential secretary, Luc had intercepted a letter to the King from Ivan, Tsar of the Russians. Catherine was almost overcome with mirth to read of the Russian leader's indignation at the barbarity and excessive brutality of the recent massacre. Here was a man who had laid waste to a complete city, and whose own cruelty rightly earned the nickname *"The Terrible"*. Such irony caused the Queen Mother great amusement.

♦

A special envoy from Pope Gregory in Rome bowed low as he presented the King with the famed *"golden rose"* statuette. The priceless gift was bestowed only on those who rendered a great service to the Catholic church, and Gregory had felt moved to honour the French King following the destruction of so many heretics. The courtiers assembled, broke into light applause at such a gift bestowed by the pontiff.

Charles, his mother at his side as was usual, barely acknowledged the beautiful golden ornament, and apart from a brief, vacant attempt at a smile, he stared morosely at the floor.

Wisely sensing what, could so easily be interpreted as a snub to Rome, the King's brother Henri glanced at Catherine, and stepped in to marvel at the beauty of the object, questioning the envoy about the long history of the golden rose as well as extolling the virtues of the Pope and the high esteem in which he was held by all French Catholics.

The Queen Mother was moved at the sight of her favourite, stepping in to save the honour of his family while the King did nothing but slouch sullenly in his chair. Catherine could only pity him; there was little left of her son's sanity, and each day she felt him drift more and more into a world of his own.

The court that had for so many years been seen as the European centre of display and majesty; was becoming a nest of vipers, the court balls and entertainments that

Catherine and the court had delighted in were rarely held now, and the Queen Mother had heard how the Valois were insulted throughout the courts of Europe. Their pathetic, weak King who, it was felt, had lost complete control was now openly mocked, even in Paris itself.

Catherine sensed enemies as she had done so many times. All hope now rested on her darling Henri; only he could bring order from chaos. He would be strong where Charles had been weak; he would charm and enchant, where his elder brother had been dour and serious.

As she glanced at the King she had worked so hard to protect and nurture; she saw only a pathetic man with the weight of too much responsibility. Surely he would not live to see out another year. For a moment she thought back to her early years of marriage; how strange that she who had spent hours begging to be blessed with children, now sought to be rid of one of them.

Navarre and his cousin Condé endured the presentation with much rancour. They had been instructed by the Queen Mother that they must be in attendance, it must seem by all in the papal envoy's entourage that the Royal family were united, even those who had only recently returned to the true religion. Indeed, this must be the impression for many of Europe's ambassadors recently returning to Paris now that the killings had more or less ceased.

While Navarre could look on with feigned disinterest, his cousin found the occasion almost beyond endurance, and could not even be chivalrous to the fawning Clarice de Moulette, one of the most beautiful members of the Queen Mother's *escardon* who silently approached him.

A scent of lavender perfume, had already alerted the Prince, before with a touch on his arm, Condé turned to see the young woman who had recently been introduced to him. "Madame, forgive me" he began, slightly embarrassed at greeting her. He, who had been so recently wed to Marie, Princess of Clèves, should no longer act as a single man, and yet he was drawn to Clarice most strongly.

The Queen Mother had also noticed the two of them drift away from the crowd. It certainly did not appear that Condé was bewitched by the lady. Indeed, Catherine suppressed an urge to laugh aloud. The man was a religious zealot. He and his prim wife were too busy considering their immortal salvation to fall into a trap set by the lady of the *escardon*.

Nevertheless, the situation should be watched closely. Such was the perversity of the Queen Mother's domestic policy where the ladies of the *escardon* were concerned. Any private arrangement her ladies made without their mistress's permission would be closely watched.

♦

The Huguenot stronghold of La Rochelle had remained steadfast in its defiance of the crown. The port, on the western shore of the country had resisted attempts by the King and his mother to install a Catholic governor within the city.

By the end of the year, Catherine had insisted that the Catholic army should lay siege to the city. What had not been anticipated was the valiant resolution of the citizens to defend their stronghold. Vastly outnumbered though they were, the Rochellais fought with all their resources, even women and children were employed to throw large stones at their attackers as part of their spirited resistance.

With an army consisting of some Royalists, as well as the recently converted Navarre and his cousin, Condé, Henri, Duke of Anjou commanded the force sent to La Rochelle. Catherine had insisted that Navarre, Condé and the tiresome, Alençon, should accompany the army. Catherine naturally had spies within the camp, and with Alençon proving to be more and more troublesome; it was as well to monitor his movements. News had already reached her that her youngest son was forming a growing comradery with of Navarre. Animosity inevitably caused friction between the brothers as Alençon fumed and sulked that he had been given no command of his own.

Inside the Royal tent within the army camp, the main commanders joined Anjou as they poured over plans for a renewed attack against the city walls. Alençon languished in a seat, one leg over the arm, the other gently kicking at a small stool.

Henri could bear the truculence of his younger brother no longer, and proceeded to tease him about his new friendship with his brother in law.

Navarre had, with Condé already left the tent, yet several others had stayed, and now watched the ensuing scene with dismay as Henri deliberately goaded his irritable sibling. "I see you and our new brother have little interest in plans to end this defiance of the crown." Alençon continued to stare before him. Henri warmed to his theme as he stood before his brother. "What a provincial boor he is, I declare his manners disgust me." Anjou's dark eyes glittered with the light from one of the many torches that had been lit now that the night was drawing in.

Alençon merely sneered at him, "Forgive me brother," he said, "but I can only say I find him an admirable man, a pleasant refreshing change is welcome with such tedious company as this."

Henri waved his arms to signify inclusion of all those present "Why brother, you must surely jest. Is it fitting that a man with the manners and stench of a goat herder should seek our company? No, like you, he will tag along and revel in the praise that will be afforded us once we have dealt with the Rochellais. Like you, he will make little contribution to this task, preferring to wile away his time with the wanton sluts that he enjoys so much."

Alençon stood and gazed with his bleary eyes at his brother who stood before him and chuckled. "You should live to be such a man. With your jewels, your hair, the fine clothes that you adorn yourself with, the perfumes that you adorn. Ha! Why, even our sister Margot has fewer jewels and powders. You preen yourself brother like a catamite!"

The gasp within the tent was audible, and an excruciating silence descended upon the company. Both brothers were now standing facing one another although Henri was by far the taller. Alençon glared, his cheeks flushed and hot. Henri's dark eyes held an almost unfathomable depth, and sparkled with malice.

Whilst the company waited with bated breath, the flap of the tent moved and a servant holding a tray entered, completely unaware of what was transpiring. As he came to walk past Henri, the Prince put out an arm to stay him, even though his eyes continued to bore into the grey, dull face of his younger sibling.

"Wait!" he instructed, "Hand the wine jug to the Duke d'Alençon." The Duke accepted the jug whilst the servant stood to one side nervously awaiting dismissal. A smile played on Alençon's lips, at Henri's pathetic attempt at a conciliatory gesture. He was about to fill his own goblet, when his elder brother handed an empty goblet to the servant, and his voice rang out loudly. "See messieurs," he announced, putting an arm around the horrified page, "My valet has no wine, I have no wine! But, fear not, my brother will serve us himself! Quickly brother, see to our faithful servant, and all our friends. Let it not be said that you did nothing during this campaign. come, we are waiting!"

One or two of Henri's close circle of friends, did indeed drain their goblets, and held them out towards the Duke.

Alençon did not believe he had ever been angrier and more humiliated, and after a moment for the shock to be realised, he hurled the jug to the ground, its rich liquid spreading across the Turkish carpeting. He then grasped his dagger from his belt and made to lunge at the elder brother who still stood smiling at him.

At once, there were several who stood between the brothers. Indeed, it was the Duke d'Aumale, brother to the Duke of Guise, who grabbed Alençon's wrist until he could wrest the dagger from his hand. Henri still stood smiling at his brother, revelling in the scene he had just caused.

Alençon, having dropped his dagger, pulled away from d'Aumale's grasp and feeling the heat of humiliation, could do nothing else but storm from the tent, and out into the cool night air, the roars of laughter ringing in his ears.

♦

Back in the capital, the Queen Mother groaned as she read reports from her spies at the camp at La Rochelle about the tensions between her sons. Even after all this time, and all she had tried to teach them about strength being in unity, there were still scenes like this. Tensions could so easily escalate, and there were always those who would use such disharmony for their own ends. Few could be as easily won over as Alençon, she feared.

That aside, she was sure that the whole episode had been instigated by her younger son, he who had written several times to her as well as the King imploring them to give him command of something, rather than suffer the constant indignity of being merely a shadow in the camp. How could he possibly think that she would overrule anything her darling Henri had decided. He who was her all, her very spirit, would act nobly in all things. Yet, it could not be denied that Alençon would make a troublesome enemy; he had no real power as such, but his growing friendship with Navarre could yet cause a problem. As usual, she must be kept fully appraised of the unfolding situation.

As she sat and pondered these latest domestic developments, Catherine was aware that many members of the court had kept a distance from her, indeed, several of the ladies of her *escardon* had gathered together, whispering and looking at their mistress with concern. The Queen Mother called to one of them, Louise de la Florin. "What gossip is this that has you all cackling like a group of hens?" she demanded. "Quickly girl, I do not like secrets." The chamber was silent as the young woman licked her dry lips nervously. She was a vivacious, handsome young woman with a flawless complexion and large brown eyes, whom Catherine liked, and advanced as she had almost all of her maids of honour. Louise swallowed, and at last spoke up. "Madame, it is the recent book that has been distributed throughout Paris. The author should be shamed and punished for such treason as this."

Catherine cast her gaze at the woman, her large dark eyes narrowed suspiciously. "What treachery is this?" she demanded. Louise turned to the other ladies, motioning them to give her the book they had been looking at. One of the other ladies handed to her a small book that Louise in turn passed to the Queen Mother. Having done so, she backed away nervously.

The Queen Mother took the crudely printed papers, that could not conceivably be called a book so much as a pamphlet, and began to read.

The title of the work "The Life of Saint Catherine" immediately attracted her attention. The ladies of the *escardon* waited for the torrent of fury – but it did not come; indeed, the Queen Mother suddenly gave way to great gusts of laughter, such as her ladies seldom heard. Louise approached apprehensively, as the tears began to spring from Catherine eyes.

The publication Catherine had soon realised was an ironic title that purported to be a brief character study of the Queen Mother herself; in it were detailed the crimes and schemes of Catherine de Medici from the time she had first arrived in France, to the latest horror in Paris, all deviously planned by the devil's own disciple – the Queen Mother. Eventually, Catherine was so overcome with mirth, that she had to put the book to one side.

Gradually, the ladies felt it safe to approach their mistress, who dabbed at her tears with her lace handkerchief. "Ah, my dears," she eventually spoke "a most amusing book, the author has laid many atrocities at my feet has he not? But do not think that I for one moment am concerned. How like Paris to lay the infamy of its own lust for blood at the feet of a poor mother, how easy to cast the blame at my feet. It is a burden I must carry. My only disappointment is that so much has been left out, what a much finer volume would this have been had the authors come to me first, I could have told them so much more!" And so saying she began to laugh again.

At one side of the chamber, the ageing Cardinal of Lorraine laid a hand on the arm of his servant Montague. "I too have read this work," he said "and yet while there are certainly injustices within it, I know something of the subject, and although Huguenot writings are certainly not the soundest, I would have to say on this occasion they can be said to have hit the bulls-eye of their target."

♦

The Queen Mother opened her eyes with a slow flicker. She could see only Cavriani as he leaned over her wiping the sweat from her forehead and down to her neck. How strange that she had never noticed how old he was, she could not recall ever knowing. She found it suddenly amusing that his head was quite bald, and yet his nostrils and his ears sprouted tufts of wiry hair.

He smiled down at her suddenly, and in that passing moment, she saw what she had never seen in any of the looks that people had ever given her – pity! The observation made her suddenly sad, and she felt a hot tear run down her cheek, she who had never exercised pity, and had certainly never received any.

It was indeed strange, that although she told herself she would wipe the tear away, her arm did not move, she looked down at it – motionless.

The brief period of lucidity would not last, and even as she thought of it, the lights and shapes began to change again.Henri, her beloved son, ah, that darling boy! She saw him again, his blurred image came again into view, the silence gave way to voices, and excitement......yes, there was joy and excitement. News.... important news. She could see him now, King.... a throne at last.................!

◆

News had reached the court that Sigismund, the King of Poland had died. Both Catherine and the Charles were thus thrown into a flurry of political activity.

Despite Henri's reluctance to accept the nomination as the heir to the now vacant throne, Catherine had sent one of her most trusted envoys, Jean de Monluc, Bishop of Valence to Poland to argue in favour of her darling son. The Queen Mother had made it her life's work to promote her children in any way she could, and this was surely an opportunity to obtain a crown of his own for her beloved Henri.

Whilst acknowledging that the massacre in Paris had certainly not helped the Valois cause, Monluc was nonetheless a wily and persuasive diplomat. The Poles enjoyed an almost unique position in that they enjoyed a religious harmony within their realm, and would, as a result be wary of electing a religious zealot. However, it was the assurances from the French King that he would not only pay Poland's debts with the wealthy income from the Anjou estates, but that he would offer them military support against the constant threat from Russia, should it be necessary.

As many as forty thousand Polish nobles assembled to consider the candidates and decide on their next King. Meanwhile, Charles instructed Henri and the other generals at La Rochelle to begin negotiations and end the costly siege that had been nothing short of a humiliating disaster.

In the moments before they would leave the antechamber for the arrival ceremony of the Polish delegation, the Queen Mother sat and considered her two sons. Charles made a sorry elder brother to her darling Henri. The King looked so much older than his twenty-three years. His hair had started to thin, and his pallor was grey and drawn. His large eyes appeared sunken and dull, the dark rings beneath them bore witness to his growing insomnia. The horror of the St Bartholomew massacre haunted him in his waking hours and made restful sleep almost impossible. He would spend many hours in the night stalking the long corridors of the palace looking for traces of blood on walls or floors, sometimes on his hands and knees crawling, muttering incoherently. At such times now, only his mistress, Marie and his faithful Nanon could soothe him, and persuade him back to his bed.

For any mother, his suffering would be heart-breaking; but Catherine could do no more for him. Life had taught this Queen that there was nothing to be gained by regretting what was past and done, life must move on, and to survive, one must regret nothing, there must be no steps backwards. As she watched her eldest son now, she saw him not as the King, but as an old man that could do nothing further to keep his dynasty alive and secure their future.

Henri, by comparison had flourished since news had been brought that he was, bar an official ceremony, King of Poland. Now, as he paraded in front of large mirror, dictating alterations on his new wardrobe, every turn seemed to boast to his elder brother, "Here I stand, a King as a King should be." His personal tailor, a small and busy fellow, fussed around the fashionable Prince.

Catherine felt such a sense of pride as she watched him preparing for the ceremonies, studying himself, inspecting the small drop-pearl earing, or his finely-shaped eyebrows. Here was her son, her pride and joy who was now to finally be a King, her maternal ambition for him almost realised. She recalled her nervous anticipation when the vote of the Polish nobility was being decided. One of her own dwarves, Krassowski, was from that same country, and the Queen Mother had lost no time in sending him to use the contacts he had in that land to tell her which way the vote would go; indeed, she would have to know whether more monetary help might be made, although on her insistence, and Charles's eagerness to be rid of his haughty, arrogant sibling, the treasury was all but empty.

It had been late one evening when Krassowski had insisted on being taken to the Queen Mother, and where he had fallen to his knees with the joyous news that he "saluted the mother of the new King of Poland!"

How she had warmly embraced her son, who was finally a King in his own right, albeit of a nation about which he was still perturbed. He had heard rumours, he told his mother. "I am led to believe they indulge in barbarity, and little gaiety. Indeed, there are no masques, mock hunts, no ballets, balls or feasts of any kind unless they are for religious occasions." Catherine had embraced him, which he secretly disliked and assured him, that he could suggest the introduction of such pastimes as those he would miss. "Are you not their King, eh?" he would smile at her, and she would again stroke the side of his face. "That is good, my most dazzling of Kings. Remember this too my son" now she kept her voice low. "Your absence will only be temporary, for much as it pains me as his mother to say so, your brother grows weaker by the day I will send for you as soon as his end draws near."

Catherine felt no guilt over this, Charles was the past, and Henri the future. He will be King, and his mother will be there beside him, together they would remedy all ills.

It was sometime later that the Polish delegates finally arrived at the Louvre to be presented with their new King, and he to them. Each side must have found the presentation a surprising experience.

The deafening noise of fire from a thousand or more harquebusiers heralded the arrival of the Polish envoys. The tall men, dressed in rich long-flowing robes of gold and silver brocade with fur-trimmed necks, wide leather boots, and carrying jewel encrusted swords at their sides. The men themselves were mostly tall with hard features, slender yet muscular and with their heads shaved to the nape of their neck, and their beards long and straight. The men of the court found this of particular interest, contrasting as it did with the French fashion of keeping the small beard short and manicured.

The Duke was certainly a dazzling looking spectacle, and this was just the impression that he had intended to give to the delegation. Henri stood straight and elegant, his somewhat haughty features gave a certain nobility to his face. His mouth, straight and red slightly raised at each corner as if fighting amusement. His aquiline nose, prominent in all of the Valois, gave a symmetry to his soft angelic complexion, his skin of alabaster colour was flawless. His firm chin was dusted with a short cropped beard, exquisitely shaped in the latest fashion.

It was, however, his eyes that one was drawn to; like his mother's, they were almost black in colour, and stared out, glittering, – one could never tell from pleasure or displeasure, yet his long, dark lashes, almost gave them an innocent appeal. Their almost sinister gaze could entrap as well as discern. Many who associated with him, chose to do so because he was not only heir to the throne, but also the favourite son of his mother.

Yet, it was easy to be drawn to him, such was his magnetism. Also from his mother, had he inherited the most beautiful hands, delicately shaped, with long fingers that were set off by the most valuable rings. His slender figure was perfectly proportioned, and whilst his mother chose to ignore it as nothing more than a sensitive side to his nature, he was most assuredly effeminate.

The Polish delegation were somewhat transfixed by their new King. His appearance was quite dazzling to them, and it seemed almost at once that they talked of leaving as soon as protocol allowed, so that they might then display this new and fascinating man to his new subjects.

The days of ceremonies, meetings and ratifying details came to an end sooner than the new King of Poland had hoped, and now, faced with the reality of his departure for the stark, and reportedly inhospitable place, Henri began to delay proceedings by feigning illness, or claiming that his entourage had not been properly selected, or that he was unhappy at certain details not having been discussed properly.

To his mother, he ranted and railed about the injustice of this impending doom. How could he say goodbye to the refinement, luxury and intrigues of the French court for the provincial severity of the Polish one. Moreover, he was expected to take a wife, the intended bride was none other than the sister of the deceased King Sigismund. Here though, Henri complained to his mother, that she and Charles had agreed to everything in order for him to be gone from their sight.

For Catherine this was a cruel charge; even her favourite, he who was now so close to fulfilling all she had wished and worked for, even he was not satisfied. Yes, she remonstrated with a somewhat over-dramatic son, the vacant throne that they both coveted was the throne of France, but while Charles lived there was little they could do. Both were fully aware that Charles was determined to have Henri out of his sight, and would agree to anything in order to see him depart the realm.

Finally, there was to be Henri's official entry into Paris as the new King of Poland. Following this, Catherine had personally organised an official celebration to take place at her magnificent Tuileries Palace.

Named after the tile works that had once occupied the site, the deeply superstitious Queen Mother had heeded warnings from the Ruggieri brothers about her fate should she even spend one night in the fabulously ornate residence. She nevertheless continued to use the palace for celebrations and official events.

The elaborate creation that Catherine had commissioned in 1564, was composed of several long buildings, and exquisite gardens were being still being laid and formed. The famed architect, Philip de l'Orme worked under instruction from the Queen Mother herself.

Here then, the palace was used to entertain the soon to depart Polish delegation, many of whom were still intrigued at the sight of their new sovereign, with his vast array of jewels, and a rather disturbing penchant for dressing in a manner more suited to a woman.

Catherine's *escardon* were present, and the entire court were decked out in sumptuous gowns and richly jewelled doublets. All manner of French cuisine was beautifully adorned with elaborate decoration, and followed course after course.

The Queen Mother watched the players in this drama carefully. Her spies were all around, and anything of note would make its way back to her. Her eyes cautiously followed Alençon; Margot too was not to be left to her own devices. Catherine picked out Navarre and Condé, and there was Madame Clarice who had drawn Condé to one side of the great state room. With the knowledge that the lady was in possession of a potion that would surely be used to ensnare the Prince, Catherine would need to give her a warning that it was not wise to indulge in any personal dalliance when one worked for the Queen Mother. Arrangements for the departure of her beloved had kept her occupied, and she must remember not to lose sight of the many dangers within her midst.

♦

The Queen of Navarre studied herself in the ornate Venetian mirror that one of her ladies in waiting held before her, and nodded her approval at the reflection.

Her husband the King was expected at any moment, and she was indifferent to whether he found her pleasing or not, there was no denying that a compliment, even from him was nevertheless, accepted. Indeed, she had often thought, that maybe she would remind him that he was now married to a beautiful Princess, and yet chose to fornicate with the lowest serving wenches and maids, even those in the Royal palace itself. Naturally, of course, his advances towards her were met with horror and refusal, nothing had changed there; she still found herself repulsed by him.

Navarre and she were as different as it was possible to be. She was fastidious in her hygiene, and personal attire, sometimes spending many hours of indecision over which of her many gowns to wear to a ball. Her black hair must shine, her lips must be rouged, and her eyes must sparkle like the stars in the sky. Her perfumes were various, but always subtle. The Queen Mother's own perfumer, Monsieur Rene, would create the most delicate fragrances, especially for the Queen of Navarre.

Navarre, by comparison, was less than scrupulously hygienic. Margot closed her eyes suddenly and shuddered at the thought of his unwashed body too close to her own; his skin was rough and smelled of sweat, leather and wine. His hair, continually unkempt and dirty, and his breath was almost unbearable He would often be seen in the same clothes for as long as a week at a time, even then there was no thought or imagination in how he should look, it was as if he merely told his valets to hand him anything they liked.

His one exception to his unwashed, unkempt manner was the day of their wedding, when he had somehow managed to arrive for the occasion dressed cleanly and appropriately, his beard trimmed and his hair washed. For some days at least, he was not wholly repellent to her, but even then, she did only as much as duty demanded. Navarre wore the suit for several days following the nuptials. Many ladies of the court appeared to find it quite becoming.

How often, as much as she hated herself for thinking it, did she not make the obvious comparison to the Duke of Guise? His appearance was always clean and elegant, yet masculine.

His hair.........She shook herself from her reverie; she would not allow herself to think of him, even though her heart secretly yearned to be his. The time since she had last kissed him seemed a lifetime ago; they had duties to their families, and those they had learned, must be paramount. Guise, she was sure still felt something for her, and while she chose not to notice him at all, she felt his eyes upon her. She dared not return the gaze.

Margot dismissed these thoughts, no good could come of them. She instead diverted her attention back to her boorish husband, and there could be no denying that whilst as a husband he was totally unsuitable, she found him a happy and often amusing company. He was one of the few who could match her temperament and cunning; she was not in the least deceived that behind the careless laughter, and riotous behaviour, beat a noble heart, and a quick brain. It was almost impossible to dislike him, such was his carefree manner. His eyes missed nothing, his thoughts may be hidden deep, but there was the instinct of a survivor, one who would do what, for the moment, must be done, and look to better times.

A third guest was expected to join the King and his Queen; Margot's younger brother – Alençon. While she allowed her servants to arrange the table and ensure that there was plenty of wine; she allowed herself some time to consider her younger sibling and how best she might stop him from getting himself banished from the realm, or worse!

News had reached the Queen Mother and the King that the Duke d'Alençon was causing trouble and unrest. He had argued constantly with Anjou during the infamous siege at La Rochelle, keeping counsel with only Navarre and Condé, both of whom resented their inclusion. Alençon had been more than happy to fan the smouldering flames of discontent; indeed, reports suggested that the Prince had gone as far as to try and gather enough malcontents to break away and form a new army.

Having failed in that attempt, he had then hatched a plot whereby he, accompanied by Navarre and Condé would escape from the army and keep as far away from the French court as possible. That particular plot had been uncovered by Catherine's own spies, although the secret could not be kept for long. It was, as a result, rumoured that the only person unaware of it was King Charles himself.

All this gave Margot plenty to consider as she welcomed her husband, who spent more time than was necessary thanking the female servant that had let him into the chamber. Margot shot the girl a fierce look, and the King was quickly ushered towards his wife. He lingered over her delicate hand for some moments, and when he looked up at her, it was with that familiar glint in his eyes. "Madame, my Queen" he proffered with a sweeping bow. "You are enchanting as ever Margot," he said "you appear as radiant as the sun, the goddess of...."

Margot interrupted, his mockery of the gentlemen courtiers with a wave of dismissal. "You are a just a provincial boar." she told him "Such fine manners are of no meaning when spoken by you, they are only coarsened, please be seated."

Navarre laughed loudly, and pulled his chair closer to that of his wife. "Ah, Margot, should you not welcome me with open arms, and let me warm your bed at night instead of denying yourself the pleasure a real Bernais can give you?"

The Queen glared at him, "You have had my welcome, and my bed is warm enough, it certainly has no need of a Bernais oaf to warm it." Navarre threw back his head and roared with laughter. "Ah, yes," he teased, "I am told that you have lovers, Madame, fine young gallants who would replace me as the most important man in your life!"

"Ha!" Margot started, her eyes already beginning to blaze. "And you who shun the company of your Royal wife for the bed of countless harlots, there are a score of men more important in my life before you!"

The pair of them sat silent for a moment as though the repartee had been merely a means of introduction to one another. "You still have your innocent poetic court boys."

"And you your harlots, although I understand that Charlotte de Suave has become passionate about you. You are fortunate indeed, she is certainly a most beautiful companion."

Navarre laughed," Ah, surely Margot, you will not play the outraged wife and demand that the lady is banished from the court?"

Now it was Margot who chuckled "Your affairs are of no interest to me, you must surely know that. I will say however, that I hope you realise that she is my mother's creature."

"I know she serves the Queen Mother it is true, but there could surely be no further interest in me, I am turned Catholic, and a prisoner of the King. Everything I do is known to all. Charlotte is a delight – I do not believe for one moment that she loves me, it matters not." Navarre smiled at his wife, she was far from perfect herself. He settled himself into a chair opposite her, resting his boots on the arm of hers.

"Yet, I now hear that a gentleman serving your brother Alençon, is known to be in favour with you at present. Joseph Boniface de la Mole. A pretty boy, yet he seems like a sound enough chap. Ah, how beautiful you are when you are embarrassed." Margot blushed furiously; it was true that she had recently been in the company of the handsome Comte, and was enjoying a liaison with him.

The two of them looked up at the sound of the outer chamber door being opened, and into the room marched the Duke of Alençon, He bowed stiffly to his sister before kissing her on each of her rouged cheeks, and nodded at Navarre, who threw one leg over the arm of his seat swinging it childishly as he took a long draft from his wine, holding it out to be refilled by another charming young attendant who he was sure he had not noticed on his arrival.

Alençon slumped into the chair opposite Navarre, and took the jug of wine from the servant once it had been filled. In two mouthfuls he had drained the glass and proceeded to refill it as much as he could. before putting the jug down and sighing deeply.

Margot allowed him a moment, before she berated him. "What could you have been thinking brother, to consider escaping from the army at La Rochelle? You must surely have been aware that our mother has spies throughout the armies of the King? I thank God that you were warned in time before you could commit a greater folly."

For once, Navarre agreed with his wife, and was more serious than usual as he added his voice of reason. "Margot is right, my friend," he said. "I long for freedom from this court as much as you do, but this is not to be hastily arranged."

Alençon had risen from his chair and now paced the room. "I can no longer bear this stifling court with its arrogance and duplicity, I am treated no better that a common foot soldier, even our mother's dwarves fare better. No, I will be rid of this place as soon as I can, with you and Condé or by myself. I will start a new faction, I will give a voice to those who opposed to this court, and its rulers. The devil take them all!"

Margot sniffed with disapproval, "Have a care," she warned, "Your folly will lead you to an uglier prison than this." Our mother will soon learn of your loose words. Remember, that you are already seen as a rallying figure. Your Royal status is seen as a legitimate head for those dispirited at their treatment since the massacre."

There was an interruption, as the chamber door opened and Margot's attendant slipped into the room making her way to her mistress and whispering in some urgency. Margot dismissed the lady, and turned to her brother. "Our mother is on her way here. Quick brother, you must not be found. Your presence will arouse suspicion. Here, take this door to my bed chamber, and hide yourself lest she decides to enter there." Alençon allowed himself to be ushered away, while Margot sought to make the scene as innocent as possible, although she was aware that presenting her mother with a picture of marital bliss would almost certainly meet with derision.

No sooner had her brother been unceremoniously pushed out of one chamber than the Queen Mother, followed closely by one of her trusted dwarves, swept into the room. Her eyes were met with her daughter and new husband apparently enjoying a convivial game of chess.

Navarre stood respectfully, and Margot inclined her head to her mother. Catherine allowed the moment to linger whilst she took in the scene before her, missing nothing as she cast her dark eyes around the room. Finally, she broke into a wide smile before seating herself. Both mother and daughter noticed the third chair that had been drawn up by the fire in between where husband and wife now sat. Catherine said nothing, and Margot desperately prepared an explanation should she need one.

Catherine waved the dwarf away in dismissal and settled into the recently vacated chair.

"I rejoice in seeing your attention to your wife, my son." she smiled tightly at Navarre. "Indeed I had begun to think, as have others, that the two of you were most unsuited. Yet I joyfully find that the two of you are of an accord, and that there is harmony between you. Ah, that your mother, whom I still weep for, could only have lived to see your joy of one another." Navarre's smile tightened at the mention of his mother, he still refused to believe that Catherine had been the cause of her death.

However, more and more, he had begun to view the Queen Mother as most of the French court did; as a dangerous adversary. He had heard it often said hat she was synonymous with the dark arts, and poison just one of many means she had employed over the years to rid herself of any physical threat to either herself or her children.

"I am told, my son," she continued "that you have often failed to follow mass as directed. Allowing your servants to interrupt the service with messages that you then insist need urgent response. This is folly, my son, the King and I had believed these reports to be scurrilous, and yet your priest himself complains to me that he is exasperated at what to do with you."

Navarre turned to her with an expression of complete innocence. "Madame, I am still learning to embrace the faith as you would have me do. I am but a sinner. I will endeavour to apply myself more fully. Forgive my......."

Catherine held her hand up towards him "There is nothing you need say to me in your defence, my son, but speak to your priest, inform him that you will apply yourself more diligently than has previously been the case." She breathed in as though drawing strength and seemingly dismissing the subject. She then turned her attention to her daughter. "I hear my child, that you have taken pity on your younger brother, and are often in his company these days." When Margot merely smiled at her mother Catherine continued, "You do not deny that you are often seen in his company?" Margot looked spiritedly at her mother. "Should I need such a denial? I am his sister; why would I not enjoy his company? Are we not brother and..."

Catherine looked cross "Have a care, girl" she interrupted "I have a heavy hand for insolence." Margot and her mother stared hard at one another for several seconds, but it was Margot's eyes that dropped first; almost frightened to become drawn into her mother's deep black stare.

When the Queen Mother continued, she was calm again. "I mention this, child, because as you are no doubt aware both he and your dear husband here had a mind to leave the Royal armies at La Rochelle and desert the court with the intention of rallying a mob army together, to indeed become the focal point for all dissidents."

Navarre glanced quickly at his wife. The statement had been made to her, and yet in that brief moment of her hesitation, he spoke. "Alas Madame, you have been misinformed by your agents. The boy is wild of course, and given to fanciful ideas, but his words were in jest, indeed he was heavily in his cups when he uttered the throwaway words about leaving the army."

Catherine looked to her daughter who now spoke up. "Indeed, it is as my husband says, these are no more than the rambling words after too much wine, and the frustration of the ongoing siege."

The Queen Mother arched one eyebrow and her placid, heavy face broke into a quick and false smile. "Of course, daughter, you will assure your brother when you find him, who knows where he could be hiding from his mother, tell him that all will be well whilst the preparations for your older brother's departure. I want none of his sulking and tantrums. Tell him to bear in mind that I have worked long and hard to bring about Henri's election to the throne of Poland, and I will show him no tolerance if he plays me for a fool!"

Catherine smiled again, rising to her feet. "Well, my dears, it warms my heart that we have had this little discussion. I know that I am at fault, that all these recent talks with the Polish deputation have taken up much of my time, but, never fear, I am well informed." So saying, Catherine took up her walking cane and made for the chamber door. "I suggest, my dear," she said to Margot that your brother is not kept away from his wine for too long, he is seemingly unable to function without it."

Margot looked again at the table, quietly cursing at the full third goblet, but when she looked up to make some excuse, her mother had silently left.

Navarre, allowed himself a chuckle at the farce of the previous few minutes, and lazily moved his chair backwards and banged his booted foot loudly on the adjoining door before declaring,

"It's alright monsieur, the danger is past, you can come out of hiding!" Margot sighed at her husband's behaviour; would he never grow up or take anything seriously? She grimaced as she too relaxed in her chair, letting out a sigh of released tension once her mother had left. Why did she, even now a married woman, indeed a Queen herself, feel so nervous in her mother's company? It had always been so; theirs had never been an easy relationship. Something in Margot irked her mother she was certain, but what, she did not know. All she did know was that, try as she might, the two of them could not enjoy the company of each other – always there was suspicion between them. She watched her brother saunter into the room, kicking aside Navarre's outstretched leg, and taking up the tell-tale goblet of wine.

Margot shook her head at her brother "You do know of course that you cannot avoid her forever" she stated to him" Alençon sighed deeply, and shut his eyes as though the action would go away if he did not consider it.

Navarre seemed to be enjoying the whole episode, he leaned over and tweaked the Duke by one of his ears. "You will be sent to your chamber for being a naughty boy!" he said laughingly. His infantile gesture, did however lighten the mood somewhat. Alençon knocked his hand away, but grinned; even Margot could not help but smile.

"Remember, brother," she nevertheless warned, "should anything happen to Henri in that barbarous country, you are premier Prince of the realm; the most important man second only to the King himself. It would be sheer folly to follow too bold a path away from the court. Even the most reliable of informants are not always to be trusted; and however secretive they may think they are, our mother is aware of all of them.

Her own spy network is quite quite unbelievable. Nothing is secret."

Alençon huffed, "and yet still I am treated like a child, a man of no consequence; just there to be humiliated and taunted by Henri and ignored by Charles. There is nothing for me here – nothing. Yet, they will all listen to me after...."

He got no further before before Navarre tipped the contents of his goblet straight into the Prince's lap. "Mon Dieu!" Navarre attempted a sincere apology, and drew out Alençon's own handkerchief from the top of his doublet, proceeding to dab at the wet red stain. Strange, thought Margot, that although her brother had been about to fly into a rage, something passed between the two men; something understood by them that she felt was being kept from her. "Listen to you after what?" she spoke straight to her brother. Alençon paused, but it was Navarre who with consummate ease, spoke for him. "After the reopening of talks to marry the boy here to the Queen of England."

"Ah yes," Margot stated, "I have heard that there is again talk of pressing your suit to Elizabeth Tudor, that must surely give you some hope, you will be away from the French court you hate so much, and as King of England, you would certainly not be ignored then."

Navarre let out a loud bark of laughter. "Indeed, my boy," he clapped Alençon hard on the back as he rose to pour himself some more wine. "And I've heard that she is a fine woman, ripe for the marriage bed. Why reports say that she is most comely. Apart obviously from the rotting, black teeth, the foul breath that none dare tell her about. Oh, and the withered breasts of course..." Alençon could not help but laugh.

"I'll never be married off to that old baggage, let no-one say I will. Mother will again order and we must obey, but she will not find me so willing to dance to that particular tune."

Margot sniffed with impatience. "You will get nowhere if you act with defiance. Be seen at least to be open to the idea, present few problems to be overcome. You do not know what is held in the future. Would King of England really not be worth the indignity of bedding an older woman?"

She glanced at her husband who leant against the wall. "One sometimes has to do what must be done, however distasteful that may be." Navarre made a sweeping bow to his wife and laughed again. Margot shrugged and chose to ignore the barb. Strange, that she found she could actually enjoy his company, even though of course, they were an ill-matched couple.

The young Queen of Navarre had enjoyed several dalliances since her affair with the Duke of Guise; she was even now, uncertain if she would ever love any man in the same way again. Of course, her closest attendants and friends who had been aware of the relationship, had assured her that in time, her heart would mend, and she would meet another. Yet what had happened was that she was now married off to this provincial bore, for no matter how civil they chose to be to one another, the facts spoke for themselves – this was not a marriage of equals as far as she was concerned.

Her husband was a scruffy and uncultured man, who looked to bed any woman who smiled at him, although that was not a prerequisite to a liaison with the popular young King. Navarre was more than happy to overlook the fact that his lust might not be reciprocated. He laughed at life, and his role in it; very little appeared to anger him, or frighten him. Yet, Margot had at times seen another side to him; he could be serious when the occasion called for it, and she knew too that he offered a front to most people.

His valour and bravery were beyond question, and those lazy eyes of his missed very little.

It was indeed, because of his popularity that he enjoyed the friendship of so many – and who in this court could boast the same?

Time, however was pressing, and Margot was entertaining again later, the handsome Comte that she knew served her young brother. Indeed, the young man had a prominent role in the early discussions with the English Queen, that Alençon had railed against. How much Alençon knew of the affair she was unsure, but it mattered little; Joseph Boniface de la Mole was an extremely favourable companion, and she was enjoying some entertaining evenings in his company.

One of which would be this very evening if she could only get the now slightly inebriated pair of men out of her apartments. Margot caught the eye of her attendant as she entered to bring in more wine as her brother had demanded. A knowing glance was all that was needed. The lady left the chamber, but returned in some agitation a moment later. "Well, Marianne what is it?" she enquired innocently. "the Queen Mother Madame, she is coming this way again."

Alençon almost chocked on his drink in his eagerness to stand and bow to his sister. "Madame, my sister," he uttered uncertainly, "I must be out of here when she comes......yes, out of here, shhh." He held a finger to his lips. Navarre slapped him playfully on his back, nearly knocking the shorter man over. "Come my brother," he stated "let us be gone before we are trapped." He laughingly bent to kiss the hand of his wife. "Madame, I hope you and...whoever... enjoy a convivial evening."

Margot felt herself blush deeply as the Bernais King winked knowingly at her, before putting a strong supporting arm over Alençon's shoulder, and stumbling out of the room amidst giggles and, for Navarre, a chance to smile at the quite charming Marianne, who closed the chamber door behind them.

Margot smiled at the young attendant, "Bless you Marianne. Heaven only knows how long we would have had them here. Luckily the thought of a second visit by my mother is enough to clear the room." She sighed and stretched in her chair as she looked forward to the evening ahead.

♦

The ladies of the Queen Mother's *escardon volant,* sat with their mistress during a much welcome respite from all the latest balls, galas and entertainments that had been put on for the Polish delegation. The envoys from Cracow were enjoying some time to view the city. That in itself had necessitated cleaning up the dirty streets, the open markets that sold the most exquisite fare, but were surrounded by filth. The open drains throughout the city centre must be cleared, and for a while at least, Paris would be seen as a clean, sweet-smelling capital of culture and opulence. Such was the Queen Mother's policy of presenting a façade that would fool all but the most cynical visitors.

The morning was dull and gloomy, and outside a sharp breeze served as a chilly reminder that autumn would soon give way to winter. From the window of the chamber, the Queen Mother gazed out over the view of Paris. She watched with satisfaction as the lavish entourage of the Polish delegation could be seen being led in a large cavalcade of dignitaries. It was good that Henri entertained them all himself. He would undoubtedly find the whole morning tiring, and would no doubt complain of a headache and fatigue and take to his bed. Charles had remonstrated with his mother that Henri's excuses were both undignified and dis-respectful. What could she do? She would visit him, but invariably she would justify such occurrences He had been under a great strain, she would argue. His behaviour was certainly a talking point with the Polish nobles, and yet, they seemed to be so enchanted by this young man, bedecked in costly jewels, earrings, bracelets, his long slender fingers almost covered in costly rings.

Whenever she thought about all she had done to secure a throne for her darling, she was saddened also that he would be leaving her and travelling so far away. Nevertheless, it was important that she did not let other issues continue to distract her; there was much to consider.

Catherine pondered on her brief visit to Margot the day before. She could not help but chuckle at the sight of the couple seemingly so innocently employed. Never was there such an ill-matched pair, and yet, there was some connection between them, she was sure. It certainly was not physical; she was certain of that. The thought of their wedding night and the repulsion she was sure that Margot had felt, had privately caused the Queen Mother great amusement.

The extra – marital affairs that both conducted however were something that must be watched; Margot in particular, let her heart rule her head, and was seldom without a love interest. One had to be so careful, she constantly warned her youngest daughter; there were plenty of men at the court that would be happy to lead Margot astray, and unfortunately, Margot seemed to be quite happy to be corrupted.

Catherine had done her best to be aware of what all her offspring were doing. With her eldest daughter, Claude, the Duchesse of Lorraine, she had far less to concern herself with. Claude was, by comparison to her siblings, a gentle natured woman; she was a dutiful wife and mother, and generally preferred to stay away from the court as much as possible.

No, it was the rest that were a constant cause of mistrust; and with a rather cruel irony, her children were never so dangerous than when they were on harmonious terms with one another. The only affection they all shared was towards Claude. Other than that – Charles appeared to tolerate Margot, but could not stand the sight of either of his two brothers. Henri, thought his elder brother and King a pathetic imbecile, and as time went on, was finding it harder and harder to disguise. He did not appear to have the slightest regard for Alençon at all, and made no secret of his distrust of Margot. Alençon hated them all without exception. Whichever could be useful to him was abided, and when their attention waned, he gave them no more consideration. That left Margot – and it was this child that Catherine believed could be almost more dangerous than the rest; she had wit, cunning and a sharp brain, and her brothers ignored her at their peril. Like the others, she felt merely pity for Charles, yet such pity upset her rather than disgusted her.

Margot bore no great affection for Henri, but then would someone like her, attracted to virile men, feel at ease with a brother who consulted with her only on matters of fashion and make up? It appeared that, at present anyway, Margot's familial affection had been cast on Alençon. She saw in him the sadness of being the youngest in a brood that enjoyed honour and recognition. It was as though Margot would provide the encouragement that his mother should bestow on him. Now there was a situation that must be closely watched. There was no way of knowing how much unrest could potentially be caused by that pair.

Of course Alençon had been with Margot and Navarre, when she had called at her daughter's chamber. It amused Catherine to imagine her youngest son being forced into a wardrobe or pushed under the bed. Naturally, she could have searched the chamber next door, but it had not mattered. Had she wanted to know the extent of their affection, Margot's evasiveness told her all she needed to know.

As troubling as all this was, Catherine wondered why Margot's latest lover, Joseph Boniface de la Mole, continually cropped up in her thoughts. She knew little of him despite him being one of the deputation who had acted on her son's behalf during the last abortive attempts to marry him off to the English Queen. She recalled noticing him at the time. He was a Huguenot, and had been in Alençon's service some time; but something alerted Catherine's instinct that there was maybe more to him than the handsome, genial gallant he appeared to be.

With these thoughts in mind, it was maybe time to look more closely at these recent developments, la Mole may well be as benign as he appeared, but only time and sharp observance would tell.

♦

With great pomp and ceremony, the Royal party escorting Henri, King of Poland eventually reached the moment when farewells must be made. Catherine felt she would be overcome with emotion as she embraced her favourite son. She had worked long and hard to bring this moment about, and yet she could not bear to see him go.

Charles, who had been persuaded, to virtually bankrupt the Kingdom in order to have his brother successfully installed in Poland, would willingly have paid twice the amount. Never had he disliked his brother more than he did watching him cling to their mother, weeping uncontrollably. Henri had used every stalling tactic to delay the moment he must depart, but even he could see that he would have to go. Catherine had quietly whispered to him, "Leave, my son, you will not be there long."

As the party made the grand procession on to Poland, Catherine finally broke down, and had to be helped by her ladies, sobbing loudly that she could not bear to see him go.

Charles looked upon the scene with some emotion. Not for his scheming brother, who would have done anything to cause him personal anxiety. It was their mother's distress that caused him to fight back tears of his own. He would not have those present believe that his tears were for his brother.

Finally, he rose from where he had sat watching the moving scene. A spasm of coughing overtook him, one of many in the past few days. He held his handkerchief to his mouth, while he waved away all offers of help. When he finally drew the cloth from his mouth, it was red with blood.

◆

Charlotte de Suave was still a great beauty, and had served the Queen Mother well. Her pale skin and beautiful dark eyes had captivated so many. Indeed, her beauty was undiminished from the young girl that Catherine had used to ensnare Antoine de Bourbon. In recent months, she had been a great success as the mistress of Margot's husband – the King of Navarre.

The lady, however, had never really provided Catherine with any information that was not already court gossip, but it had not hurt to have one of her own *petit band* within the intimate circle of her son in law. Now however, it was a rather different task that the Queen Mother had in mind for Charlotte.

Catherine called the woman to her. "Sit here, my dear," she invited. Charlotte curtseyed, and nervously sat on a stool beside the Queen Mother. On her other side sat her dwarf and fool, known as *Petit Chaton* who sat and played with a small cage containing a tiny brown mouse, that she fed with little pieces of cheese from a silver bowl.

"Now, Charlotte, I have a new duty I wish you to carry out." Charlotte licked her dry lips and swallowed nervously. "Ah child," the Queen Mother continued, "Is it not the case that the King of Navarre showers you with gifts and seemingly adores you, wicked Charlotte, stealing all the men's hearts at court."

"I am ever at your service Madame" Charlotte replied with downcast eyes.

"How goes your affair with the Bernais King? Charlotte confirmed reports that had reached Catherine that Navarre was quite captivated by the countess, buying her costly gifts. Catherine noticed the younger woman's discomfort, and heaped further embarrassment on her by enquiring about their more intimate relations. Charlotte hated this aspect of the Queen Mother's interrogation; it was acutely uncomfortable to discuss such things.

Nevertheless, it was unwise to withhold such details, one never knew who else may be watching.

Catherine laughed aloud at some of the revelations. Although she was rarely shocked, she professed to be scandalized at such behaviour.

Having satisfied herself that the seduction of her son in law had been a complete success, she now set out a new task. Charlotte felt her stomach sink at the Queen Mother's new instruction. "But Madame," she eventually stammered "The Duke of Alençon.... he is your son."

Catherine looked coldly at the woman's manner. "I am well aware of who he is, girl. You are to bring an end to your affair with the King of Navarre in favour of the Duke d'Alençon, or is the exchange of a King for a mere Duke too much of a come-down for you?"

If there was one man at the court that Charlotte had nothing but repulsion for it was the Queen Mother's youngest son. Aside from the fact that an attack of smallpox as a child had badly marked and pitted his face, he was surly and a bore. He had a reputation for what one of his mistresses had described to Charlotte as "unnatural". His vices were well known.

Catherine had now lost all pretence of good nature and spoke coldly. "It is enough that I can still find your services useful. My instructions I believe are clear enough, you are to end the relationship with the King of Navarre and pay attention to my son, the Duke! Bring me word that this matter is dealt with. Remember, my child, that I will know if my instructions are not carried out successfully."

Catherine dismissed the woman and sat back to consider her next move. Charlotte had caused some concern by leaving the chamber quickly, and all eyes turned to the Queen Mother.

Clarice de Moulette was another lady that seemed to surround herself with Huguenot gentlemen, many of which served either the King of Navarre, the Prince of Condé, and even the Duke d'Alençon. Yet, it did not appear as though the young woman enjoyed the company of these men for their looks and courtly charm. Their conversations seemed to be more intense than merely honeyed words and admiring glances.

It mattered little to the Queen Mother that Clarice was not a religious fanatic like many of her attendants. Her lack of interest in religion was not to be held against her; indeed, hadn't Catherine herself always been regarded as having a very benign attitude to religious observance?

However, news reached the Queen Mother that clandestine meetings were held, some away from the court. Earnest speech, hushed voices and darting eyes, all suggested that the situation must be closely followed. Nevertheless, she felt an urge to laugh aloud – it certainly did not appear that Clarice was enjoying the results of the potion the Ruggieri had sold her.

It seemed that her fellow countrymen were not averse to selling a 'false mixture.' Catherine was unconcerned. She had to smile as she wondered, would the young woman realise that the mixture was nothing more than a harmless tonic, a remedy for an aching gut, or even an emetic that would render the poor innocent victim helpless enduring a looseness of his bowels?

Even though the misery of some others never failed to keep her amused, there was still an atmosphere of tension and now, as much as ever, her spies and informants must be ever vigilant.

◆

Dark, forbidding clouds had settled over Paris. Though the hour was late, the city still hummed with activity. Inns and taverns were still illuminated, and patrons sat carousing and discussing the current events. The guards posted on some of the main streets were a token presence rather than a threatening one, and few worried about them.

Meanwhile, in a dark and filthy backstreet, the Ruggieri brothers were entertaining two gentlemen of the Duke of Alençon's service. Joseph Boniface de la Mole was a tall broad-shouldered young man with dark hair and bright green eyes, His well proportioned features were of perfect symmetry, and his beard worn short and neatly trimmed. He was, to many females at the French court, considered to be the most beautiful of men, but with a rugged, masculine countenance.

His companion, Annibal, Comte de Coconas was the most eloquent of men. Of a similar height to his comrade, he was fairer of complexion, pale blue eyes, and thin lips. His own beard was less defined, being merely few wisps of blond that barely covered the end of his chin. These two Huguenot courtiers served the Duke of Alençon, but, in the case of la Mole, the Duke was not the only member of the Royal family whose favour he enjoyed.

Joseph was the current lover and favourite of Margot, Queen of Navarre. Whilst such an attachment was fraught with danger and consequence, he claimed that he was completely bewitched by the sister of the King. Good fortune and careful planning had afforded Coconas the welcome attention of Margot's close friend and confidante, the Duchesse of Nevers.

This particular evening, they had sought the assistance of the Queen Mother's faithful necromancers. The four men had been in earnest conversation, sat by the dim light of a candle of fat, that omitted a strong odour but spluttered against the draughts of wind that seemed to swirl around the room.

Cosimo Ruggieri held the glittering gaze of la Mole as he handed over a small carefully wrapped packaged, no more that five inches in length. La Mole exchanged a quick glance at his companion, nodding to him. At this signal, Coconas reached into his tunic and drew out a large velvet bag which he then placed on the table, before sliding it across to Cosimo, who satisfied weighed the bag in his hand before appearing satisfied that the contents were correct, and slipping the purse into one of the wide pockets of his old tattered robes. He had, during this slick mechanical manoeuvre, not taken his gaze from the courtiers face; their eyes almost locked in a battle of dominance. Eventually, Joseph looked away.

It was the other brother, Lorenzo, who eventually broke the silence and, whilst he and his brother had kept up an almost constant stream of deference to the courtiers, he now spoke with almost threatening severity. "Remember, messieurs, that none of this business is to be traced back to our humble door. The discovery of what we now give you is treason if discovered." He cast la Mole a wide smile, displaying his decayed grey teeth, "And even the highest in the land will not be able to save you!"

La Mole shot the brother a sharp look. "You have been paid well, the price was to include an assurance of your own discretion. It is well known that you are not without allies at court, and enjoy the favours of the most powerful in the land." Cosimo arched an eyebrow at this, but then smiled and nodded.

A sudden spit from the candle broke the uncomfortable silence, and the two courtiers rose to leave. They gave the brothers a last look, drawing their cloaks around them as they turned swiftly out of the dark building and away into the night.

♦

News had reached the King and Queen Mother, whilst the court was staying at Saint Germain, that an audacious plan had been hatched for King of Navarre and Alençon to flee the court and to move northwards at the head of a Huguenot army.

Catherine had been horrified at this betrayal by her own son, but was not entirely surprised by it. Alençon was a weak boy still, nothing would change that, indeed, his indecision would always be his worst enemy. Navarre, in his turn was, she believed, far too lazy to have conceived such a plan.

The Queen Mother's spies had informed her that the Prince and Navarre were to have been met by a Captain who would help them to get out of the palace. Apparently, a misunderstanding about the timing of their deliverance had sent Alençon into a confused panic, and he lost all nerve for the plan.

Instead, he had raced to his mother, and confessed everything. Whilst Charles, who had again been taken ill, was happy to let his mother discover the full facts, and those guilty of its conception, had raged at this fraternal betrayal.

Alençon presented himself before his mother and brother, and cut a desperate and contrite figure. It was, he said a foolish plan, that he had felt honour-bound to defend himself against the Guises, his plans had been to strike at that family rather than his own. He had been misunderstood, he claimed. His foolish action resulted from his holding no formal position in the Kingdom. Surely, with Henri his brother being elected King of Poland, Alençon should have been conferred with the office of Lieutenant General of the Kingdom and yet, he was overlooked. Catherine had sighed with exasperation, to imagine that he had the bearing and discipline for such a role.

Alençon's pouting and posturing amused Navarre, who stood lazily to one side with an ever present smile on his face, but with very little to say. When examined by Catherine as to his motives, he merely stated his wish to be free of the court. "Forgive me, Madame," he stated, "if I yearn for the freedom that should be afforded every honest man. I long to return to my own people, to my sister, my Kingdom."

Catherine discussed these troubles with Charles and some of his ministers, several of whom wanted Alençon and Navarre charged with treason. Catherine was inwardly horrified at the very thought, and well into the night, she tortured the King that he could not treat his brother so. Eventually, Charles agreed that the two men were to be held under even stricter bounds at court. One issue he was most adamant about was that, even though he be the King's brother, Alençon would not be created Lieutenant General of France.

Catherine watched as the King staggered to his feet, his attendants immediately at his side, helping him as they had to, for he was weakening by the day. At only twenty-three, his youth had all but gone, and some days he did not even rise from his bed, and yet often he would be overcome with energy, and spend a whole morning at his forge, or hunting until exhaustion took him and he had to be carried back in a litter.

Catherine was certain that Margot had had a hand in Navarre and her son's plans. She was certainly devious enough, and without doubt, more courageous and clever than all three of her brothers. Had Salic law not prevented females from women from ascending the French throne, Margot would have the makings of a worthy ruler. That did indeed make her a clever adversary, and now the Queen Mother set her informants to be her eyes and ears, all must be watched and heard – treachery was everywhere.

The departure of Henri for Poland, and the constant threat of more trouble from her son-in-law and youngest son had wearied Catherine, and she departed on a visit to her estate at the Chateau of Chenonceau. Here, she spent quiet days, walking in the picturesque gardens, with the beautiful lush and tastefully styled lawns.

The Queen Mother came upon a small seat at the base of a large tree at the far end of the gardens, so she sat and enjoyed the rare opportunity of a refection on recent events, yet she seemed unable to concentrate on the present, and instead found herself considering days gone by.

How strange, she thought, that she should come to this place, when she had any number of other retreats she could have retired to. Chenonceau had of course, been given as a gift to Catherine's greatest enemy, Diane de Poitiers in the days when she had been the mistress of the late King Henri Deux. How the Italian Queen had hated her rival, although of course, she had been able to hide the resentment of being herself offered the dark, imposing Chateau de Chaumont. No sooner had Henri died so tragically, than his widow had banished Diane from court, after instructing her to arrange to vacate the beautiful chateau in exchange for that of Chaumont.

Catherine was surprised at how she could still smile in satisfaction at an episode from so long ago. Diane had been dead for many years, yet she could still feel hatred for her. Nevertheless, in her thoughts, she realised that she was no more loved by her children than she had been by their father. The fact saddened her, but she could not consider that, she must move forward – never look back.

It suddenly amused her to consider how her daughter Margot would have dealt with such a situation; ah, but Margot was different, she loved spontaneously, passionately. She could endure Navarre's affairs by having her own. They were agreed that their marriage could never be a conventional one.

She considered her children, how would their lives have been different had their father lived? Would they have been happier, or would they have been foolish, arrogant, spiteful and passionate? All those emotions that were so evident in her brood. A smile played upon her lips as she considered how they would have fared at the hard school of the Medici. How would they have endured the tyrannical discipline of Clarissa Strozzi?

It suddenly occurred to her then, that she had not thought of her stern, hard kinswoman for many years. How she had hated her. She recalled too, the fear of those terrible days of her orphaned childhood, when the mob had rebelled against the Medici in Florence, and the young heiress had been lowered out of a window inside a stout wicker basket, and smuggled out of the city, away from those that would not have pitied her youth, but merely slaughtered her.

From there of course, she had been taken to the nuns of the Santa-Maria Annuziate della Murate. The imposing convent would at last be a refuge for a while. How strange that now, as her age advanced, she should give any thought to those harsh years again.

She shook herself from her reverie. The cool wind was becoming fiercer now, and the sky looked grey and ominous. She drew her light cloak around her tightly as she made her way back into the warmth of the chateau. Once back in her apartments however, she was greeted with urgent dispatches from Paris – a further plot had been revealed.

Within the hour, the black carriage of the Queen Mother tore through the countryside. Catherine's nerves were tingling, but her mouth was dry at the thought of this latest plot. It appeared that it was a further plan to aid both the King of Navarre and the Duke of Alençon. Catherine re-read the details, and angrily cast the letters to one side.

This now, of course, threw her plans into total disarray. How could she and the King, for all the use he was, move forward with the sound policies that were needed if the Valois were to rule? Her determination to maintain a stable Kingdom for her darling to return to; her plans all jeopardised because of a stupid boy, and a wily young fox, who may well yet have the final laugh.

Once she arrived back at the court, she hurried to the chamber of the King. No sooner had she dismissed his servants, than she vented her frustration on the sick and drawn man. "Well, here is a pretty state of affairs, my son. Don't just sit and stare at me, Charles, we must make plans! Are the ringleaders even rounded up?"

Her son turned tired red eyes towards her. He look-ed dazed and so very worn out, his thinning hair fell in straggled strands across his face. His wide mouth sagged and a sliver of spit hung from his bottom lip. His shoulders were even more hunched than when his mother had last seen him. After giving her son one of her most withering looks, she called for his advisers; the council must be immediately convened.

Further details of the planned uprising were emerging, and it was reported that the men who had concocted this daring and audacious plot had been Joseph da la Mole and his constant companion, Coconas. There would be consequences for all concerned.

A force of Huguenots, that had the sanction of both the King of Navarre as well as Alençon, was to invade Normandy. The man at the head of this force was to be a name familiar to Catherine, and for whom she bore unadulterated hatred, – Gabriel, Count de Montgomery. This had been the same man who had, so many years before, jousted with Catherine's beloved husband and been the cause of his most tragic and painful end. At the time, Henri Deux had, in a brief moment of lucidity, ordered that no blame should be levelled at the Count, who had been doing as his King had instructed.

Catherine however, bore her grudges deeply. It mattered not how it was done, but she had promised herself that one day, she would be the instrument of Montgomery's downfall.

After the jousting accident, the Count had fled to England and had lived his life in constant anxiety that the Medici Queen would arrange an unfortunate accident, or he would choke on a goblet of wine, or even feel cold steel in his back. He had almost cried with joy when he had been informed that a personal plea from Catherine to Elizabeth to extradite him back to France had been refused.

His torture would have been less if he had presented himself at Catherine's feet and let her vent her hatred against him. As it was, he lived in constant fear, and only now had he become embroiled with Navarre and Alençon, and had played a large part in these recent events. As he waited for further information and instruction, Montgomery had a sick feeling that all was not well.

♦

In the charming privacy of her bedchamber, Margot remonstrated with her lover. The Queen of Navarre's pale features, were coloured as much from their love making as her rising temper. She wore her hair unpinned, its gloss off-set against the lights from the many candles that lent some intimacy to the room.

She had risen from her bed, and had slipped on a light gown that accentuated her lithe figure and generous curves. Her scent was as bewitching as her body, and Joseph, Comte de la Mole wanted to further enjoy both. His Royal mistress stood tantalisingly close, but still out of reach. "Why," she demanded "must you involve yourself in these intrigues? Why would you risk everything you enjoy merely to serve my brother?"

Joseph sat up, running both his hands through his dark hair. He was exasperated. He and Margot had spent a great deal of the evening arguing over the soundness of a plot that he had devised with his friend Coconas. The plan was an audacious one, and it was true, the element of risk was great, but so were the rewards. Alençon would climb higher than others had believed possible, and the star of Joseph, Comte de la Mole would rise with him.

"Your brother has been good to me," he spoke softly after an uncomfortable silence. "He is a good man, Margot. Your family slight him, mock him for his appearance; but he is a gentle spirit I believe. He will never be a King of England, despite all the foolish play-acting. He may never be King of France, and yet..."

Margot sat on the bed beside him, and took his handsome face between both her soft hands, "He will never be anything if you pursue this course," she said earnestly. "This plan will fail, and you will be sacrificed before my mother and brother look to punish a man who does not have the wit to realise that he will never be smart enough to outwit our mother. This plot to assist the Huguenots is wild and ill-conceived, how can you hope to succeed?"

"Have you yourself not aided our scheme?" Joseph retaliated. "You have known about your brother's plans as well as those of the King, your husband."

Margot opened her mouth to speak, but no words came and she rose and stood staring at the dying embers in the large fireplace. Joseph rose from the bed and stood behind her wrapping his strong arms around her and kissing the nape of her neck. She eased herself reluctantly away and turned to him. "How can I let you hasten your destruction when...." she paused, collecting herself and controlling her fragile emotions "When I have fallen in love with you?" There, she had said it; the words she thought she would never utter again after her juvenile passion for Henry of Guise. He faced her, wiping a solitary tear from her cheek, her sparkling eyes glittered from the candlelight. "I could never live with myself if I let your brother down, sometimes honour must come before all else."

Margot smiled sadly as she looked up at his face. He hadn't said he in turn loved her. Perhaps that was too soon for him, perhaps he didn't feel it, maybe that was why he found it so easy to risk all. "I beg you to take care, my love," she implored as he pulled her towards him. Joseph buried his face in her black hair, breathing in its fresh smell, "I will always take care, my Queen," he spoke softly as he slid the gown from Margot's shoulders, letting it fall to the ground.

The lovers had slept for barely an hour, when a loud banging on the chamber door roused them both. Joseph, with instinct, reached for his sword, as a harsh voice called to him through the oak door. "Monsieur de la Mole, you are to surrender in the name of our most gracious Majesty the King!"

Joseph had already leapt naked from the warm bed, and was struggling to clothe himself, while Margot knelt on the bed, clutching the silk sheet around her, too shocked for a moment to take in what was happening. The banging continued. "Monsieur!" the command came again. "You are to surrender immediately, or we will break down the door!"

Margot had now come to her senses and dressed herself hastily in her light gown. She could stall the guards, but it would be impossible for Joseph to escape; he had already looked hastily at the window, an impossible drop, and too far from any ledges to hope he could reach one. Their eyes met suddenly, a realisation that try as she may, it was pointless to prolong the inevitable. Joseph de la Mole would not be found under a bed, or in his mistress's closet. He put down the sword he had taken up, and motioned to Margot to unbolt the chamber door.

Within moments guards burst in to the chamber and secured Joseph's wrists. He stared at her right up until the soldiers escorted him from the room. Both knew that they would never see each other again. The escort marched steadily away, as Margot sank to the floor and wept.

♦

The Duke of Alençon paced his apartments, desperate for news of the plot that had been uncovered. Surely now, he could expect no mercy from his brother. He cursed both Charles and their mother. Any other mother would be expected to protect her sons, even the one she did not love. And why in God's name did Charles not simply die, as many had believed that he would at any moment?

His manservant brought him wine, which he gulped down greedily, its strong, heady flavour giving him some measure of fortification. He held the goblet out to be refilled. He drew the drink to his lips when the banging came, loud and startling. "Your Royal Highness, you are bidden to attend his Majesty, the King!" Alençon nodded to his manservant, who opened the chamber door, as the waiting guards stepped aside.

The King of Navarre was serious for once; in the hours since la Mole had been taken, he had sought out Margot. Despite their obviously unsuitable marriage, they had been able to at least be allies. He was unkempt, loud, brash, but impossible to dislike – and Margot had certainly tried to hate him. However, her hatred never lasted long, especially with him who would always laugh at misfortune and boast that nothing was so bad that he could not extricate himself. Now, however, there was a problem, and in his uncertainty, he had turned to the one person who could help him.

Margot, for all her romantic dreams, was a realist. She knew enough of her husband and her brother's plotting to be drawn into the affair. She also knew that Joseph was a prime instigator of this new plot. However far it had gone, she knew it would take a miracle to save him now. Her beautiful lover, she wept every time she recalled the look he had given her as he had been led away, she suspected all was lost.

Nevertheless, she could probably help Navarre. One look at his eyes, and she saw that he was at this moment, no longer the clown, but a man desperate to save himself. She quickly made him sit. "Take the pen, I'm assuming you can write?" she said waspishly "We must write your argument, and let us pray, to whatever God it is that Huguenots pray to, that it saves your life."

♦

Rene de Birague was a wily, astute man, with much cunning, and a strict observer of the rule of law. An Italian patrician, he had been a long standing councillor to more than one King. He was not tall, and yet he had a noble bearing,

A bald head, and a thin, drawn face held dull humourless eyes. His long nose ended in a point, and his thin, stern mouth gave him an evil countenance. Now, as he sought to advise the King and Queen Mother on how best to act in light of what he described as "delicate and alarming new evidence," Catherine was reminded of the man's rather annoying habit of coughing lightly after every few words.

"Your Majesties," he began, walking around, his head bowed as though choosing each word carefully. "I have advised you that I would act most severely with both the Duke and the King of Navarre, ahem!"

"No!" Catherine stated sharply, before laying a hand gently on the King's bony shoulder "What, I mean monsieur, is that the King and I would act with caution in this matter, you and those who work for you have uncovered this plot to free these two, but there can be no Royal blood spilt. Nay, monsieur, I know that you would argue severe measures, but that has never been my policy with my son."

Birague arched one of his thin eyebrows at the statement, but Catherine continued as she seated herself on a chair next to Charles. "To proclaim both Navarre and my youngest son traitors would be a rash and foolish step, we have culprits enough surely, tell us of them."

Birague coughed, bowing his head slightly in deference. "There are indeed others embroiled in this recent plot, ahem! We know already of course that Montgomery had been at the head of a force of Huguenots that were to invade Normandy, ahem..! The names are familiar to us all, the brothers, Montmorency, Turenne...ahem!"

"What of the Prince of Condé?" Catherine asked.

"Alas Madame, reports reach me confirming that the Prince escaped our men at Picardy, ahem...it is believed that he has fled to Germany." Birague cleared his throat, and seemed slightly nervous. "Which brings us...ahem! to the main protagonists in the drama – the Comtes de la Mole and Coconas."

"They have surely confessed?" Catherine snapped.

"Indeed they have, Madame," the Chancellor answered her, "and, ahem!, while searching la Mole's belongings, an alarming discovery has been made."

Catherine leaned forward, and Charles fixed the man with a steely gaze. "A discovery?" The King spoke softly but sternly "What type of discovery?"

Birague made a few strangled noises with his throat and continued. "I ordered the house where the two traitors slept to be searched and found this." He then produced a small package, about five inches in length, and wrapped carefully in parchment.

Birague had his Royal master's full attention as he proceeded to undo the parcel, revealing a small wax doll. Catherine recoiled as though the object would bite her. The reason for her horror was not only that a small pin had been embedded in the doll, but that the figure wore a small gold crown upon the head.

Charles was the first to speak, a confused look on his vacant, honest face, as he looked first to the Chancellor and then to his mother. "What does this mean Rene? Is it meant to resemble me? I... I don't understand – what?"

Catherine recovered within moments of her initial shock "Of course it's meant to be you! There has been some devilry here! It must be destroyed... burn it !.. Burn it!"

Birague hastily re-wrapped the wax figure and placed it in the pocket of his robe.

The Queen Mother was visibly shaken, desperately trying to comprehend the consequences of this macabre discovery. "You have questioned la Mole?" she asked with as much composure as she could muster.

"We have, Madame," the Chancellor confirmed. He sniffed with an air of derision; "he claims that it is not an image of the King, but..."

Charles let out a sigh, visibly relieved, but his mother looked sternly at Birague, waiting for his conclusion.

"The accused says that the image is meant to represent the Queen of Navarre." Catherine breathed in through her nose, desperate to quell the growing anxiety she felt as the minister continued. "He claims that he was desperate for Queen Marguerite to be enamoured of him, and that he had the doll formed by......ahem!"

The Queen Mother held her breath – "the Italian necromancer Ruggieri." Birague could not help but look to Catherine whose mouth was set in a hard line, her large eyes seemed set to burst from her fleshy face.

The Chancellor had to privately admire the ease with which the Queen Mother stifled her anxiety and retreated to her more familiar persona.

"Have the Ruggieri brothers brought in," she commanded. "I will question them myself first...nay Chancellor, do not seek to overrule me on this matter. It weighs on a distraught mother as well as a Queen. Bring them after it has fallen dark."

The Chancellor bowed in acquiescence. "And the King of Navarre and the Duke? Surely now, you would see the need to imprison these men, this plan runs deep and dangerous."

Catherine interrupted Charles as he leant forward to speak. She again placed a hand on his shoulder, leaning slightly on it so that her son was in no doubt that he was to be silent. "This will be decided by his Majesty and myself, Chancellor, you will leave us now."

The Chancellor looked slightly annoyed at such a curt dismissal, but he bowed stiffly and turned to leave, clearing his throat quite vigorously. Catherine stayed him as he reached the door.

"Birague, the gentlemen la Mole and Coconas are to feel the full weight of the King's wrath, there is to be no mercy." Birague nodded again and left the room.

♦

The King was exhausted after the activity of the day, and Catherine left him to rest while she considered these latest alarming developments.

The Ruggieri brothers would feel the full force of her fury; how could they have been so foolish as to become involved in such a deception as this? Why had they not sought to bring it to her attention? She had understood that their services were enjoyed by many at the court for various reasons, but a wax image wearing a crown? It was infuriating, given that all knew of her interest in the occult.

Of course it was widely known that she had a great interest in the astral movements, and even black magic, as it was rumoured. Nevertheless, as furious as she was with her fellow Italians, she could not afford to make enemies of them – they knew too much. No, she must deal with the problem of their punishment. Of course it must be seen that there was no favouritism towards these fellow countrymen.

Navarre and Alençon were a different issue. As keen as she knew Charles was to be rid of his brother, he was fond of Margot's husband, and one could not be guiltier than the other. Navarre had already made his own representation by a cleverly worded document denying any knowledge of all that had occurred.

When Catherine had read the statement, she again heard Margot's clever words, for surely Navarre himself could not have compiled such a document by himself. No, she must make certain that both the foolish men were constrained as much as possible, away from the court, Vincennes perhaps. She would ensure that they were more closely confined.

If there was to be any good to have come from the episode, it was the capture of Montgomery. The Queen Mother had sworn to be the means of his death for many years, and so now at last, she would have her revenge.

It was several days later that Catherine de Medici looked into the eyes of the man who had-so far as she was concerned – effectively, murdered her husband. He had not looked towards her as she had hoped; she wanted him to see her smile, for hers to be the last face he saw before he was decapitated.

Margot and her close friend, the Duchesse of Nevers held one another's hand as the men they loved were executed. Margot barely recognised the beautiful and gallant man to whom she had lost her heart. Two soldiers had to carry his broken body to the executioner; his face was a mass of bruises, blood caked one side of his face, his legs and arms broken, his perfect nose shattered and disfigured. Margot wept openly, desperate for the executioner to have the job finished and end her lover's misery.

Margot shut her eyes as the axe fell on that slender neck, and hot tears ran down her cheeks.

◆

In his purpose-built forge in the seclusion of a cell down in the dungeons of the palace, the King of France laboured heavily at the glowing red-hot furnace. He would hammer furiously at whatever metal object he had at the anvil with no specific creation in mind but would adopt an almost hypnotic stare as he then plunged it into a large barrel of water causing a loud sustained hiss and a brief billow of steam. This was no blacksmith's with the traditional smells of leather and burning and a powerfully strong man wielding a large hammer, pummelling the metal into a well made item. The heat from the forge down under the low ceiling made the air stifling and almost unbearable.

Nevertheless, Charles had adopted this almost excessive exercise as a way of channelling the rage and violence he felt inside himself at times of tension and stress. When the demons that plagued him became too much, he would storm out and work at the labour until he was exhausted and would sometimes need to be carried back inside. His white, puny body thin and gaunt, stripped to the waist, gleaming with sweat.

His attendants would look pityingly at their King. An actual blacksmith would be in attendance to ensure that no unnecessary risks were taken, although, in truth, none would dare approach him. His ever attentive hounds would lay nearby, watching him dutifully. Occasionally, they would rise restlessly, turn and relax again with a deep sigh from a cooler distance, but never moving too far away from their master.

Eventually, too exhausted, Charles staggered away from the fiery heat, almost collapsing from the punishing ordeal. His attendants helped him to a seat nearby, offering cooling water to slake his furious thirst.

He pushed away his servants. "Do not attend me, leave me be!" he broke off into a heart-breaking sob and sank to his knees. "Dear God!" he wailed. "What have I done? So many people, so much blood...and Coligny, my dearest father...*mea culpa!..mea maxima culpa!*" He crawled along tearing at his hair, pulling it out in clumps. "I will be avenged on her...my mother! My mother!"

His attendants stood watching his distress, yet all they could do was follow him as he rushed from the workshop.

♦

As time went by, the Queen Mother had begun to feel that the strong, French wines did not suit her palate, and, as she had been warned by her physician that her fondness for rich food and wine were contributing to her weight gain, it was far easier for her to dilute her wine with water. It was this same refreshment that was brought to her at times during the day. One of the palace servants thus carried the drink on a tray with goblets and a full jug.

Catherine had dismissed all but two of her attendants, as the day had been tiring. The reports from Poland were frustratingly slow, and she longed for news of Henri. She realised her anxiety stemmed from the lethargy of the situation. Charles was by now so alarmingly inept, that at times she had to exercise restraint from physically attacking him.

All her work in ratifying treaties, arranging conditions and overseeing details during the past few months leading up to Henri's departure had given her such pride. The dream of a throne for her darling was now realised. Nevertheless, she missed him terribly.

Such was the lot of the nobility. Her eldest daughter, the late Spanish Queen Elizabeth had similarly left France to begin a new life in another country. Indeed, had she herself not been taken from the land of her birth and sent to France at such a young age? The lives of herself and others were sacrificed for the greater good. She would rest for a while, she announced, and stretched out on one of the couches in her room.

Outside the chamber in an alcove looking out over the ornate palace gardens, Clarice de Moulette felt almost as though she would be physically sick as she waited for the servant that would, at this time bring the customary refreshment for the Queen Mother. As she fingered the small bottle in the pocket of her gown, she reminded herself that she and her aunt had agreed this was the best way, despite some misgivings.

She would have to flee the court, that had needed planning, and now her only concern was that she had to leave her ailing aunt behind, for the time being at least. She well knew that as long as the poor King lived, her aunt would never leave him. Now, at last, time to turn words into deeds. The hour was upon her and yet she felt a strange detachment.

She started as she heard the approach of the young page who carried a tray containing the customary jug and goblet; Clarice moved towards him holding out her hands and took it. Once he had then turned and walked back the way he had come, Clarice moved swiftly to the alcove. She fumbled in the pocket, and removed the small bottle from it. Her deft, delicate fingers shook as she removed the small stopper, and carefully poured the contents into the jug and swirled the liquid around. Once done, she briefly shut her eyes in an effort to control herself, before turning back to the chamber door.

The Queen Mother's favourite female dwarf, was known to all as Petit Chaton. If her real name was known, it was certainly never used. Some suspected that she was a vagrant that the Queen Mother had saved from the streets of Paris. There had even been a vicious rumour that she was Catherine's own child, and had been born with a deformity that prevented her growth, and she had needed to be locked away until her mother had deemed it safe for her to simply "appear." She amused the Queen Mother, and like all Catherine's dwarves, was loyal in every respect to their mistress, and would do all she asked without question. It was Petit Chaton that opened the chamber door at the same moment that a small bottle fell from Clarice's hand as she turned away from the alcove opposite the chamber door. The small bottle was made of thick glass, and had therefore not smashed as it hit the floor where it rolled around briefly before the dwarf picked it up.

Clarice put the tray down on a table just inside the chamber, and snatched the bottle away from the small woman, and waving her away impatiently. She took up the tray again and moved it to another table nearer to where Catherine rested. Clarice felt sure that the sound of her swiftly beating heart could be heard by all, and she could feel the blood pumping in her head, racing as though she would faint. The Queen Mother lay undisturbed, and indeed appeared to have slipped into a mild sleep.

After what was only a matter of seconds but which felt like minutes, Clarice swept away from her mistress almost running to the chamber door. There had been so few in attendance that no-one realised her hasty departure.

Meanwhile, Petit Chaton sat down cross-legged on the carpeted floor at the Queen's feet.

No sooner had Clarice left, than the dwarf climbed up onto the Queen Mother's couch shaking her awake. Catherine was understandably cross at the intrusion. "Whatever is this Chaton? Why would you disturb me thus, I....?" the Queen Mother stopped mid-sentence, as the dwarf whispered into her ear. It was some moments before her mistress could properly comprehend what she was being told. Was Chaton quite sure that Madame Clarice had tampered with the wine in the jug? The Queen Mother looked over to the small table where the wine tray had been left.

That Clarice had hastened from the room was a clear indication that there was some intrigue and danger afoot. "Quick," said the now lucid Queen Mother, "she must be followed." Suddenly, she smiled. "And I think I know where Madame will head for." So saying she took up her walking cane and, with the dwarf in tow, strode along the passageway.

♦

The King of France bounded up the great staircase, his shirtless body shivering now. He appeared a pitiful sight to the startled men and women that gathered as usual near the Royal chambers. Charles pushed aside attendants, ignoring the fawning courtiers who bowed and curtsied as he stormed past.

Clarice had reached her aunt's chamber, she was surprised that her legs did not give way, such was her nervousness. The room was fusty and smelt damp. Some flowers that she had only recently bought, were now lank and lifeless, drooping over the side of their ornate vase.

As though she could smell her niece's lavender scent before she opened her eyes, the old woman was roused, and Clarice rushed to the side of the bed. "It is done aunt, it is done." She spoke as she caressed the cold hand of the elderly woman, stroking the delicate skin soothingly.

"The mixture will take but a few hours to work, and then your beloved Charles can at last be rid of his evil nemesis. It is God's work that has been done this day, and......" she paused suddenly. Was that a creak she heard? No, she must be hearing dangers where there were none. The wind outside was getting up now and this end of the palace was certainly the oldest aspect of it, and everything seemed to make a noise.

"Madame Serpent will no longer enjoy the slaughter of innocents, and her rule of terror will at last be at an end. But I must hurry my beloved, once my part in this episode is learnt, I must be nowhere near Paris. I have made arrangements, my people are well paid for their help, but I must make haste."

She kissed the woman who smiled up at her and gently nodded. Clarice wiped a tear from her eye, she would send for her she said, although the old woman knew as surely as her niece, that she would not live many more weeks. Clarice kissed the upturned palm of her aunt's feeble hand, and turned quickly away. Nanon breathed in once more that powerful scent, and then drifted back into a calm slumber.

♦

The Queen Mother and faithful Chaton swept purposefully along the long passageways,

And up a small flight of steps before arriving at a door where Catherine turned to her companion motioning to be silent. As they neared the chamber she did so without the use of her cane so as to be able to approach her goal without being heard.

The room had a simple curtain that crossed just inside the entrance, allowing one to step into the room without being seen. Catherine cursed her luck as the old door made a small creak as it inched open. It was nevertheless sufficient for her to hear what was being discussed, and as she did so, she felt her blood turn to ice.

♦

The King burst through the door of his mother's chambers, calling for her as he did so.

None of her attendants could say where she had gone. By now he could feel himself tiring, and only his fury and distress kept him on his feet. Nevertheless, he had a raging thirst, and after pouring himself some of the wine from the jug by his mother's couch, he felt sated, flinging the goblet down which in turn upset what remained in the jug. Now shouting for his mother, he tore out of the chamber, his attendants as always attempting to keep up with him.

♦

The Queen Mother had reached her chamber again, and had sat down, such was the weakness in her legs. Throughout her time in France, even knowing she was so unpopular, it had never occurred to her how she would meet her end.

She wondered at her own surprise, she who had faced death almost daily as a child. Throughout all her pregnancies, the most vulnerable time for any woman, Queen or commoner, she had never believed that she would not survive. Yet now, she was faced with the fact that dangers were still at her shoulder.

The stupid girl, curse her and her fool of an aunt, did they really think that they could.......? Her thoughts were suddenly interrupted as she glanced to one side, where Chaton was picking up an empty goblet from the floor. Its contents had been dashed to the carpeting and a stained it.

One of her other servants had at that moment arrived to attend to the mess. Catherine, still pale with shock watched as the boy knelt to wipe up the damp patch.

"The contents of the wine jug are to be thrown away at once!" she commanded. Then she paused in puzzlement. "Chaton?" she asked looking down at the dwarf. "The wine was at the table there was it not?" She motioned to where Clarice had left the tray nearby. Some of Catherine's ladies were gathered, not knowing what had transpired. She called to Isabelle. "Quickly girl!" the Queen Mother commanded. "Which one of you touched the wine in that goblet, quickly!"

Isabelle, continued to look confused. "Why no-one has Madame, there has only been us – oh, but, yes the King came looking for you, he seemed highly distressed, it was he who threw the goblet down once he had finished it......."

The Queen Mother felt as though she would faint, Charles had drunk the wine.....Charles had drunk..! All her maternal instinct screamed at her to hasten to the King, to call his physicians, to have him induced to vomit, bled, anything to purge him of the foul poison that would surely be erupting within his frail body. And yet something stayed her; something she was unable to fight against. Her heart told her that she could not ignore this deadly threat to her son, and yet her good political sense told her to hold back.

Was this then the will of God? Might it be that this was to be the end of her son's reign, that he could at last be at peace, and then her darling...! She could not help but feel almost relieved that perhaps this could be the only way. She was aware that Chaton was staring up at her her large blue eyes staring; did they accuse? Petit Chaton would be the only other witness to this potential tragedy. Catherine studied at her for some moments before speaking. "Go, my friend, and find your little comrade Krassowski, bring him to me, and tell no-one of this." Chaton nodded her head obediently, and ran off pushing her way through the ladies in waiting.

Catherine's hands shook, and she cursed her nerves for failing her at such a time as this. No word had come to her that the King had been taken ill, that would suggest that the poison – if indeed it had been poison was too diluted to act as swiftly as a neat potion would do.

As she sat alone, she forced herself to consider this predicament; never had she longed more for her darling Henri. He would talk softly to his mother. He would know what must be done.

The faithful dwarf, Krassowski arrived with Chaton trailing after him. Catherine sent the little woman on an errand and once she was gone, the Queen Mother gave him some strict instructions, and only when he had left to carry out her wishes did she then make up her mind what must be done.

♦

Clarice made as much haste as she could. It was impossible for her to take her aunt with her this night, but she would return for her. With the impending commotion she was sure would now ensue, she was certain that no-one would raise objection to the old nurse being attended to by her niece.

She had slipped out of the palace unobserved, and was nearing the pre-arranged meeting point, where a companion would meet her, and transport her out of the city. Her anxious journey took her down a small alley and past some shops now boarded up for the day. Clarice felt a trickle of sweat run down the back of her neck. With each step she told herself to be calm; this was God's work she had done this day. She clutched at the crucifix in her pocket and tightened her grip on it.

Suddenly, she was aware of a shadow, just a quick shape that ran across her path; she gasped, when she saw the long tail of a rat disappear into a doorway, she sighed with some relief. However, in the effort of navigating her steps away from the rodent, she was uncertain if she had turned in the right direction. The alleyways appeared like a maze; she had been able to see a dim light before, but now all ways seemed to crowd in on her. Her legs felt weak, her stomach churned as tension seemed to spread throughout her body.

Just then she was aware of being pulled from behind, she lost her footing, and felt herself falling, she cried out but her scream was muffled by a sharp pain on the back of her head. She was stunned for a moment, but she was aware of someone prising her mouth open, she wanted to scream, but the small hands that held her were too strong. She felt a bottle being forced between her lips and then a bitter liquid in her mouth. She tried to spit the liquid out, but a hand on her throat forced her to swallow, and suddenly, she could no longer struggle; she could feel the horrific numbness as she was aware of her body losing sensation. She was unable to focus now, the numbness had reached her arms, her fingers......

From that point she knew nothing more, but sank into blackness.

♦

Madeleine, the former Royal nurse, was unsure what had woken her. She had lain, sleeping fitfully. Her weakening strength made any effort difficult, she had not eaten for some time now; not really aware whether the servant that usually attended her had come or not. The pain in her chest was continuous, although resting as she did, on several pillows made the discomfort less acute.

As she peered out from the warmth of her heavy bedclothes, she was aware that the room however was very cold. The small fire that was usually lit provided enough heat for her comfort, yet today she could see that the grate was grey and dead. Even the spring air seemed to howl ferociously around the chamber, bringing with it a biting chill.

How long would it be before Clarice came to her? The plan they had devised had been carried out. Clarice had said it was so before she left, she had said she would return. Once the deed was done, Charles, her dear Charlot, would be safe, his suffering would cease – he would be free.

She was unsure if she had slept again, for when she next awoke, the room was lit with two candles, illuminating the bed and throwing shapes against the walls. She smiled suddenly, she could smell it surely – lavender! Clarice was here then, she had returned, the scent was so strong, and she wanted to call out, Clarice had surely sat waiting for her aunt to wake. Something drew her gaze however, towards the window. A dark, portly figure could be made out approaching her bed. "Clarice, her voice was rasping from thirst "Have you come for me? I am weak, but I will crawl if I......"

Suddenly, the figure loomed into clearer view. Madeleine had wanted to scream out – it was the dark and unmistakable form of Catherine de Medici.

The Queen Mother smiled down at the woman, the blaze in her eyes caught by the light of the candle that she carried, her heavy features casting a grim apparition. When the Queen Mother spoke however, her voice was quiet and caring. "Ah, dear Nanon, you are awake at last. You must have needed the rest my dear, I swear it does my heart good to see you. Although, it seems that you are shocked to see me. Ah, but yes, you had surely imagined me writhing in great agony from the draft of poison that your foolish niece attempted to kill me with!" Catherine's voice had become harsh and brittle. "You weep silently now old woman, because your plan failed, as you can see. This is no dream I am most certainly alive!"

Madeleine struggled to raise herself up from the pillows, but she was pushed back down by the Queen

Mother who now glared at her with venomous hatred. The aged nurse felt her heart racing, she felt a nausea, that she could barely contain. Catherine now held the woman down with force, her voice now almost hysterical. "Ah, but surely you do not imagine I would fail to have the girl followed and have her answer for her crime? Foolishly, I had believed that she was merely trying to ensnare a Prince, ah, but your stupid Clarice had another plan in mind did she not? Well, she has paid the price for her infamy."

The old nurse fell back against her pillows, tears streaming down her withered cheeks; the Queen Mother was relentless. "The final horror of what you tried to do revealed itself when my son, the King drank in error that which had been prepared for his mother. Ah yes old woman, I speak the truth. You sought to eliminate me, in the hope that Charles would be better without his mother's hand to guide him. Consider then, in these last few moments that the one person you hoped to save you have most probably killed."

Madeleine sank back, sobbing. What had she done? Murdered the King? She was barely aware of where she was. If Catherine was speaking to her, she was no longer able to hear anything. It took but a moment for Catherine to pull out one of the pillows from under the old woman's head. The elderly nurse looked up as the cushion covered her face. The Queen Mother was strong against a weak, feeble old woman, although the nurse struggled against it for a moment or two, she could not catch her breath, and eventually went limp. After only a minute, Catherine withdrew the pillow and stared down at the now lifeless eyes of the former Royal nurse.

For a moment, she looked down at one who had seen all of the many trials and tribulations that Catherine had suffered down the years; death, despair, heartache. Ah, but was she not a creature of Diane de Poitiers? She shook the memory away and carefully tucked away a rebellious streak of her now greying hair back under her black skull cap, and smoothed down her gown. Then with another glance at the dead woman, Catherine felt a hot single tear on her cheek she wiped such a foolish emotion away and then silently left the chamber, the door creaking as she drew it shut.

Having returned to her apartments, she retrieved her cane, and composed herself before setting out for the Royal chamber of her son, announcing to her attendants, that the former Royal nurse, her son's dearest Nanon, had taken a turn for the worse, and was much more breathless today, adding that she was to be regularly updated on her condition.

♦

By the time the Queen Mother's cane could be heard tapping along the passageway to the King's chamber, servants had already been sent to find her. She gasped at the news – the King was taken extremely ill, he had been vomiting for over an hour, and was now being bled in an effort to rid him of whatever had caused this sudden onset. The Queen Mother had delayed getting to her son's bedside, she had hoped she would be too late. Now, she would have to be with Charles until the bitter end.

Catherine entered the darkened chamber that was lit only by a few candles. The sight that met her eyes was one that no mother should see, and as she hastened to her son's side, she barely recognised him.

The King's eyes were bloodshot, and had sunk further into their sockets, his face now took on a hollowed form, his cheekbones sharp and prominent. His face and neck seemed to be seeping blood. Indeed, cloths used to wipe his feverish face lay beside the great bed in a red heap, and servants were being ordered by his physicians to change the sheets that were becoming soaked. He had collapsed earlier following what was assumed to be a particularly robust few hours' activity at his forge. Over the past few days his doctors had warned against such activity. The man had grown so thin of late, at it was impossible for him to take any sustenance, yet he coughed up large quantities of blood, and his breathing was becoming very laboured. Every couple of minutes he would cry out and arch his back as though trying to rid himself of the gnawing pain in his stomach.

The physicians were thankful that at last, the King seemed to be sleeping, even though the rattling of his lungs suggested it would not be long before he would breathe no more.

The chamber was warm now, the doctors would allow no windows to be opened, the fire must be banked-up. The sheets were changed again, and Catherine glanced around the room, taking in the pathetic scene. Charles's Queen, Elizabeth, sat dutifully to one side of the bed. A strange, devout girl that Catherine had never really taken the trouble to become acquainted with; she had made little fuss and was happy to be at mass from dawn until dusk. Charles's mistress, Marie Touchet stood weeping just behind the Queen.

Catherine liked the girl, whose simple good nature and genuine love for Charles had endeared her to many.

Both Anjou and Navarre here in Vincennes, were in attendance, as indeed, Catherine had insisted they should be.

With the situation now seeming hopeless, the Queen Mother believed it imperative that the throne be secured for Charles's brother, the King of Poland; therefore, a document was hastily drawn up appointing Catherine once again to take control as regent until Henri could return. Both Navarre and Alençon witnessed the document, and it was then that Charles opened his eyes and with laboured gasps asked for his brother. Alençon stepped nearer to the bed. "I am here, brother," he said quietly, feeling as though the emotion would overcome him. Charles moved his head to one side then the other "No," he rasped, "I mean my brother Navarre." Alençon, humiliated again, stepped away as a tearful Navarre came forward and kissed the dying man on his forehead, ignoring the bloody sweat that now streamed down off the Kings rotting body. Navarre wept openly, whispering gently, "My brother, my King"

Charles tried to raise his head but did not have the strength, he seemed to want to say something, but the moment was lost and again the breath rattled within him. He raised a withered bony arm, and his weak hand brushed the King of Navarre's head gently.

The King's priest, Sorbin had arrived some time before when it had been agreed that the King may well not last the night. The next few hours would be a crucial indicator of whether his strength would hold out. His doctors, however, saw little hope.

Some hours later, one of the Queen Mother's ladies reported that the old nurse Madeleine had passed away peacefully in her sleep. As if the suffering of her son and his imminent demise were not enough, the passing of the old nurse would be an upsetting development.

Then, as though a blow upon a bruise, the dead body of Catherine's favourite female dwarf, Petit Chaton had been found at the bottom of a stone staircase at the back of the palace. Her neck was broken, her crumpled body stone dead. Why she would have been in that particular part of the building was unclear. The news of these events must wait for now, these tragedies would be too cruel for the Queen Mother to bear at the moment. A sad finale was being played out in the apartments of the King.

♦

When he was afforded the luxury of even the briefest spells of sleep, Charles was tortured. Within moments of closing his eyes, all he could see was cadavers and bones, piles of them. When he was awake, he felt death all around him, the room was awash with blood, dead bodies lay on the floor by his bed, their throats cut, their limbs hacked off. When he awoke, he would see the blood on his hands, taste it in his mouth. He seemed to imagine his old nurse was in the chamber "Nurse, nurse," he croaked with a sob, "So much blood....so much.... is it this much that I have shed?" His breathing became more shallow from the effort of speaking. Catherine bristled at the mention of the nurse, she had almost forgotten her.

A long haunting night finally gave way to a crisp May morning, although the light was shut out by the heavy drapes that remained drawn in the dying King's chamber.

All efforts to alleviate the dying man's rattling chest had met with little success, and the physicians in attendance could only offer grave looks to the Queen Mother, who sat on the opposite side of her son's bed to his Queen. Elizabeth's tear stained face was heart breaking to see. At times she would lean over her husband and gently kiss his brow, allowing her lips to linger for several seconds, her red eyes closed as tears spilled from them; laying a trembling hand on her husband's chest as though such an action could stem the noise from within his frail body.

The Queen Mother with her customary grasp of reality, however painful and distressing it may be, knew that there was only one outcome here. Like the Queen, Catherine had not moved from Charles's bedside for several hours, clutching her rosary beads tightly in her hand. The King's confessor was aghast to notice that the Queen Mother occasionally also allowed her fingers to caress her talisman bracelet, an evil amulet to be handled at such a moment as this. He was horrified. No wonder so many doubted Catherine de Medici's adherence to her faith.

She continued to watch her son, the rattle of his every breath sapping what little energy he now had. Then, having not moved for some hours, he turned his head slowly to face her, managing a slight smile as a single hot tear trickled down from the corner of his eye, coursing its way down his blood-sweating cheek.

Catherine heard his crackling, hoarse whisper. "Ah, ma mere, adieu ma mere!"

His bloodshot eyes seemed to widen as he stared at her. She did not meet his gaze, but looked down to her lap, drawing her handkerchief to her mouth to muffle the sob that threatened to break forth. Her resolve not to betray her feelings or emotions was almost too much to bear.

And then, something changed, the aura within the chamber was altered, Catherine drew a short breath and held it before closing her eyes – the rattling had stopped.

♦

PART TWO

♦

"The Prince who encourages the rise of another ruins his own"
—Machiavelli

♦

A glorious bright sun shone down on the French capital. The air was stilted, and despite the cloudless sky, a storm felt imminent. The Royal court, so long in mourning for the late King was now beginning to show signs of activity. The wheels of government had ground slowly, but anxieties and pressure did not abate merely for a passing of a King; indeed, it should surely be especially vulnerable at such a time.

In the gardens at the Louvre palace, the ageing Cardinal of Lorraine walked with his young nephew, Henri, Duke of Guise. The Cardinal was beginning to grow frail, his proud bearing of old had begun to give way to the weaknesses of the body, and he now walked unsteadily, his shoulders rounded with the onset of rheumatism.

Resting on the younger man's arm, he could shuffle along, but age set his speed. Still dressed in the rich red robes that he had worn for so long, his cardinal's hat covered the thin strands of grey hair that were just evident around his ears. His parchment-like skin was a strange shade of grey and yellow, his cheekbones, protruded sharply from his withered face, his thin, cruel lips were set in a straight line, apart from the occasional twitch. His foul breath could be smelt from some feet away, made no better by the state of his rotting teeth.

His nephew held out a strong arm for support, inwardly cringing as the Cardinal leant closer to him to speak. The older man stopped after every few steps to cough, or to spit. A pitiful, old parody of a once noble figure. The Cardinal was of little consequence now in the affairs of France, a country he and his brother had virtually ruled, through their niece, Mary Stuart many years before.

Well, much had changed, Mary now languished in England as a prisoner of Elizabeth Tudor, the Cardinal had always said that his niece was a woman led by her heart rather than her head, and alas he had been proved correct. The woman had simply made her way from one tragic mistake to another, and had been rather disloyal to her family in France, by spurning their help and advice. Ah, well, there was nothing he could do now, her fate had always been in her own hands.

He thought often of his brother, the great Duke, assassinated by an agent of Gaspard de Coligny, the former Admiral of France, now also dead thanks be to God; slain, rightfully so by the strong arm that now supported his frail body.

Henri de Guise had grown up a great deal since the massacre of Saint Bartholomew's eve. His self-belief had grown, as indeed had his tendency to arrogance; he knew well that he was of the most noble blood, greater even than the Valois. With his lean, athletic body and strong, handsome features, square jawed and with bright green eyes, he was a great favourite with the ladies at the court. He could be both charming and amusing, was a fine dancer and excelled in most games and sports, was an expert horseman, and dedicated scholar.

The Cardinal saw his brother whenever he looked at his nephew; he would be so proud of what he had become, everything his father had wished. Now though, the son of the man the Parisians called *Le Balafré* was facing an uncertain future. With the death of a King came a period of change and upheaval.

Religious unrest still raised an ugly head; treaties were signed, pacts arranged; all easily made and just as easily broken. The Cardinal had no qualms about his nephew's commitment to the Catholic cause. Like his father, he was proud of his family, his heritage and an even fiercer defender of his faith.

The Cardinal continued, "I hear news of our illustrious new King. Word has reached me that his Polish subjects watch his every move, and would keep him a prisoner rather than see him leave." The Cardinal began to wheeze as he chuckled, until he could barely take a breath. At length he recovered himself, dabbing his watering eyes, and spitting to one side, before continuing. "Nevertheless, the serpent Catherine, who has guarded his throne like a she-wolf protects her lair, has made an error. In spite of her best efforts, the Huguenots are stirring once again; the Medici has failed to notice the likes of the Danville and Montmorency factions strengthening their ties with the heretics. It is even planned to attempt to convene a general assembly. We must be sure to be prepared for this my son, it is you who must play a significant role in the months ahead. The new King may be a coxcomb, but he is clever and devious, the Florentine blood in him is strong, he is pure Medici!" The Cardinal uttered this damning assessment with a sneer.   Guise nodded sagely "I believe I despise this new King more I did his pathetic brother. He sickens me."

The Cardinal was well aware that there was bad blood between the two young men, their relationship as boys had been uneasy at best. The old man looked at his nephew, and permitted himself a smile; "You may need to disguise your hatred my son. Whether you like him or not, remember never to trust him, and certainly be wary of his mother. You know that Philip of Spain is eager for a Holy Union, as he calls it. A Catholic League, an organization that will be triumphant throughout Europe. Soon even the Catholic force in England will flock to our banner." They stopped at a stone seat beneath an ash tree, where the Cardinal sank gratefully down, wincing slightly as his limbs objected to the hard surface. Guise sat next to him, only on the edge of the stone, restless at having to be still.

The Cardinal's bloodshot eyes glistened, as though his own words brought him elation. Guise, although eager to play a significant part in this development, had learnt as he had grown up, that it was so easy to stumble. Could he rely on Paris for instance? Surely yes; had they not flocked to do his work on the night of Saint Bartholomew? Paris was his, he knew that, as did his uncle, who somehow could read his nephew's thoughts. "You surely do not doubt your popularity my son? You know how the Parisians cheer you when you enter the city. They would follow wherever you would lead them, have no fear of that." He patted the young man's thigh, allowing his hand to linger there a moment. Guise felt suddenly uneasy, and stood up abruptly; he was far from happy with the affection his uncle sometimes showed.

As they rose and walked again, Guise tried to turn away as his uncle's words came in wafts of foul breath. "Work quietly, work secretly. On no account divulge any plans to anyone whose loyalty is questionable. Remember, my son, Catherine's spies are everywhere, trust no-one, work discreetly. Do not forget, this is her favourite son who will now occupy the throne of France, the Valois serpent will be even more venomous in making certain he stays there."

The Cardinal cackled suddenly as he recalled another item of gossip from his own spies. "I am told that our new King has for some time declared himself to be passionately in love with the Princess de Condé, yes – wife of that heretic Bourbon. He declared, I understand, that he could not bear to be parted from her when he left for Poland, and had stated his intention to arrange a divorce from her Prince in order to marry a King." The old man noticed his nephew's look of curiosity and elucidated; "There is come to court this week, news that the said Princess has a disease of the lung, and may well not live to see the new King crowned, that leaves us with an open opportunity. One must naturally assume that the Medici does not favour such a match and I for one would not be surprised to be told that a *"morceau Italianise"* had been added to the physician's tincture." His thin frame shook as he paused to control a further rasping cough. "Nevertheless, this does open up an invitation for us. Such a chance as we seized upon during both the reigns of Henri Deux and the sickly François."

The old man looked around to ensure they were not being overheard and continued in a lower, conspiratorial tone. "I speak of course of Madame de Valentinois, and our captive kinswoman, Mary Stuart." The Cardinal arched an eyebrow as he leaned towards his nephew. "We might yet provide another who will appeal to our new sovereign. I have in mind Louise de Vaudemont. A beauty, whose virtue is unquestioned, and who I am told had attracted the attention of the Valois fop before he swore undying love for Condé's saintly wife.

Moreover, the King met the lady when he visited his sister on his journey to Cracow. It is believed that they appeared to enjoy each others company. Think on this, my son, a Queen of France from the house of Lorraine would see us rise again as the premiere family in France. We might also hope that the girl being a devout Catholic can keep her husband's ever wavering commitment to his faith under greater control."

The Cardinal was silent for a moment before enduring a further, violent bout of coughing.

He had spoken for too long, and had become too animated in his excitement and vision to return to the days of former glory that he and his brother had once enjoyed.

Eventually, the prelate's breathing and coughing were under control, but his nephew insisted that he should now return to his chambers and rest. The Cardinal gripped the younger man's arm with his bony hands, the joints of his arthritic gnarled fingers enflamed, his long yellowing nails brittle and chipped. He leaned heavily on him as they turned and retraced their steps. There was much to consider.

♦

In his Polish palace, Henri, the new King of France relaxed back onto the sumptuous velvet cushions of his vast bed, where he reposed in great fatigue. It was a usual place for him to be once he had dealt with the tedium of the Polish secretaries. The King, at twenty-three years of age was a handsome figure, inheriting both his slender hands and his sharp, dark eyes from his mother. His pale skin and flawless complexion was his great pride, and he was conscious of his appearance in every respect. His bath water must contain only the costliest fragrance, his soaps he had specially sent from Castile in Spain, nothing else would do. His hair was not long, being cut just above his perfectly shaped ears in which he sported a diamond stud, one of many jewels that he adored.

It was little wonder that the Polish people found their King both fascinating and frustrating. He could be dazzling in appearance, yet they found him both unpredictable and lazy. Neither could they understand his reluctance to learn their language, relying on translators or explaining that as their King, it was for them to understand *him*! Their recent frustration concerned the prospective Polish bride that they would have him marry, the Princess Anna de Jagellona. Often official functions dictated that they must be at the same occasions, but Henri could charm and smile, knowing that to the plain Princess he must seem like a God, bedecked in jewels from head to foot, with the costliest silks and velvet doublets, slashed with vibrant colours. He would nod to her and smile at his most dazzling, whilst in private, laugh with his friends about her pallor, lack of grace and style. His duplicity would have made his Medici mother proud.

Even now as he read the many letters that his mother sent him, he was preparing to flee as soon as he could. While he did of course, find the Poles and their cold, serious ways all rather tedious; he had to admit that he actually did very little other than make compulsory official appearances, sign reams of documents that he did not fully understand – his translators made every effort to make sure he understood what he was signing and why, but Henri admitted to one of his close attendants that he could easily have signed his own abdication and not been aware of it.

He sighed again as he took up his mother's latest missive, holding it in his slender hands. In it, she advised him to act cautiously where the manner of his departure from the Polish court was concerned. Catherine held great misgivings about how the Poles would react to this news.

Henri sent for his Master of the King's household, René de Villequier who would mastermind the delicate operation of ensuring the King could leave Poland before any of his council were aware of it. How his mother had cautioned him about becoming too *"removed from his subjects"* and it was true, that after an official meeting with his council, and the greeting of dignitaries or special audiences, the King invariably complained of fatigue, and would retire to his apartments to rest. Thus he could be often undisturbed for most of the day. With these retirements an almost daily occurrence, who would notice if the King had not been seen outside of his chambers?

France's ambassador to Poland, had, upon the death of Charles, been officially relieved of his duty, and therefore sent ahead by Villequier to prepare the route of the planned departure. Fresh horses at each of the planned stops as well as any other provisions that would be needed during the flight ahead. Already charged with letters for Catherine, was the messenger who had brought Henri the news of his brother's death – Chemerault, one of his mother's trusted officers.

The evening of departure drew near, and Henri became immediately alert. Gone was the lethargy that he complained of each day, and instead, a man of decisive action, and eager to make good their plans.

There was, however, a threat to all the arrangements. The King was informed that his Polish chamberlain, Count Tenczin, had urgent need of an audience with him. Were Henri to refuse, suspicion would be aroused, so he therefore instructed that after a short wait, the Count could be admitted. The King hissed at the gentlemen in the room to make themselves scarce, or at least to behave as though nothing was afoot, guilty as they all looked. Whilst his heart beat faster and harder, Henri donned his nightcap, and appeared to be dozing peacefully when the chamberlain entered.

He was a man of average height, with a bald head and sharp stern features, his black bushy eyebrows were knotted sternly as he took in the scene that met him. He had expected to find his sovereign booted and preparing for flight, but instead was greeted by a weary King who barely seemed awake enough to talk with him. "Forgive me my good Tenczin," the King yawned, "I am barely awake, yet you would disturb me at this late hour. Nevertheless, I, as you know am always prepared to serve my dear subjects. Come sit with me here, on the bed, I insist." If Henri had wanted to unsettle the chamberlain, he had achieved his goal; the King was notoriously remote in every sense, and an invitation to sit so close was surely unheard of. He was therefore taken slightly aback as he addressed the King, in French as he was one of the few in Poland that did. "Your most high and mighty Majesty," the chamberlain began.

The King snapped his fingers to an attendant. "Some wine, my dear Count?" he asked vaguely. The Count was caught off guard, but rallied. "Mighty King –" he began again, raising a hand to the ready servant. "Are you sure you won't sit?" the King said. The now slightly irritated Count shook his head, "My most gracious King," he testily continued, "I am sent on a quest from your council to allay some fears we have over your Majesty's plans, now that the King of France, your brother is dead."

Henri pinched the bridge of his nose, closing his eyes as he looked away, before stifling a sob. Eventually, he took a deep breath and sighed, "Forgive me Count, I am still in some distress over my brother."

The Count now felt rather uncomfortable, shifting from one foot to the other, and casting his eyes down to the floor. Eventually he broke the uncomfortable silence. "My King, we your council insist on being made aware of your immediate intentions in light of some recent behaviour by your Majesty's closest advisers"

Henri looked up at the Count with a dangerous glint in his black, fathomless eyes.

"My council-*insist?* He emphasised the word with an incredulous tone. The Count was beginning to wish he had not rashly volunteered to approach the King who was now looking at him with a cold gaze that was extremely unnerving.

Tenczin bowed his head. "Forgive me Majesty, I have spoken carelessly. Let me explain if I can." Henri said nothing and the Count continued. "Majesty, we have heard this day, alarming news, and we your council –"

"For heaven's sake man, speak your mind!" Henri interrupted crossly. The Count licked his dry lips. "Your exalted Majesty, we have been advised of a train of horses and baggage under your herald, heading away from this city. There is alarm that you will soon follow them. Word has even reached some of the citizens, and a crowd is beginning to form outside the palace itself."

Henri made a mental note that he would personally box the ears of that careless, stupid Villequier. Discretion was paramount, he had told him, all must remain as though nothing of any importance was taking place. Wear no livery that could be identified, and give their plans away. God's death, were all his attendants fools?

When at last he spoke, it was with warmth, but also determination. "Count Tenczin, report to my council, not only that I am distraught that they should trust me so little but also that they should see their King as a fool who would steal away by night like a common thief." He raised a hand to silence the chamberlain who was about to interrupt. "That I should have so little regard for my own honour, that I would not hold council with them, and fully discuss and be advised as to what should happen now my dear brother has passed away and I am expected to wear his crown."

The Count was humbled slightly by the obvious offence his words had caused. He bowed again before speaking quietly, "Shall I inform the council that you will discuss this further with them in the morning or should…?"

The King interrupted him crossly, irritated by the man, and furious that the kinsman he trusted could have been so indiscreet. "Enough now! You have been a bold petitioner Tenczin, but I am tired, tired of your questions and false accusations. Leave me now!" With a wave of dismissal, he then turned onto his side, grumbling with oaths and curses that the Count could easily translate.

The chamberlain stepped backwards to the door of the room, bowing several times. As soon as he was outside, his stern manner returned, his mournful, concerned expression replaced with a hard, steely sombreness. He was immediately approached by several of the council who had waited, eager for news of the audience. He looked firstly to them and then to the waiting head of the palace Tartar guard. "Have all exits from the palace sealed off and guarded" he commanded. He then turned his attention to his fellow councillors. "I do not believe that the King will attempt to leave, but I fear his attendants might. Something is most certainly going on, but I believe he values his honour too highly to slink away in the night. He is sleeping now, we shall attend him tomorrow, and I believe all will be well."

Henri lay waiting for a reasonable time to elapse before he got out of bed, and marched swiftly to the adjoining chamber. Here were his closest friends who had travelled to Poland with him, and who were as eager as he was to be away from the city, and heading back to France. These followers of Henri's were a dazzling sight; each of them dressed in the lavish expensive fashions, abhorring the plain, rough and unsophisticated dress that men at the Polish court favoured. The Frenchmen wore large expensive jewellery, their fingers weighed down with enormous rings with precious stones, pearls and gold necklaces adorned their slender throats. Their caps had elaborate plumes, and their expensive Spanish leather shoes had gold buckles that shone brilliantly. Their hair was also a wonder to the Polish men; curled immaculately and worn quite long. Their ears were usually decorated with pearls or diamonds. To many, they were a wonder to behold, but the Polish men found them disgusting; they fawned on one another giggling and whispering to their master.

In contrast however, they were also fine swordsmen, quick and agile and surprising the court with the displays of prowess that their King seemed to enjoy so much. Their obvious pride and bravado was a curious contrast to their general foppish behaviour.

Now the King had quickly thrown off his lethargy, and was eager to put their plans into action. The danger and excitement of the risks involved seemed to breathe new life into him, and he gave quick sharp instructions. The main items of importance had been sent earlier with Villequier, now it was necessary only to collect together a few other items that would have been noticeable had they been missing any earlier.

Henri's concern was primarily focussed upon the large wooden treasure box at the foot of his bed. Any jewels that had been brought from France had gone ahead, but he had no intention of leaving the contents of the box. "Quelus," he instructed one of his closest favourites, "help me with these" He opened the chest. Inside were gems, diamonds, rubies in all forms and sizes. Henri reached in and taking out a handful, stuffed them into the pockets of his coat. Quelus and a couple of the others did likewise, leaving almost nothing at all. It was a wise precaution the King said, "It might yet take many bribes in order to get out of this godforsaken land."

Two of the King's gentlemen had been sent to establish whether there were guards at any of the easiest exits, and when they reported back, it was with the bad news that almost all the exits had been placed under guard, with the exception of the kitchen, where a small side door led on to an alley that ran down towards the quieter area of the city. A rendezvous had been planned at a small chapel on the outskirts of the capital, where horses and the rest of his men waited. The palace was quiet, and the King had dressed plainly like a servant in order not to be identified. He thanked his sound policy of not staying around the court too long and thus, he was certain that most of the courtiers had only seen him from a distance, bedecked in jewels and finery.

At last they reached the steps that led down to the kitchen. Mercifully, they had met no-one other than a few servants, and were soon at the small door, horrified now to see that a guard stood just outside in the alley-way. Obviously he had left his post earlier and had now returned. The King looked to Quelus and nodded, there was no choice. The Frenchman's swift approach from behind was unheard until it was too late, Quelus's dagger slit the guard's throat before he could call out; blood spurted from the wound as the soldier collapsed. Henri did not even look down as he stepped over the body.

Once away from the palace, the party almost ran towards the chapel. Horses and refreshment awaited them, but it was decided not to linger for too long; the King's absence could be noticed at any time, and if a crowd had indeed gathered at the front of the palace, they too would set out to pursue the escapees.

Mounting quickly set off at speed, heading for the town of Osświecim, thirty miles away from Cracow. The night had drawn in, but fortunately another of the party, Pibrac, had travelled and then memorised the route several times, saved them from becoming entirely lost.

Meanwhile, the King's disappearance had been discovered, when a change in the guards on duty at the small alley outside a kitchen door, revealed the dead figure lying in a vast pool of blood. The chamberlain was alerted, and he at once marched straight to the Royal chambers – they were empty, as were the contents of the treasure chest at the foot of the King's bed. Orders were quickly carried out, with a vast number of the Tartar cavalry setting off at a thunderous pace in pursuit of the King's party. It would have been impossible to stop a gathering mob of citizens from taking to the road themselves, and a large mass joined the soldiers and set off to drag the King back to Cracow.

Before the escaping men realised it, they were now being closely followed by the mob and the Polish cavalry. They could almost hear their approach, clearly their superior knowledge of the terrain had allowed the pursuers to make up much ground on the French party. Further frustration ensued, when it became apparent that in order to cross the river Vistula and onward to the relative safety of Plessy, they would need to navigate the narrow bridge, a crude construction of wooden planks the width of which only allowed for single-file. They were half-way across, with the mob and cavalry in sight, when Henri stopped, and shouted to those behind him to tear up the planks behind them and cast them into the choppy waters below. With the bridge successfully destroyed, they could afford the risk of stopping to see the baying mob screaming at them, and the imposing figure of Count Tenczin whose horse joined those at the head of the Tartar soldiers. For one moment the eyes of the Count met those of the King, and even from the distance, Henri could imagine the malice in the chamberlain's eyes. Rocks, small stones, arrows and all manner of objects were hurled across the river, most landing short of their target, and splashing into the cold water. It was almost dawn now, but the French could not afford the luxury of a slower pace, they must press on further; but not until Henri pulled up his mount and turned back one last time. He smiled, he was no longer King of Poland, but he was King of France – and he was going home.

♦

The new King must leave a French figurehead in Poland that was for sure, Catherine suggested in a recent letter that this personage could even be his younger brother Alençon at a later date, when they could be satisfied that he would cause no further trouble. Henri had scoffed as he read. Surely his mother didn't believe that such a day would ever come, any more than he did. Ideally, the Poles could elect one of their own for the honour, aided by a French commissioner of course.

Henri was advised not to be too generous with his favour, at least until he had spent time with his mother and been made aware of those who deserved to be recognised by the new King. The Queen Mother was aware that her son had surrounded himself with some *"less than honourable"* characters, as she chose to describe them. That must cease. It was never wise to have more than one or two close friends. The King's companions were excitable and sometimes headstrong there was bound to be jealousy and discord before too long.

Many of these young men came from great families of course, but that was, naturally, where the most ambitious ones were tutored. Early learning included how to make your way at court. Catherine had met too many of them not to be wary of their ambitions.

Above all, it was Catherine's intention that her beloved Henri would be advised by her in all things, for surely she had suffered to successfully hold the throne for his brother, and would do so again for her "darling boy" – indeed, they would rule together. Catherine would of course be regent until the new King's return, and she would use the time to ensure that all was in readiness.

Upon Charles's death, the Queen Mother had kept to her apartments in the Louvre, and although she hid away to grieve in private, there was much to do. Firstly, there was the lying-in-state of the deceased King, and his funeral to arrange. It must be a lavish affair of course, and with the treasury almost emptied by vast amounts that Catherine had used in order to ensure that the Polish crown was offered to Henri, loans would need to be negotiated. An immediate advance of 30,000 écus had already been despatched to the new King, for his "personal enjoyment", as word reached the Queen Mother that her fugitive son and his exhausted retinue had at last reached the safety of Vienna having been met by an advance group of officials sent by the Emperor Maximillian, headed by two of his sons.

The Royal party was met with three gondolas; canopied with golden silk, one in violet coloured velvet and finally one in black velvet, all trimmed in costly golden thread, and peppered with small jewels. Henri naturally chose the golden one as being the most suited to a King. He stepped into the craft, that boasted eight gondoliers wearing Turkish turbans. Behind followed a dazzling flotilla, sumptuously decked out in all manner of adornments. The gondolas were then uncovered, much to the delight of the large cheering crowd.

Henri drank greedily from this nectar of pomp and elaborate celebration. He had several times disguised himself, and leaving the Foscarini Palace, he would wander around with his closest companions incognito, mixing with wealthy merchants, travelling artists and trawling the large markets buying costly scents and cloths.

Artists vied to paint his portrait, and indeed one of his impromptu visits had been to the celebrated artist, Titian. Glass blowers from Murano set up their own gondoliers outside his Palazzo Foscari on the Grand Canal, and the Henri was enthralled by their amazing creations. Everywhere he went, he was cheered and adored as the most spectacular of Kings. He was guest of honour at so many fetes and balls that he lost count.

Having delayed his departure as long as he could, and the letters from Catherine imploring him to return to his capital becoming more desperate, his departure for France was inevitable. It was, therefore, with a sorry heart that he eventually heeded his mother's entreaties, and headed out for France.

Throughout his homeward journey, more letters arrived from Catherine. Henri had at first told many that he wished that his mother could have joined him on his celebrated entry into Venice, and been with him to enjoy the many delights that had greeted him there. To Catherine, he dramatically declared, he owed a debt of gratitude for bringing him to such honour. His secretaries noted nonetheless, that he had curiously omitted to write personally to his mother since before he left Cracow, preferring to leave that onerous task to one of them.

The Queen Mother's letters to her son arrived with alarming frequency. And with each letter, Henri took less and less interest. There was time enough for France he told his followers, and besides, as King, he could surely be his own master and behave as he wished. For her part, Catherine felt an uneasiness as news reached her from her spies, as much as she hated to have them in her son's entourage, that the new King had been busy distributing honours and wealth to those he felt were deserving of his largesse. The Queen Mother's concern grew when it was reported to her that her son had spent all of the money she had sent to him, as well as a further debt of 19,000 écus. She had been informed of the misappropriation of money and jewels that he had taken when he left Poland, and whilst deploring such covert embezzlement in one of such high office, she had felt it better not to enquire whether any of this additional wealth had been saved, as she well knew the answer.

♦

The Queen Mother felt exhausted, and was taking a much needed rest from another day of anxiety over her son's reluctance to return to the capital. At fifty-five years of age, she was getting older, but her famous indefatigable energy was admired, even by her many enemies. Now however, she felt that she could do no more about hastening Henri's entry to his capital. It was clear that her beloved was being badly influenced by his companions; young men who sought to fawn and lavish praise on their master for their own ends rather than support him in his duties. Had she not already warned him against favouring such men?

As she had mourned Charles, she was, in the many private hours she spent, acutely aware that events had sapped her energy. She had watched him grow into a hysterical man who could be given to many moods. A man whom she had become unable to trust and deal with; but his passing had affected her more than she had expected. In the days following Charles' death she had questioned all that had occurred. Now she dismissed the past as of little relevance, one could not mourn forever. Moreover, she was also aware that she had been unable to relinquish the power she had enjoyed.

Initially of course, her influence had been necessary; Charles was a mere child when he ascended the throne. Now there was Henri, a man she believed to be a King that would rule with strength, power and wisdom. It was true that he was despised by many as being fickle, extravagant and, most deplorably, was considered the most Italian of all her offspring. How the populace still hated her. Even after she had sought to find a peaceful solution to the ever growing number of religious wars. If she advocated tolerance, she was maligned as a heretic, yet to add her support to her fellow Catholics was to arouse further suspicion among the Huguenots. The wars had brutally ripped apart the country she had known as a young bride.

She must shake off this lethargy, she must again be her son's eyes and ears, she must watch, and help to avert any threat to her beloved, for only a mother knew what was best for her son.

Much as she wished it were not so, she had come to realise that she had no wish personally to retire from the cut and thrust of the most dynamic court in Christendom. Forever the realist, she knew as well that her brood was not strong, either in mind or body with the exception of Margot. What cruel twist of fate had determined that by far the most agile minded, quick witted and personally brave and compassionate of her children should be a daughter, one that could never rule in her own right? Whilst she was enough of a traditionalist, and a believer in the Salic law that prevented females from becoming Queens by birthright, she could nonetheless cast some envy at Elizabeth Tudor, who was Queen of England by divine right, and indeed, one that would certainly never share power.

Catherine had admitted to herself that the episode with Charles's former nurse had taken its toll. She had never really seen herself as her son's tormentor. Was her dominance so great that it had been thought, even if only by an old retainer and her niece, that Charles would have been better off without his mother? She could never have forgiven an attempt on her own life, which she justified may as well have been a threat to her son, as he needed her guidance still. No, the nurse had to die, and Catherine had felt no remorse in dealing with the problem. The niece Clarice had betrayed her mistress. The Queen Mother had taken time to instruct her, and ensure that she was loyal, and she had sought Catherine's death for her own ends. No, pity was not to be wasted on her, or her aunt.

Petit Chaton, however, had been another casualty of the affair. Although she had been steadfastly loyal to Catherine, was nevertheless, a witness to the whole sorry episode, and it would not have been wise keep her alive and run the risk that the fool, clever and amusing though she was, would not be tempted by either bribe or torture to reveal that the King had drunk poison that had been intended for the Queen Mother. Why, would be the question, had she not hastened straight to his physicians and tell them that he had been poisoned? Catherine paused in her thoughts, she was not sure herself why she did not do so.

Suddenly she was shaken from her reverie and fatigue; there was consternation in the adjoining chamber. It was with an irritable scowl that she nodded to her attendant to open the door. She was pushed aside by one of the captains of the guard, who marched in, and, bending to his knee, presented the Queen Mother with a letter. She at once recognised the insignia of her son, on the seal, and tore open the parchment. After a moment, she smiled, all trace of fatigue and concern gone. The Royal party was awaiting her at Lyon – the new King was almost in Paris.

♦

For Catherine, the sight of her favourite son moved her to such emotion as she had barely felt before. Here then was the culmination of all her plans, all her work. She had managed to secure the throne long enough for this most adored of all her children.

In a rare demonstration of humility, the Queen Mother fell to her knees before the new King. With his own tears streaming down his pale but excited face, he raised her up and embraced her tightly. To her, he declared, he owed everything; she had given him life, she had nurtured and protected him, and guarded this crown that he now was called to wear.

After the Queen Mother had wept as she embraced her darling son, she presented his brother and sister to their eldest sibling and the new King of France. She was aware that the ceremony was little more than show for the watching courtiers and more importantly, ambassadors, who would report to their masters that there appeared to be harmony within the Valois, and a new era of trust and friendship. Catherine had always wanted her children to trust one another, to be above schemes and plans of destruction – strength was only in unity, she had told them so often. Now as she watched the King embrace his sister Margot, there was little warmth in their greeting. Where there had once been goodwill, there was now caution, and no small amount of fear.

Alençon and Navarre were presented before their sovereign, and every fibre of the youngest Royal son screamed at the injustice of being presented like a courtier. He barely made contact with his brother's offered hand, and was surprised when Henri drew him forward and embraced him. Similarly, Navarre was greeted like a long lost friend, and was held in the King's arms for some minutes. Margot smiled cynically at the spectacle; here they now embrace warmly, but Henri would in time seek her husband's destruction. The Queen of Navarre turned to find the cold stare of her mother upon her. She shivered as she always did when she believed that Catherine could read her very thoughts.

Henri appeared to put betrayals and rumour behind them and had addressed his brother and Navarre. "The past is forgotten my brothers, I set you at liberty and wish only that you assure me of both your love and fealty." Catherine watched their bowing heads, and despite this attempt to start this new reign with magnanimity and friendship, she could not help feeling that to grant the two miscreants the freedom to leave court, might have been unwise.

Time would tell, and there would be ample opportunity later to suggest that in future, he should maybe take opinion and advice from his mother before such an important decision was made.

She was unaware that at their embrace, Henri had whispered to his younger sibling. "Kiss the hand of your sovereign – maggot!" Alençon felt the flush of fury, and immediately stepped back, his eyes flashing dangerously. Yet, he could do no more – for now. Despite a ready audience, for once his good sense prevailed, and he merely stepped back, his jaw set tightly, his hands trembling.

Margot would later describe her feelings, as always, in her journal. *"When the King clasped me to him I trembled from head to foot, the emotion of which I had the greatest difficulty to conceal"*

The Parisians, ever a capricious crowd, cheered their new King and yet Catherine with her keen sense of drama was in no doubt that behind the waves and cheers, the citizens would be sniggering at Henri's effete mannerisms, his curled and decorated hair, his flamboyant clothing, and not least – his companions.

The new monarch's group of favourites were a dandy collection of misfits as well as high-born individuals; all copying the fashion and mannerisms of their master. The Queen Mother eyed them cautiously; their relationship with Henri must be watched carefully – any sense of their own importance could signal danger.

Catherine knew too that the Parisians muttered her name and cast her hateful looks. It mattered not to her, she had always been detested, and she had long ago given up any effort to endear herself to them. Even as she rode in a covered litter beside her son, she was aware of several people spitting on the ground before her, and some even hastily crossing themselves. Catherine could laugh at such hysteria now, but she was also aware of their power; here in Paris a quiet but determined band could evolve into a gathering and, thereafter, a mob.

For the present, all seemed well, and already Henri had shown himself well to his people, she could only pray that newfound fondness the Parisians had for their sovereign would endure.

One member of the King's entourage that the Queen Mother took special note of was the bewitching, Madame de Vaudemont who, during one of the many stops into the heart of the city, seemed to have caught the eye of her son. The girl had been at his side a few times before the entry into the city, laughing, and allowing the new sovereign to delicately coil her hair around one of his jewelled fingers. This was both welcome, and a slight cause for concern. She was happy of course that Henri was taking an interest in such a beautiful young woman. Louise de Vaudemont was a lady of average height, with shiny auburn hair which she wore loose, allowing it to tumble over her elegant shoulders. Her eyes were of the brightest green, and perfectly complimented her smooth complexion, and small but sensuous mouth.

Catherine was at least pleased to see him show an interest in the opposite sex; his pawing of his favourites and his love of fashion and jewellery had led many to gossip about his sexuality.

Surrounding himself with young men who were mere images of himself did not help. There was some concern however; Madame de Vaudemont was of the Lorraine family.

What power had that dynasty had over the Valois; Diane de Poitiers, Mary Stuart, and now a new generation. The beauty and lust for power of those creatures had broken hearts – none more so than her own. Even the young Duke of Guise had bewitched her daughter Margot. Well, this would be carefully watched; she would ensure that one of her many faithful and trusted spies became her eyes and ears where Louise de Vaudemont was concerned.

♦

In the chamber of the new King, Catherine sat with her son, patiently explaining her reasoning on various matters, drawing his wandering interest back to the issues of the day while he picked at a loose thread on his lace cuff. The tall, sinister Luc, Catherine's most trusted personal secretary, hovered at her side, pointing to previous letters, and bowing his head at her instruction, his long dark hair falling over his face as he did so. Henri watched him, unable to prevent the look of distaste at his mother's creature. As Catherine continued to discuss the various dispatches with Luc, it did not escape his notice that at one point, one of the letters they attended to was hastily inserted into some other dispatches. Both Catherine and her secretary glanced straight at the King, catching his eye. His mother was adept in masking her feelings so that none would guess her thoughts, but

Luc flushed slightly; the heightened colour sitting strangely on his white alabaster skin.

The King cast an uneasy glance at the pile of documents and, uncomfortable at this other man's presence, motioned him to leave. Catherine looked sharply at her son, before she too nodded to her servant that he was to leave. Henri looked sulkily at the gaunt figure as he bowed low and departed. "That man stirs an ill feeling in me," he stated, to which his mother merely smiled.

"He is as loyal to me as...." she began, but Henri interrupted, "It is to his King he needs to be loyal" Catherine cast her eyes downwards, and folded both her long-fingered hands in her lap as he continued. "I have listened long and hard to your instructions Maman. Your advice, sound as always, given I know in your love of me, and your wish to see France once again the greatest nation in Europe." Catherine smiled at him. It was true that she had discussed with him as she had with Charles, the need to surround himself with faithful men, and be ever available to them, as their dear father and grandfather had been.

"There are customs and decisions that I will change," he stated in a tone that brooked no contention. "The old custom of approaching the King with requests will cease. How am I to hold my dignity as King when anyone can just approach me with demands while I am dressing, eating or even bathing! This must stop forthwith, and bring to an end such an outdated concept, indeed the whole charade is an insult to Royal dignity." Catherine listened calmly, but knew better than to interrupt and incur his petulance. "Moreover," he stated "such an audience with the King must be presented in writing, my secretaries will, thereafter, present the King with a list for consideration. Furthermore, no person shall just just enter the Royal chamber without permission."

Henri glanced quickly at his mother. Her thin mouth was set in a fixed line, her hooded eyes attentive. He continued, "A rule will be prescribed for the manner in which I shall eat and I will decide which of my nobles will present to me my napkin, and each course of my food. I have discussed this with my closest friends and I agree with them that these former practices are outdated, and indeed an affront to my Majesty."

Catherine's heavy features sagged. She breathed deeply as she sought to explain why such customs were important and not to be openly dismissed, but her son continued. "I have been giving the question of the Huguenot threat some serious consideration also." His mother waited; she could imagine what some at the court would make of him discussing the question of the Huguenots *after* he had questioned domestic issues. Henri, distracted for a moment, inspected an outstretched hand, moving the rings on one of his jewelled fingers and smiled at its brilliance.

"I have, with my dearest and closest comrades, he continued, "been discussing the *Brotherhood of the Battus*-do you know of it maman? No, I did not think you would, but it is certainly the most honourable institution. I shall tell you of it." The King had become suddenly eager to discuss this latest fascination. He sat himself at his mother's side, eagerly explaining that the clothing of the sect was not, as she had suspected, rich and garish, colourful and above all – expensive. No – quite the opposite...but, he declared with delight, he would tease her for a bit longer. She and the court would all see when he and his closest circle would carry out their first "observances" later that evening. "We clearly cannot entirely eliminate the scourge of these Huguenots by force alone, so we must therefore trust in God to do it for us....do not interrupt me! Suddenly the jewelled hand slammed hard on the desk where she sat.

Catherine was startled by the ferocity of the action "I will not be interrupted by you or any other!" he shouted suddenly. She had been about to remonstrate with him about such folly.

Catherine waited with patience for him to continue after his sudden outburst. The King stood and wandered to the large window, looking out onto the carefully edged lawns and abundance of colour and imagination that gave the Royal gardens such beauty. He watched several of the courtiers strolling back to the building as the heat of the earlier sun ebbed, giving way to a cooler air as the day drew towards dusk.

"I shall purge myself, and the court if need be," he eventually continued. "We shall learn to suffer as our Lord did, and we will be victorious in our endeavours. God will see how we are repentant, and give strength to our cause." Henri could sense his mother's distaste for such things, which he sought to counter. "Remember, Madame, that you yourself hold the trickeries of the Italian brothers in great esteem; surely if one can trust them...." The accusatory intention was not lost on the Queen Mother, but before she could counter the insinuation, the King had taken up the pile of letters and documents that she and Luc had been going through. With the advantage of height, Henri laughed as he held the papers high above his mother as she unsuccessfully reached for them before he had chance to go through them.

"Ah," Henri laughed, "a letter from our governor at Le Havre, that old rogue! Gossip, nothing more. Another from the armouries, and here another pathetic message from Mary Stuart......" The King stopped as he uncovered the letter that Catherine had tried to conceal from him. His mother sat down slowly as he took in the words. When at last he spoke, it was with a sob "She is dead they say, Marie, my Princess is –" and with those words – he fainted.

♦

There was consternation within the French court. The new King was ill, dying some had said. The death of the Princess of Condé had caused such a shock that already there was great debate about what would happen if, as feared, he was to pass away.

In the apartments of the Queen of Navarre, Alençon, the heir presumptive, paced nervously, his mood varying from elation and excitement to nervous apprehension. Only the previous week he had been devising a way to depart the court without raising suspicion about his intentions. Now, he might well be about to inherit the one thing that he had longed for; to be regarded, to be an absolute ruler of France. His brother's malady may well now be his finest hour to do the decent thing and die and it was not without a cold heart that the youngest of the Valois awaited the death of his elder brother.

Margot sat and watched Alençon while she also considered the ramifications of their elder brother's untimely death. She of course could not inherit, but she was astute enough to believe that Alençon as King would prove more disastrous than Henri, or Charles before him. Yet, the only other candidate would be her own husband. Margot smiled, what would he make of the role? And yet his accession would of course mean that she would be Queen of France, a far richer prize than Navarre.

How different were any of them? Alençon would keep his eye on the throne and make life sheer hell for any that had crossed him before he became King. She smiled, the ever youthful Charlotte de Suave would no doubt find her lover much more attractive once he was a King rather than a mere Duke. If, of course, he did indeed become King. Margot however, had other distractions.

Bussy d'Ambois was a gentleman in Alençon's intimate circle, and a man of great interest to the Queen of Navarre. Bussy had come to her attention a short while before and had, inevitably, become her lover. He was tall and dark, with the most perfect features she had found in anyone since La Molle. She sighed at the memory of the beautiful man she had lost. Bussy was every bit as virile, and with the most impeccable manners. What had originally begun as a flirtatious amusement became something more special, and as was her usual nature, she allowed herself to be courted and adored by this wonderful slave who worshipped her as much as she did him. Care must be taken nonetheless. Margot knew that Bussy's squire was currently a favourite of her brother the King; although for how much longer it was hard to say. Nevertheless, she must be cautious Her mother was ever ready to believe the worst, and it was certainly advisable not to draw the attention of Catherine de Medici.

So Margot sat and allowed her mind to drift to the pleasantries of her most recent suitor, while Alençon paced, and drank and waited earnestly for the summons that would surely arrive, that the King was dead – Long live the King!

♦

In the presence chamber of the King, Catherine listened to Henri's faithful attendants as they described the malady that had completely overtaken their master since the news of the Princess of Condé's death. The King they stated, was bereft. He continued to see no-one but these few men on whom he doted. The Queen Mother looked again at these favourites, all from good solid backgrounds, and with wealthy families. They copied their master in everything; already they chose to dress like the King – although not so similar that they would outshine him, that would invite disaster. In Henri's eyes, that was tantamount to treason.

These gentlemen were effete, their manners quite feminine, their clothing bright and colourful, their fingers, heavy with gold rings of diamonds, and precious stones, pearl earrings swinging as they turned their heads. A cloud of expensive scent filled the air wherever they went. These dandified followers did not readily impress the King's mother; Catherine had seen too many men and women attempt to cling to the cloak of the powerful for purely selfish advancement. These lap-dogs loved Henri now, but they saw their stars rise only with him; if the worst were to happen, their ambition would die with their King.

That same King was now lying in his bed, prostrate with grief, and claiming his life to be at an end; it was not worth living now the Princess was gone. The Queen Mother almost beyond all reason herself, consulted Henri's doctors, and – of course the Ruggieri brothers; this was surely the work of some evil influence, some dark spirit that would take the one person who she loved above all others.

On the Ruggieri's advice, she instructed one of the King's most trusted gentleman. "It is said that the King wears a cross and chain around his neck that had belonged to the late Princess, it must be removed from him. While he wears it, he will be tormented by his grief." Catherine's superstitious nature, receptive as ever by advice from the Italian brothers.

The following day, Catherine felt that it was surely time to take positive action about her son. She had fully believed that his heart was broken by the death of the woman he adored; who knew better than she how deep that longing went, how brutal was the grief that was left for the living to bear. Despite this understanding, she was in truth, becoming irritated by the histrionics and melodrama. Henri needed to put a stop to the rumours that he was dying of a broken heart, he must show himself to his subjects, allow his brother to see that the rumours of his terminal illness were purely that – rumours!

Three of Henri's companions stood at the chamber door, as though defying anyone to approach. Besides that, the King had locked his chamber door the previous day, and claimed that no-one was to be permitted to enter. On hearing that he was still refusing to open the door, the Queen Mother therefore gave orders that it was to be broken down. She would personally ensure that the King would cast no blame on any but herself.

Two strong guards thereafter drove heavily at the door until at last, the hinges gave way, and with a loud crack of the splintered wooden frame, the thick oak door swung wildly for a second or two before it crashed to the ground in front of the startled King's bed.

Catherine immediately took charge. Henri was at the centre of his large bed, a tumble of expensive silk sheets and costly bedcovers, all now a tangled mess. The chamber was cold and dark, the heavy drapes shut out any penetration of light, and candles gave little illumination, many of them burnt almost down to their ends lending the room an air something akin to that of chapel.

The King was unshaven and wearing only a night-shirt; his effeminately long finger nails had clawed at the skin on his chest, and tell-tale signs of blood coloured the silk garment. Much of the vigour he had enjoyed in his youth was already starting to fade, and this was obvious from his demeanour; his eyes, usually dark and bright like his mother's were now dull and lacklustre as sadness sat heavily upon him.

Catherine noticed to her horror that her son cradled a miniature portrait of the dead Princess, and his slender fingers held it occasionally to his lips, where he would whisper to it as though her very spirit was contained within it.

"My son," the Queen Mother stated, a sternness in her commanding voice, "you must desist with this melancholy, no good will come of it. We have your coronation to organise, your court need to have you amongst them. Why I myself am all but despairing of your very life, a life I have endured all to preserve." The Queen Mother broke off and turned slightly away, but not so far that her son could not see her clutch her handkerchief to her lips, and that he could fail to hear a strangled sob. There was silence for a moment, Henri did not react in any way, but glanced at her and looked away. "All is lost without her, I cannot take on this great burden alone."

His mother moved towards the bed, reaching out her hand which he took in his. "My darling son, how could you ever think you are alone? Why, I devote my very life to make yours happy and content. I am here always to guide you, to advise you. Have I not toiled to protect you, often at the risk of my own life? I have sworn to stand with you as you work to make this France a great power once again. Moreover, I also knew much of the Princess, and I believe she loved France as you do, and had let it be known that she saw a country reunited now that you had taken the throne." This was untrue of course, but it did illicit some response from her son.

"She would have been my Queen," he moaned forlornly. Catherine knew of course that such a thing would never have happened, these detested wars of religion had been fought for much less than a Huguenot Princess marrying a Catholic King, not withstanding the lady in question was of course already married.

Catherine sat on the bed beside him, tenderly brushing his hair from his pale face, swollen from hours of weeping. "My son, there will be others in your heart, the pain will become more bearable, and in time, you may not forget, but you will of course find a new reason to live. You are a King, you are young and strong, you have great physical beauty, and the love of your court. So much to help you."

Henri, she noticed, was paying attention now, he wiped his eyes, and his demeanour steadied. Now, wondered Catherine, she would play the one card she believed would trump all others; she patted his hand gently, and stood up. "My son, if you still feel that this burden is too much, then I must advise your council, your ministers. I will now have to prepare your brother, for this burden will now of course rest with him. I hear that already he is planning the day when you relinquish your birthright to him. I shall of course retire to my own estates, he will care little for his mother's guidance, I who have…"

The desired effect was greater than even Catherine could have hoped for. Henri's eyes flashed, their old sparkle rekindled. "Brother? You say my brother makes ready to take the crown? What plans has the traitor made? He will no sooner mount my throne and give orders than a knife blade will be buried in my back. That maggot!!! He shall not inherit! Never! Never!"

As though he had been woken from a deep sleep, Henri began to stir himself and before his mother's own eyes his vigour seemed to return, he shouted for his attendants, ordering that the heavy drapes be drawn to let in some daylight, blaming them for shutting out all the light. His band of gentlemen that upon hearing his voice, had all but raced into his chamber, and now were bearing the brunt of their Royal master's displeasure. Surely it was their fault that all the time he had been virtually dying of his grief, that they had not warned him that his brother was covertly planning to launch a coup.

What a lucky escape, as usual he had his mother to thanks. He turned to speak to her, but Catherine had left the room as the the heavy door was picked up and taken away. She felt happier than she had been for days. The tensions within her family were a constant worry to her, and yet how useful on this occasion. Power was still the one thing that they all coveted more than anything. She had played a dangerous game. Even as she wearied at the disharmony between Henri and Alençon, it had been necessary to twist the dagger of their mutual hatred a little more in order to safeguard the situation. She prayed that she had not overplayed her hand.

The recovery of the King from his dark illness was welcomed throughout the court, certainly by his immediate entourage, but not by his brother Alençon who almost cried when he learned that the King was seemingly back from the very brink of death. The Prince's servants had kept their distance from his, such were his infamous rages.

Whilst Henri had indeed shown himself again to his court, he exchanged the broken-hearted King for an extremely repentant one. The brotherhood of *"The Battus"* was an ancient movement dedicated to self-flagellation, punishing themselves for their sins. The King was fascinated by this and it appeared that he found it a mystical transfiguration. He declared that henceforth, he would join this dismal following, dressing in black monk's habits, their faces concealed by large cowls. Naturally, his faithful gentlemen, slavishly following his lead in all things, took to parading barefooted, dressed only in sackcloth in a procession held at night by torchlight. The ceremony would culminate in a thrashing of bare skin with birch wood.

Among many of the court who followed this strange directive, was the ageing Cardinal of Lorraine, who, not wanting to risk being ostracised by the new regime of young hopefuls that surrounded the King, joined in the processions, barefoot and penitent. Catherine could allow herself a smile of derision at such a sight, but for some reason, the observation of the Cardinal was much on her mind for sometime afterwards.

Perhaps this could be explained by the continual presence of Louise de Vaudemont who was, the Queen Mother had to admit, certainly an amenable young lady, she had now been introduced formally to the King by the Cardinal, and it was obvious to all present that Henri found her much to his liking. Catherine had at first been alarmed at such a prospect as this, but, the fact that her son should be observed to take a mistress would please both her and the nobility. His love of fashion and make up and styling had begun to make him a laughing stock behind his back.

The Queen Mother's spies reported that gossip from the more virile men within the court, was bordering on treasonous; their new King's behaviour suggesting a comparison to the English King Edward, the second of that name. Catherine instructed one of her secretaries to undertake some research into this distant English figure who, she later learned, had lost his throne by favouring young male friends. Henri was enjoying his mistress, and that would not harm his reputation with the virile members of the French court. Indeed, it was expected.

The King's marriage must be immediately arranged before any distasteful gossip began. Naturally, a match with a Princess of Europe would be favourable, and Catherine congratulated herself on discreetly approaching the family of the Swedish Princess Elisabeth Wasa, for certainly only a member of Royal blood could be considered fitting for her son. Preparations for the Princess to visit must begin at once.

♦

In the apartments of the Queen Mother there had been a pleasant evening of music and song. Outside the rain had raged throughout, the sky was heavy with dark forbidding clouds, and a strong wind howled around the palace. While the Catherine ate from a dish of sweet meats, she seemed happy enough until, for no apparent reason, she let go of the goblet of wine that she held to her lips. The goblet hit the edge of the table at which she sat, and clattered to the ground. The noise alerted the women in the chamber, but their mistress was standing hesitantly and staring ahead, as though transfixed.

She then rose unsteadily, her whole body trembling, her face suddenly drained of all colour, her large eyes now wide and fearful. With a trembling arm, she reached out, pointing to the corner, where nothing but a large candle sconce stood, and in a tremulous voice cried out. "Do you see him? It is the Cardinal, the Cardinal of Lorraine, he is – he is dead! See him there, he passes through this chamber in his journey to the other side. See, he reaches to me…" and with that, she sat down heavily and burst into tears.

The ladies within the chamber stood aghast, looking from the Queen Mother to the corner that she alluded to in puzzlement. Several crossed themselves quickly. Catherine continued to stare, horrified, until she allowed her ladies to help her from the room. Her terror remained as they supported her into her bedchamber. It was felt better to put the Queen Mother to her bed, appearing as though in a trance, she showed no sign of her normal composure. Even as she lay in her bed, she continued for some hours to stare into the distance as the night sky rumbled with thunder and flashed with bright lightning. At times she would draw up the bedclothes to her face, clutching them within tight fists. The storm outside raged for the whole evening, and Catherine insisted that extra candles be lit and that she was not left alone, as she spent a troubled and disturbed night.

A particularly severe flash of lightning lit up the oppressive apartments of the ailing Queen Mother. The female attendant who had been watching the storm from the window, jumped with the shock and redrew the heavy curtains. In her bed, Catherine smiled slightly as she recalled the death of her most hated adversary – the Cardinal of Lorraine. Yes, she recalled, a night such as this, the devil did not take its souls quietly, it arrived with a fanfare of noise and light, almost lashing out as it guarded its prize.

Catherine could see the irony of his death and hers; each of them had nursed a hatred and distrust of the other, yet they would both enter the darkness of death with the same legacy of failure. The door of the chamber opened suddenly and through the haze and delirium, she could see her son, the King.

Ah, my beautiful boy, my darling. He had come to weep at his mother's piteous state, he would beg her to live, but each hour that passed drew more of her strength away. The talisman bracelet that she was never without still clutched in her hand. She could not hear what was being discussed by Henri and the physician, but her son glanced over to her only once before offering his limp hand to the doctor to kiss, before turning to the door. He paused a moment, looked to her again, and then was gone.

A great sadness set upon her. Cavriani had watched the King leave and stared at the closed door, before casting his eyes down. "Ah, monsieur," she wanted to say. "Do you not see that this is the price I pay for having given everything to my son?" She was abandoned again as she had been as a babe. Hoisted down the walls of the city in a basket for her own safety, and yet now at the end of her life the basket would instead be a coffin.

She was tired now, the brief moments of lucidity exhausted her. She sighed again and surrendered to the dark

One of Catherine's ladies in waiting relayed the news to her mistress that her great adversary, the Cardinal of Lorraine had died the previous night. The response from the Queen Mother however was annoyance. Catherine rounded on Madame de Maily with irritation. "What news is this to me?" she queried with rising impatience. "Did I not foresee it myself? Were you not all in attendance when I saw him as he appeared to me before he crossed over? You tell me nothing new! Ha, the devil take that vile old prelate."

Later, however, the Queen Mother summoned the Duke of Guise to her to offer her commiserations on his family's great loss. "He was a great man, a true servant of God, his piety was well known to all," she spoke sadly "and all of France have suffered a grievous loss at his passing." Once or twice, the Queen Mother broke down, and bemoaned that all her generation were dying around her. Privately however, she laughed loudly at the details of the Cardinal's death. He had, according to her faithful dwarf Krassowski, joined the King's "fashionable" Battus group, insisting that he also would walk barefoot and wear a common sack in his devotion to the Almighty. It appeared however that he had inevitably caught a severe chill and had died from it.

Krassowski's own informant in the service of the Cardinal had also revealed that whilst he donned a rough hessian sack, he wore a silk garment underneath. The Queen Mother laughed loudly; how little that surprised her. She for one would give personal thanks to God that she had been spared the further scourge of the man once called *"le tigre de la France."*

The French court as a whole, made very little of the Cardinal's death. Whilst many knew him, he had lost most of the power he had once enjoyed at the time the Queen Mother had become regent, and his advancing years allowed him to act as adviser to his nephew rather than be the figurehead of his family. It was noted some time later, that he was so little spoken of that one could have thought he might never have existed.

♦

There was excitement within the court as preparations for the King's coronation continued at a pace. The occasion was to be an elaborate affair, costly and extravagant. Catherine had cautioned against such expense at a time when many in the capital were taxed far more than they earned, and as a result many starved, and resentment grew. Of course, Catherine would be blamed as was generally the case, but she could refuse her son nothing, and he delighted in arranging his wardrobe and that of all his gentlemen or *mignons* as they were now known. They were becoming notorious even on the streets of the capital. Bawdy and distasteful songs could be heard about them in the inns and taverns throughout the city.

Meanwhile, prospects for the Huguenots were on the rise; they had in their leader, Damville, of the

Montmorency family, one who was both brave and cautious. The Queen Mother did as best she could when faced with a deputation who presented their main grievances. Their demands were not over zealous; they asked that the new King grant them equality of worship, and yet, most alarming to Catherine, they asked him to remove the Italians that surrounded and guided him. The wording was not lost on her, she even declared to the deputation that "You Huguenots are like cats, and will always find your feet again"

The situation nevertheless caused concern, yet the most worrying aspect was the King's complete indifference to it. How long ago, Catherine thought, were those days when Henri had valiantly earned respect for his bravery at Monluc and Jarnac? Now that same man was only interested in pomp and growing extravagance, a former general who now gave himself up to fashion, make-up and complete decadence. The Queen Mother reproached her son again as to the expense of the forthcoming coronation and all the accompanying masques, balls and galas that the King was personally supervising.

Nothing was to be left to chance, it must be the most spectacular occasion to be remembered in history. The King's view was merely that as Parisians loved a spectacle, so must they pay for it.

Catherine had been horrified, but her son grew irritable at the constant warning to control his spending. "Am I to be continually bothered with this?"

"My son," Catherine began "I have to question –" Henri swung round from the mirror he stood before, judging the jewelled velvet suit he had just had made, "You question me maman," yet I am *your* King am I not? I will not be questioned. Remember that while I rule here there will be one master and no mistress!"

Catherine stood horrified for a moment. Henri almost immediately lapsed back to his former mood. "Pearls or diamonds with this doublet do you think?" His mother declared herself a bad judge of such things, and as two of Henri's favourite mignons entered the room and gasped at his image, the Queen Mother may as well have not been in the room as the sycophantic courtiers marvelled at the ethereal image that was their Royal master.

At Rheims the day of the coronation arrived, crisp and cold, but with a clear blue sky. The King, whether realising the upset that his harsh words had caused his mother, insisted that she accompany him in his carriage, decorated as it was in silk cloth and adorned with gold fleur-de-lis. Henri sat excitedly, eager for the ceremony to begin, but the journey was to prove an ugly one.

Groups of Huguenots lined the path taken by the procession, and mutterings soon turned to shouts and insults were hurled as much to the "painted and perfumed catamites" with which the King surrounded himself. Looking as though he might well cry, Catherine called guards to ensure that the crowds were kept back.

The ceremony itself was not without dramatic incident either. No sooner had the crown been placed on the new King's head than he immediately complained that it hurt him, and indeed it had nearly slipped from his head on more than one occasion. To a gasping audience, this was not seen as a good sign at all, and the ever superstitious Queen Mother had felt unnerved at the whole ceremony. However, Henri was her most beloved son for all his moods and fancies, and her heart had welled up in pride as she joined the chorus praising the new monarch. The day she had worked and longed for had finally come, and the son she knew could be one of France's greatest Kings would now realise her dreams and aspirations. There was much to be done, and she prayed that Henri had the health to endure it. For the love she felt for no other, she wept quiet tears of joy.

An exhausted Queen Mother welcomed the end of the day, and declared that she would spend the following one quietly working on state business. She had welcomed the many ambassadors and envoys that had gathered for the occasion, and now felt that the amusements and entertainments that had been arranged could be safely left for the younger members of the court to enjoy. It was therefore a day or so later when the King visited her in great excitement. He hugged her warmly, drawing her attention from the pile of letters and correspondence that littered her desk. As usual at such times she felt joy in his happiness; the endless celebrations had taken much out of him, and thick make-up hid the tell-tale signs of tiredness from his large eyes.

"Mother," he said excitedly, "you must come amongst us again, you must dress in your finest gown, for we are to celebrate. There must be extra entertainment, my Queen would wish it. Truly, I can deny her nothing." Catherine felt at once a little dizzy, and her face drained of all colour, her mouth hardened into a straight line. "Your Queen, my son?" she asked almost in a whisper. Henri clapped his hands together, and drew his mother from her chair to stand in front of him. "My darling Louise, she is to become your daughter. We are to marry tomorrow maman, you must come and greet my Queen."

It was to Catherine's credit that she did not show for one moment the most incredulous shock that she felt, and as the King talked on excitedly about his new Queen's virtues, his mother saw, like dust in the wind, her plans for a great match, celebrated throughout Europe, lay in ruins. Of course, she had known about his newfound interest, and moreover, had welcomed the idea that he would take a mistress; even despite her own experience she had to agree that men expected their King to be a robust male with an eye for a beautiful woman.

Eventually, the Queen Mother had recovered enough of her wits to speak in as controlled a tone as she could. "But my son, you have been aware that for some time I have negotiated with the great families abroad. Why, indeed the Swedish Princess Elizabeth has been most..." The King cupped his hands and gently placing them on her chin, drew his mother to him and kissed her forehead. "Ah yes," he said "but nothing formal has been agreed, we can still put an end to talks. You will know how best to deal with it maman. Ah what excitement we have, all has gone so well with my coronation, and now my marriage." Catherine barely heard him, and she remained seated as he twirled around like a child, even clasping one of her ladies in waiting and dancing with her in his gaiety.

There were occasions during his life, that merely the sight of this man laughing would have brought tears to his mother's eyes, her maternal pleasure in seeing him so elated and happy would melt her heart. This particular time was not one of them, and while she watched him, she fought an impulse to shake him and implore him to realise that everything she did was for him and her wish to see him become a wise and powerful monarch. She had tolerated the extravagance he showed, indeed, she was known herself to have run up considerable personal debts, yet that did not concern her, that could be managed.

This sort of decision, however, was one he should have shared with her first. The house of Lorraine would welcome this, she knew. That detestable Cardinal of Lorraine – even from the grave that man seemed to mock her. She was certain it was his doing; how could she not have realised their plans, been cautious as she had always been? Her lessons were always hard ones to learn, but learn from them she would. She must be always alert for the greed of men who lusted for power; her notorious spy network must be ever vigilant. A curse on the scourge of the Guise and their constant ambition to control affairs. The King may now dance for joy in the brief elation of marriage, but at what cost to him and indeed herself? She felt she would scream at the foolishness of this man, her son, who revelled more at his costly preparations than the hard work his mother was undertaking on his behalf. The situation was intolerable. When at length she could bear his over-excited behaviour no longer, she sharply clapped her hands; signalling for her women to leave her. Immediately the dancing King stopped, turning his head and fixing his eyes on his mother's as her ladies stepped dutifully back, hanging their heads and only remaining where they stood as the King raised a hand, stopping them from leaving. Henri's smile remained, but his dark eyes locked with those of his mother and Catherine caught a flash of menace. He turned to the ladies with a mock bow and, stepping over to where she sat, he leant down to kiss his mother's pale powdered face. She felt his hot cheek against her own, but his voice was like ice as he whispered, "Remember maman, it is I who will say who is dismissed. I the King."

Henri kissed her other cheek, then turned and marched out of the room calling for his tailors and servants. Once he had gone, Catherine sat for a moment and then suddenly stood and drawing her arm across her desk, swept all items to the floor with a roar of fury that made her ladies jump. Inks, quills despatches, letters and books all scattered. A nearby flagon of watered wine, an arrangement of beautiful flowers, all were cast to the ground until, after ordering everyone from the chamber, she swiftly slammed the door after them and, leaning against it slid to the floor and sobbed.

The spectacular celebrations that accompanied the wedding of the new King and his bride were the most spectacular that many had ever seen. Days of lavish entertainment, dancing, mock battles, masque balls and beautifully crafted ballet displays had followed, and while the court entertained themselves on a grand and expensive scale, the Queen Mother sat lightly tapping her nail on the elaborate hilt of her walking cane and cast her large, black eyes over those who flocked around their King.

Henri looked a devastating sight, and even his detractors at the court could not deny he cut a dazzling, if unconventional figure. The King had set a trend that those of his intimate circle followed closely. The sleeves of their shirts and jackets were elaborately padded, while cloaks were worn across one shoulder, and breeches slashed with vivid, dazzling colours. No expense was spared with the richness of his attire.

From her chair, set back from the main throng of the large chamber, the Queen Mother cast an assessing eye over the players of the merry, extravagant celebrations.

Word was everywhere that the *mignons* were hated throughout the court, although few voiced their objections for fear of word reaching their Royal patron. Catherine's hooded eyes came to rest on the group of favourites of the King: Maugiron, Quelus, Livarot and du Gast. A group of almost twelve young men in outrageously painted faces, hair frizzed and decorated with small jewels, earrings and a manner of dress that stopped just short of complete imitation of their beloved master.

Whilst Catherine could not have wished for more loyal attendants and companions for her son, these particular gentlemen did not not represent a body of wise, trusted and worthwhile men of court. Moreover, they were mocked at every opportunity behind their backs, and in some cases – to their faces. Any slight, however small, was reported to the King, and all at court knew that to retain any level of closeness to the sovereign would mean tolerance of these pampered creatures.

For Henri, a selection of these individuals was made by exception in three particular regards; their physical beauty, their complete adoration of their master above all else, and their perfect swordsmanship. These young men would strive to outdo one another in attracting the attention of their beloved King, be it by a unique gift, a song perhaps, or any feat of valour, and it was in this respect that the animosity between courtier and *mignon* began to boil over.

The Duke of Guise in particular had made all too clear his dislike of "these fops" as he termed them. He, who should be held in high regard by his sovereign and have regular access to him, as well as being a trusted advisor, was almost ignored by the King. Henri would wave him away, and the group of mignons would smile at the Duke's discomfort, happy in the knowledge that it was they with whom the King would spend his time. They mocked Guise with false laughter, imitating bows, and whispering to their Royal master, who would turn and glance at Guise before they all giggled together.

Whilst the Queen Mother could ignore the pretty boys that surrounded her son, forever assuring him of his wisdom, wit and physical beauty, she was beginning to resent the time that her son spent with them. He could laugh and joke with them enjoying the frivolity, but as she knew only too well, those who had the ear of the King could do much harm. Their power must be limited. She knew that the Duke was humiliated by his treatment. Perhaps it was time that she discussed with him some means of curtailing the influence of these court popinjays. Naturally, she could not be seen to be involved in whatever action Guise wanted to take. She naturally abhorred violence and therefore could not condone, say, an argument that could so easily get out of hand. How quickly these men drew their swords rather than taking a peaceful, rational course. She smiled inwardly at her own thoughts, and was still smiling when she slipped her arm through that of the Duke of Guise and drew him away for a more intimate discussion.

◆

The bright moon that earlier in the evening had cast a vivid illumination over the rooftops and walkways of

Paris, was, as the evening drew to a close, becoming faintly obscured by the darkening clouds that heralded the threat of stormier weather than the balmy stillness of the daytime. Across the back alleyways, four figures stealthily made their way to an area of the city, where the more popular taverns and inns were grouped. Even though the hour was late, revelry and music could still be heard emanating from the larger of these as the Parisians made what little cheer they could in such sorry times.

The four men stopped at the end of one street, shielded under the overhanging buildings that almost touched at their tip, so high and distorted as they were. They had waited only several minutes before the subjects of their particular interest appeared.

It was impossible not to recognise the foppish favourites of the court, who on this as many other nights, had spent a ribald evening of dicing and gaming, and even – discreetly, enjoying the favours of the tavern's wenches. Such men as these had become a familiar, if unusual sight around the city. Their hair curled and perfumed, their neck ruffs outrageously wide.

The group of three gentlemen of the court walked, somewhat uneasily, out onto the street, their arms entwined, their spirits high and noisy. Messieurs, Quelus, Livarot and Maugiron had enjoyed a very sociable evening. How grand life was to be a favourite of one's King, young and with good prospects.

It was at this same time that the four waiting men left the shadows of their concealment and sauntered into the path of the three mignons. The two parties stopped for a moment, appraising each other, before one of the four gentlemen, whose livery proclaimed him as being in the service of the Duke of Guise, spat at the feet of the three courtiers before he spoke to his comrades. "Ah, my friends, see here, what do we have before us, could it be a damsel fresh from his Majesty's bed? But no, it is surely one of the Queen Mother's escardon! See that painted face, the sensuous pout, such jewels and finery." The man swept an elaborate bow towards the King's companions. Another of the Guise men bowed also standing back gasping in feigned adoration at the sight before him, stepping around the nervous looking Livarot until once behind him he grabbed at the younger man's buttock. "And such a pretty arse! just as the King likes them!"

With those words he sprang back, laughing along with the other three soldiers as they then aped the mignons by pursing their lips and walking with an exaggerated manner, their noses high in the air. The faces of the King's men were masks of fury, the physical assault on Livarot alone had all three reaching instinctively for their swords, light rapiers that hung at their side, sharp and deadly. The scene was set as two sides were established, one defending honour, dignity and defence of their master, or the pleasure of the fight and, simply, following orders.

Revellers from the taverns leaving the convivial company of the inns and now spilling out onto the street, wisely hung back – this was surely a potentially violent situation.

As for the King's men, they knew that their position was now most precarious, their opponents were men from the service of the Duke of Guise; it was all too well known that in, the capital, the Guise were heroes – the mob would favour only one side in this skirmish.

All at once, swords clashed as the two sides engaged. For all their foppery, the King's men were certainly brave as well as quick and deft. Guise's men goaded them into a fight, and the mignons would not back away from it. One of the Duke's men received an early blow, and reeled away clutching his arm; the contest was equal thereafter, and blows were traded for some time before Maugiron was slashed across the face, the blade opening up his cheek as blood poured down his tunic. After only a moment though, he was into the melee again, bravely on the verge of beating down one of the liveried soldiers before a scream alerted him that Quelus had been badly injured. All fighting seemed to stop as a sword was drawn from the yellow brocaded tunic that was now rapidly turning red from the blood that seemed to gush from his stomach. Quelus sank to his knees, and with that, the soldiers stepped back, before collecting their still moaning injured comrade and retreating into the night shadow from whence they had come.

The Queen Mother had been asleep for some hours before she was being raised from her slumber by one of her ladies in waiting telling her that the King had sent for her, she was to attend him with all speed. Catherine's mind teemed with all manner of dreadful thoughts as she hastily dressed and, taking up her walking cane, made her way to her son's chamber. She could hear the King's wails of distress and anguish even before she swept through a band of courtiers and attendants, all of them standing aside to let her through.

The figure of the King was kneeling at one side of his own bed, clutching a fistful of the gold brocaded coverings in his two fists, sobbing into the material. In the

Royal bed, now lay a figure writhing in agony and distress, the premier of the Royal favourites – Quelus. It was obvious that the man had been badly wounded, the swathe of bandages that were wrapped around his body were almost entirely stained in blood. Catherine, in an instant, took in the scene before her. That Quelus was injured at all caused her little concern, though the consequences from whatever had happened might well do.

The Royal doctors she at once recognised standing to one side, their grave countenance told her that the end was inevitable. Hopeless or not, this drama should not be played out before the whole court, and with a quick wave of dismissal to the assembled throng, she proceeded cautiously to the kneeling King. "My son," she said soothingly, "What has happened here?" Henri at once looked up at her first with a sadness that she had never seen in him before. A tragic figure, bereft of all hope, and enduring the greatest heartbreak. Henri's bloodshot eyes were swollen from the crying, and yet those same dark eyes flashed menacingly as he looked up at her. "Look at him, maman – look at him! Oh, my beautiful Quelus, my darling, faithful companion. He has been slain by that whoreson! That preening, strutting peacock, he has killed my dearest one." The King broke down again, letting up only when the cold hand of his favourite reached for his own. Catherine could only be grateful she had dismissed the court gossips from witnessing Henri take the white shivering hand and hold it to his lips, and kiss it gently. "My son," Catherine began, "it is not seemly that you –" She got no further as the King screamed at her to get out. The Queen Mother stood for a moment but did not move away. She laid a soothing hand on her son's shoulder and he now turned, sobbing at her feet, holding the bottom of her gown as he had held the bedclothes. "Oh dear God! he wailed, "Heaven help my beloved Quelus, he is slain, he is slain!" Catherine now laid her hand on his head, gently stroking the fine hair that had once been so luxuriant, but was now becoming brittle from so much curling, powdering and perfuming. She hesitated to ask, but of course she must – "Who do you mean, who has done this, my son? What has taken place here?"

The answer she already knew.

Henri gritted his teeth as he spat out the words with hatred and venom. "Guise! The Guise and his band of henchmen, it is their hatred of me and their jealousy of my closest servants. Their envy of my most loyal brothers has driven them to this, they will not stop until they destroy me."

Catherine at once realised the danger of her son's words. She looked again over to the Royal physicians that had remained in the chamber. It was clear that all was lost, a barely concealed shake of the head from the chief physician had not only been perceived by the Queen Mother, the King had also seen the resignation on their faces, and he again broke down in sobs.

Quelus lingered on painfully for several days and the King barely left his side until finally the Royal favourite passed away in his master's arms.

So, thought the Queen Mother, Guise has acted swiftly following their private discussion. Catherine had immediately sent out her spies to uncover the full facts of the skirmish that had resulted in Quelus's death. Reports had already reached her that there had been several incidents where the King's mignons had goaded the Guisards into verbal arguments, daring them to touch those whom the King loved most. There had finally been enough said, and the result was violence. Catherine could see that there was a certain inevitability about the matter, and she therefore satisfied herself that all this would have come to pass eventually; but to a great extent it mattered not what she believed, but rather what Henri would do about the matter.

There had always been bad blood between the headstrong Henri de Guise and this Valois King. The Queen Mother had sent for Guise to explain his men's actions in front of the grieving King, but they were met with only a shrug, and a promise that he would have the matter investigated and the individuals responsible would be dealt with. The King had not believed for one moment that would happen; moreover, it was ultimately Guise that he blamed-it mattered little who had struck the death blow, but whose silent hand guided it. In private, Catherine laughed at the simplicity of men. She would console her son at his terrible loss – how she grieved with him declaring Quelus had become almost another son to her, whilst quietly congratulating Guise for his swift action in checking the growing power of the mignons.

It was, nevertheless, the King's immediate response that had made his mother uneasy. After emerging from his period of mourning, for which he and his remaining mignons wore black, Henri seemed a chastened man, suddenly looking old and worn, his features pale and tired, and with dark rings around eyes that seemed to have lost their sparkle and mischief. His mother looked at him sadly and pondered why all her sons had seemed to age so quickly, becoming old men almost overnight.

The King would not be drawn on his intentions regarding Guise, merely saying to his mother that he would be avenged, but not in any way suggest when or how this revenge would be exacted.

Sad news reached the court that Catherine's eldest daughter Claude, the Duchesse of Lorraine had died in childbirth, and her mother had withdrawn to her palace at Blois to mourn privately. Claude had given her no trouble during her twenty-seven years of life. She had married into the Lorraine family aged only eleven, and with her hunched back and clubbed foot, she was never considered to have the same attributes of her young sister Margot, or indeed, her late sister, Elizabeth, Queen of Spain. Whilst dynastic considerations were paramount, she had not seemed unhappy with her lot in life, and she and her husband had been blessed with nine children; the last of which had resulted in her death. Now, Catherine considered again how little attention she had paid to the private, docile daughter who had accepted without question the wishes of her mother. Had she suffered in silence while Catherine devoted all her attention on her sons? Undoubtedly so, yet it could not have been otherwise.

The youngest of the Valois sons, however, was causing unease for his mother and his brother the King. Insisting on being given his due respect by those he called "the King's catamites," Alençon was apparently under constant humiliation from Henri's mignons who teased him for his pitted complexion and short stature. How Catherine had argued with the King that he must halt this humiliation of someone who, when all was said and done, was the son of a King, and as a member of the Royal family was deserving of respect. Henri however, refused to intervene and while his gentlemen giggled in delight at every insult, Alençon had grown more and more frustrated.

It had been Catherine's idea that maybe a more responsible role could be found for her youngest son; a post with greater freedom. To this end, Alençon should maybe be free of the shackles that had once been so necessary to curtail his habit of causing trouble. The Queen Mother remembered well how the insufferable du Gast had at the time voiced his opinion, standing behind the King and whispering in his ear. It was intolerable that her policy should have been discussed with a mere Royal favourite.

Du Gast, had stated his concern, and Henri had agreed with him that it was not sensible policy given Alençon's propensity for troublemaking. Catherine's fury had been barely contained, yet years of concealing her feelings had enabled her to smile and accept the King's decision, heavily influenced though it may be.

Nevertheless, Henri was not completely unaware of the the danger his brother represented by being curtailed at court. Maybe, Alençon would learn from past mistakes and stay loyal, perhaps his mother was right and relaxing the restraints on him would show goodwill, as much as the brothers disliked one another. Either that, or, as Henri hoped, Alençon would show that little had been gained by keeping him confined to court, and his true deceit would manifest itself in some treachery and his own downfall would be almost inevitable and justified.

"I will, as you advise maman, allow my brother his liberty. If, as you suggest, he has learned from his mistakes, he will not find me unwilling to place some trust in him. He will, nevertheless, remain my subject, and he will show me loyalty. Remember however, if mine, and indeed your own, generous trust in him is misplaced I will not forgive him a second time." Word from her spies reported all manner of news concerning Alençon, but all seemed merely gossip – at the moment.

Now here at her favourite residence at Blois, the Queen Mother considered her surroundings with pleasure and satisfaction. Almost all the chambers and rooms within the Chateau had been lavishly redecorated under her supervision. Most noticeably, the walls of her own private apartments panelled in beautiful oak with ornate carvings, arabesques picked out in the richest colours of red and gold. Catherine pressed lightly on a part of one of the panels, and a click was heard as one of the sections moved. The Queen Mother smiled as she drew back the panel to reveal a small cupboard. Inside were a collection of ornate glass bottles of varying sizes, some small velvet pouches, a few jars containing powders and some ornate trinkets. She smiled after satisfying herself that all was in order and clicked the panel back in to place.

The Catherine wandered through the other chambers, the usual tapping of her walking cane silenced against the rich Turkish carpeting. She scanned the walls of her library appreciatively, satisfied in the rows of volumes in rich velum, large leather bound works, some by the great philosophers, large collections of manuscripts in Greek, Latin and Hebrew. However else history would judge her, she was sure that she would be seen as a true Medici; a lover of the arts, of architecture, design and building, whether a redesign of a Royal small chapel, or an entirely new wing to the Louvre.

She spent her days quietly, and indeed felt invigorated from them. She grieved for her late daughter, but she must carry on to prevent the remainder of her brood from destroying one another and France with them. The intolerable civil wars seemed to rage constantly. Considering the political and religious state of the realm, Catherine was ever aware than tensions ran deep, and that plots and sub-plots continued. Her vast legion of spies had infiltrated most areas, and news from them was rarely worth celebrating.

Since the massacre in Paris, the Huguenots had seemed, for a short while at least, to have lost heart in their fight for tolerance of their religion. There was no doubt that the slaying of their leaders and figureheads had set them back. However, they had not entirely abandoned their dream and there was always a new hero to lead the fight. Damville of the famed family of Montmorency could lay claim to the vast largely Huguenot province of Languedoc, and its considerable forces had on more than one occasion proved decisive in the endless fighting. To this dangerous mix was the added interference of Protestant troops from Germany under the leadership of John-Casmir, son of the Elector-Palatine. Catherine had Condé to thank for such a divisive alliance.

Here then was a new branch of resistance known popularly as the Politiques, combining their forces with the main central body of the Huguenot forces. She would still pursue her policy of religious tolerance whenever she could, but the young boys who had seemed so inept, inexperienced and foolish but a few short years ago were men now, and it would be they that carried the fate of France in their hands. The likes of Guise, Navarre and her own sons were not as easily dominated as they had been. Intolerable though it was, she realised that foreign powers held the purse strings; Spain for the Catholics, England for the Protestants. Guise, in particular, caused her some alarm. He appeared to be emerging as a figurehead for the Catholics as their King committed less and less time on affairs of state and more on his appearance, his lapdogs and spending vast amounts on his pleasures. In Guise of course, the Catholics saw his father, this brave, proud man that could trace his bloodline back to Charlemagne himself, and put his faith before all else. Catherine knew that the emergence of a Catholic League had the full endorsement of the King of Spain and this frightened her more than anything. Henri d'Guise was a young man that she needed to watch closely.

The Queen Mother had admonished herself several times whenever she looked at him wondering how things would have fared in France by now had she had such a son. Navarre seemed to be causing little concern, yet she would be wrong to dismiss him merely because of his languid and lazy attitude. Behind the buffoonery and comic bluster, she was sure, was a man of particular cunning. He had mistresses of course, her own creature from the *escardon* Charlotte de Suave, being his main obsession. One may think it strange that Catherine had set one of her ladies to ensnare her own son in law, but there was good reason in the Queen Mother's opinion. Margot had made it quite plain that she disliked her husband and raged constantly against the cruelty of being forced to marry "a provincial oaf" as she declared him. It was a sound policy to have someone close to Navarre that could report to her. Besides their overt enmity, there did exist a strange bond between the two;

both driven into a marriage that neither had wanted, each trying to survive in the hotbed that was the court of France. The intelligent Margot had, on more than one occasion, defended her husband when he had faced her brother's wrath, in this reign and the one before.

So now as she sat in solitude, her mind teeming with the many issues that faced her, she remained adamant that she would still control the King, that she could still make certain that she knew of any plots and schemes while there was still time enough to act. Alençon would always provoke, always be bitter that he had been a youngest son, with no prospect of reaching the throne himself.

One plan that may yet come to fruition however, was the reopening of talks with the English to discuss a match between their virgin Queen and Alençon. It had always been Catherine's dearest wish to live to see a crown on the heads of all her children. With the exception of the recently deceased Claude, Catherine's youngest child was the only one of the Valois sons who could not yet claim the title of King.

Catherine had written recently to her "dearest friend" expressing the hope that she might soon call her daughter. It made the Queen Mother laugh aloud when she considered the possible union. What mischief might her errant son cause for his new bride? It was said that Elizabeth would let no man rule over her. Ha, either she would have to reconsider that resolve or Alençon would have to learn to control both his tongue and his appetite for glory and adulation. One thing was certain, Catherine would feel a great deal less anxious once her youngest hot-headed son was safely over the Channel.

♦

Whilst the Queen Mother pondered over the affairs of her youngest son, he was about to reward her trust with the most flagrant betrayal. No sooner had his brother the King appeased their mother by relaxing the confines within which he had been kept than he had made furtive plans for a bold escape.

It was late in the evening and a hush fell over Paris. Few people dared to wander the streets in these times; skirmishes, robbery, brawls; all had become common enough. Paris was a city of suspicion and tensions were evident. Indeed, the only evidence of any joy and abandonment came from the Louvre, where laughing courtiers could be seen at the windows and the candelabras stay lit almost until dawn.

While the music played in the Royal apartments, a dark swarthy figure slipped quietly out of a chamber, creeping along the corridor and descending some steps to a small door. The figure knocked on the door gently three times, waited a second and then repeated the knock. The small door was immediately opened, a dull light filled the chamber. Once inside, the figure removed his cloak, and embraced the young woman who had risen to greet him. Margot, the Queen of Navarre welcomed her young brother, the Duke d'Alençon. The Prince spun around to see Margot's closest companion, Henrietta, the Duchesse de Nevers, who had opened the chamber door; he nodded to her respectfully.

Margot's eyes glittered in the candlelight, she stood proudly, her dark hair was worn down flowing over her shoulders, her dress was simple but flattering. Her brother took both of her hands in his own and met her smile. She was excited by the potential danger of a situation, and this latest enterprise was fraught with it.

"Everything is prepared?" she questioned him. "Are your men in place to meet you as planned?" Alençon nodded. "All is arranged as I have commanded. I have thirteen of my men waiting just outside the city."

With the relaxation of his confinement, Alençon would never have a better chance of gaining his freedom from the brother he hated and the mother who constantly admonished him, and treated him so shamefully. The whole of the court saw him as a fool, a bitter younger brother behaving like a spoilt child. He knew the abhorrent favourites of his brother's made fun of him, and often when he was within earshot. Well, they would all see he would not be cast aside as of no relevance, he would show them all that he too could command respect. As heir apparent, he would not be ill treated. He longed to be free of the "viper's den" as he called his brother's court. Of course it had been necessary to bide his time, it would have been foolish to have attempted to gain his freedom too soon, he must wait until his every move wasn't being scrutinised by his mother's spies and his brother's lapdogs. His only hope was escape, and it was with the help of his sister that a plan had been devised.

The Duchesse stepped forward and helped him off with his cloak, which was then substituted for a black floor-length velvet one with a large deep hood. The Duchesse was not unlike the Duke in height, so the cloak was a reasonably good fit. Margot turned him around to face her, and she pulled the cloak closer under his chin, her delicate fingers feeling the rough stubble on his throat. "Henrietta's coach is always ready at this time" she stated, the guards will not trouble you, they are used to seeing her leave at this late hour. Her driver has been instructed to take you outside the city walls. He will not betray us; he has been paid well."

Alençon's hands trembled slightly as he embraced her "God be with you, sister," he stated. Margot smiled, "May he be with all of us François. Now go, quickly!" The Prince could feel hot tears in his eyes as he turned away towards where Henrietta had drawn back a curtain to reveal a further small door which she then opened and stepped through. Looking one way then the other, and motioning the Prince, they both hurried off into the dark night.

Several minutes later, the Duchesse stopped and motioned to a gateway that led on to a courtyard. From here, Alençon could hear a horse hoof against the cobbled ground and the Duchesse smiled nodding in affirmation that the way was ahead. He squeezed Henrietta's hand and, pulling the hood firmly down over his face, he stepped out of the darkness towards the waiting carriage.

♦

The Queen Mother's normal passive features registered little of the dread that she felt once one of her trusted spies had finished the news he had hastened to Blois to relate. So, Alençon had defied her and his brother the King and made good an escape to the Huguenot stronghold at Dreux. She could not believe she had been so easily duped and her fury was almost beyond endurance. The further, more alarming news had at first been difficult for her informant to relay, but Catherine had reassured him that she insisted on hearing everything he had learnt on her behalf.

The news she had been told had been bad enough, but her spy recounted to her a strange conversation overheard between the King and one of his favourites at the moment, a man by the name of Sebastian d'Epilat. Catherine recalled to mind the vicious, arrogant individual; a small man with a slim wiry frame and a large nose, small gimlet eyes. The Queen Mother had disliked him instantly, but he had charmed the King, who valued his company and his ready wit. He adored his master and had risen quickly in his service. The conversation that her man now related gave Catherine the greatest cause for concern. The favourite was with his master when news was brought to him of his brother's successful escape. He had been there to soothe his brow, whilst whispering the vengeance the King could exact on his traitorous sibling. However, Sebastian had also called into question Catherine's part in the affair. Was the King's mother maybe tiring of her role in affairs? Was her workload too much? She was surely becoming to old for the cut-and-thrust of the political scene, and as a result was starting to make mistakes, errors of judgement that could have catastrophic consequences? Perhaps it was time for the King to question where her loyalties lay. The King, had said little in response but was heard to command d'Epilat to personally travel to Blois and escort his mother back to Paris.

Catherine shuddered at the words. She had no need to doubt them, her man was reliable. With almost a gasp of shock, she dismissed him, with a nod to one of her dwarves to hand over some coins for his trouble. Once they had left the room, Catherine broke down, sobbing into her handkerchief. This was too much. Her grief for Claude, her anger at Alençon and Margot, who the King would surely blame. More than anything, it was her anger at the King's friend, the vile whispers from one of his lapdogs. She sat for some time. The bright afternoon drifted into a pleasant early evening, and the shadows grew long through the windows of the Queen Mother's study, as she considered her next move.

She narrowed her eyes, dry now that she had spent her frustration and anger; so, the mignon was sent to accompany her back to Paris? She must afford him a suitable welcome.

It was the following day that a smart, elaborate carriage wound its way through the town and began the steep climb up to the palace. Inside, swathed in rich furs to keep out the biting cold, Sebastian d'Epilat considered his current good fortune. He was becoming highly favoured by the King, even some of those other fops were jealous of him now. He could smile at their stupidity and vanity. Of course he copied them; the outrageous clothes, the jewellery, the elaborate hairstyles. It was all necessary if he was to be closest to the Henri. Sebastian smiled, but it was at the pathetic image of his master. Henri, although still relatively young, was already showing the characteristics of old age; losing his hair, and, in all honesty also his good looks. His hands tremored slightly, unnoticed it would seem by all but his closest companions; and indeed, it was now the job of his most loyal servants to spend a great deal of time each day, preparing for his transportation from a tired, dull, almost middle-aged man to a bright, dazzling juvenile King, full of life, vigour and splendour. There were of course those around Henri who did worship him and would do anything for him, but there were certainly many amongst his inner circle that did not. Nevertheless, if playing at being a court dandy, dressing outrageously and being pawed at by a slightly hysterical looking buffoon of a King was the price to be paid on his rise to the high echelons of power, then it was worthwhile. He served a new master now, the rewards were potentially much greater than being gifted a chateau and estates for being one of the King's beloveds. He had been warned of the duplicity and cunning of the Queen Mother, but he did not heed such warnings. The days of influence that Catherine de Medici had enjoyed were at an end, and the more whispers to the King about his mother's failure in recent affairs of government, the sooner she would be dismissed from court, and the process of dragging down the last of the tainted Valois could commence.

Now, it was he whom the King had commanded to travel to Blois and bring his mother back to court. Yes, Sebastian thought with satisfaction, the time of the Medici in France was surely soon at an end.

The Queen Mother received the favourite in her study, he entered the chamber as though it was his own palace; nonchalantly, and with an air of impatience. He, like all her son's companions, was dressed immaculately, in startling dark blue breeches with a richly brocaded tunic slashed with yellow velvet. He wore a large pearl in his ear, and his hands glittered with large gold rings of diamonds and rubies. His over-exaggerated ruff made his head look smaller, and Catherine for a moment was perversely reminded of the head of Gaspard d'Coligny resting on the silver platter she had presented to Navarre and Condé following the Paris massacre.

Sebastian was known to the Queen Mother of course, but only superficially; just one of a number of faces that her son seemed pleased to have around him. She had always felt, however, that he and two other premier mignons, d'Valette and d'Arques, were not quite what they seemed. It would of course be pointless to voice her misgivings to Henri, who would have no word said against any of them.

The favourite took in his surroundings as he started to remove his fine leather gloves before he reluctantly kissed the outstretched hand. "You are welcome monsieur," Catherine said, a smile that could have masked all emotion played on her thin carmine lips.

Sebastian smiled weakly, without looking into those black, menacing eyes that he had to admit were certainly unnerving. "We must leave here soon, Madame, the King commands it," he stated, "I am to personally escort you back to Paris. His Majesty has –" Catherine held up one of her delicate hands to interrupt.

"I have had letters from my son that have informed me as much," she lied. "We will leave tomorrow after-" This time it was Sebastian's turn to interrupt "The King commanded straight away, Madame" he retorted arrogantly. Catherine smiled as though he were a simpleton "My son will allow me some time to prepare myself for the journey, I have affairs here to settle."

"The King, is not to be kept waiting Madame, not even by you"

"Yet I am his mother"

"You are his *subject* Madame, as are we all"

The impulse to take her walking cane and strike the arrogant perfumed fop before her was almost more than she could control. He had continued to stare at her boldly, without the slightest awareness that he had most certainly overstepped the boundary of protocol.

Nevertheless, years of hiding her true feelings and emotions, allowed her to remain calm. "Monsieur, you must eat and refresh yourself, you will be my guest here tonight, and tomorrow we will set off for Paris. I have been too long away and indeed the King has need of me I think. Nay, monsieur do not seek to persuade me otherwise. You will dine with me this evening. Until then you must take some rest."

Catherine smiled at the petulant young man, and once again extended her hand for the obligatory respect. He barely let his lips touch her skin, but as his eyes met hers, he felt a slight unease, her gaze seemed to draw him in, and for a moment he could understand what fear she had been able to arouse in so many. Before Sebastian had realised it, he was being led out of the chamber by one of the Queen Mother's attendants, leaving him both embarrassed and angry.

The dwarf Rodamont watched the man leave the room before leaving his position in the corner of the chamber, and approaching his mistress. Her trusty servant must take refreshment to the Queen Mother's guest, and after that – she had another task for him.

The wine that had been brought to Sebastian had been most welcome, but he feared he had drunk too freely of it as his head began to feel quite painful. He must sleep, of course, the journey had tired him; the Queen Mother had been right to advise him to rest until the following day. He would relax before he dined later, and no sooner had he lain down on the soft bed than he was in a deep sleep. Some moments later, the chamber door opened silently, and a diminutive figure moved quickly over to the bed, and after climbing up on it, deftly removed the fine small leather bag that Sebastian had carried on the inside of his costly jacket. Jumping down again, the figure left the chamber as silently as he had entered.

The Queen Mother had grown stouter with the passing years. When younger, she had been a fussy eater, turning over her food and picking at it selectively. She had however, grown to be a lover of fine wine and choicest meats, pastries and wafers. It was a vast array of food, therefore, that was presented to the King's man that evening at Blois.

Sebastian had slept well for several hours, and whilst he chafed at the delay, he had been glad of the tiredness that had overcome him. It would also afford him a better opportunity to observe the Queen Mother at a closer range than usual. Up until now he'd had little contact with her, although he had, on several occasions, found her looking at him; her gaze could intimidate, as he had witnessed earlier, but he was confident in his belief that he had mastered the difficult task of bringing the King's mother back to court, as well as enjoying her discomfiture at his relay of the King's commands.

Her double chin and heavy, pale features were like a mask, her large black eyes were bulbous, piercing and fathomless, quite her most daunting feature. Her figure was stocky and solid, yet her hands seemed delicate, with long and slender fingers which were adorned by only a single ring.

The Queen Mother ate voraciously, trying a variety of dishes, roasted peacock with almonds, hare, beef, oysters, salmon and all manner of sweets and sugared pastries. Sebastian was impressed by the spread, even though he was used to the elaborate balls and banquets that took place with such regularity at court and the

vast array of food that accompanied them. The conversation was awkward throughout the long meal, with
the Queen Mother badgering for information about the
King's affairs and whatever he knew from the court
gossips. At length however, Sebastian pushed away a
new helping of fruit before him and stood, somewhat
unsteadily. He bowed curtly to the Queen Mother, who
did not extend her hand as was usual. No matter, he
thought, he had little respect for her and was eager to
get to his chamber, he had certainly drunk too much of
the rich wine again, delicious though it was. He waved
away the assistance offered by one of the guards outside
and staggered to the comfort of his bed.

Sebastian was unsure how long he had been asleep
before the pains woke him, a dull ache at first, but soon
building to a gut-churning cramp. His throat felt
parched, and he was aware he was sweating profusely.
The pains abated just long enough for him to try and
breathe deeply and calmly, but then it was back, a cruel
stabbing pain that seemed to rip through his whole
body. At once he clutched at his stomach, desperately
retching until he vomited quite violently. After becoming
entangled in the bed sheets as he strove to get up, he fell
down to the floor on his face. The heat that rose from
the base of his guts was almost like a furnace, and he
struggled towards the small table where a jug of water
stood. He stopped again, his throat burned like hellfire,
but he could not move; the muscles in his body seemed
to be seizing up, losing what strength he retained. His
throat hurt so much, he vomited again, but this time
there were teeth within the bile, his own teeth! Blood
now-Jesu. His throat, the burning, the burning...! He
must have been delirious because through the haze of

the indescribable pain he had seen the hem of a black gown. A voice, cold and distant, spoke – a woman's voice. He was certain it sounded familiar yet it was somehow distorted through his agony. "So, monsieur, the voice said, "You would sell your soul to the Duke of Guise, whilst you fawn over your King and assure him of your loyalty? You were unwise to carry incriminating letters with you, how easily they can fall into the wrong hands. Guise and the King of Spain would have been furious to know that their secret correspondence has been so easily intercepted. How very unfortunate for them that you will not make the next rendezvous with your paymasters."

Sebastian, his body consumed in pain, tried to reach out to whoever it was, but as he did whoever wore the black gown turned and walked away. He could hear a tapping noise becoming more distant until mercifully, he finally allowed the pain and the darkness to consume him.

♦

At dawn the following morning, Catherine steadily descended the spiral staircase in the wing of the palace named after her late father-in-law, François I. She had just reached the bottom where one of her trusty dwarves bowed low to her. "It is done, Rodamont?" she enquired sharply.

"It is done, Majesty," the little man replied. The Queen Mother walked on past him and out to her waiting carriage. She sat down inside and pulled up the furs she had recently acquired, so welcoming on such another frosty morning. The dwarf Rodamont jumped onto the back of the black carriage and yelled to the horseman, "To Paris with all speed!"

♦

No sooner had Catherine arrived at the Louvre and gone to her chambers, than the King unceremoniously burst in, closely followed by two of his mignons. He was clearly in a rage; he had not presented his usual immaculate self, his hair was not its usual careful style and he wore a plain brown tunic, without the usual adornment of jewels that all the court was used to seeing. The Queen Mother nodded to her attendants, who left the chamber quietly as Henri began to shout, "You see mother, you see where your foolish misplaced trust has led us? This is a fine state of affairs, now we have lost that maggot of a brother. But he shall be dragged back here by his hair if need be, and once he is under my thumb again, by God he will not leave my sight!"

Catherine calmly sat down. "Let me go to your brother, let me talk to him. Do we know where he has gone? Could he not have been apprehended?"

Henri kicked out at a chair before sulkily sitting down on it. "I sent a band of guards to get him, but to no avail, he somehow managed to get such a head start on them, they stood no chance of intercepting him."

Catherine thought for a moment, and could almost smile; of course they could not catch him, she would have been surprised if they had.

Whatever time they had set after him, they would no doubt have tarried rather than chased down their quarry. It was obvious to all but Henri, she suspected.

They were well aware that Alençon may be the King's enemy, but whilst Henri remained childless, he was also heir to the French throne. Were something to happen to the present King, his brother would mount the throne and would certainly settle old scores – spiteful and vengeful as he was.

Two of the entourage of mignons that seemed to be forever at the King's side had accompanied their master and made no attempt to discreetly stand away or wait outside the chamber. The Queen Mother allowed a scowl to cross her otherwise passive face; these two young men were causing her the most anxiety out of all the dreadful creatures that hovered around her son. She sensed that there was something more ambitious about these two than the other fops, although a third individual, d'Epilat, had for some reason, not returned to court from his visit to Blois to accompany the Queen Mother back to Paris. Henri had enquired about him to his mother, had he not travelled with her? He had intended to visit some land and property, a gift from a grateful monarch, situated further along the Loire valley was all the Queen Mother could offer as a reason for his continue, she had seen no reason to expose him as a double agent. The matter had been dealt with to her satisfaction. Moreover, both the current favourites had surely whispered to the King the vilest things about d'Epilat in his absence. So much so that the mystery of his whereabouts now seemed to be of little importance.

Jean-Louis de la Valette and Anne, Baron d'Arques were cut from a very different cloth. Jean-Louis was tall and swarthy with black hair, a small neat beard and large green eyes. Anne, had a much fairer complexion with a large nose, piercing blue eyes and only the very slightest signs of hair on his chin. Both from minor aristocratic families, they had risen from almost nowhere, and yet were fast becoming her son's constant companions and advisers.

Catherine sniffed in annoyance at their presence, but continued when it became clear that the King had no intention of dismissing them. "We must be cautious my son," she began but Henri would have none of her advice. "Cautious?" he almost screamed at her, "no Madame, your advice to be cautious and allow my brother some liberty has led to this. Why in God's name did I not listen to Quelus? He knew better, he knew that to allow my brother any freedom of movement would lead to trouble and he was right!" Henri dramatically looked to the heavens. "And now my beloved friend you have been proved so right."

Catherine could say nothing in defence of her son's accusation. It had been she who had favoured allowing Alençon some liberty, and this was the result. "I will deal with this, my son," she eventually spoke quietly. "Indeed, your friend Quelus spoke wisely, but I will see that your brother is returned here to court."

The King glanced at her scornfully. "And why should I believe you?" Henri looked at her now with concealed hatred and distrust.

Catherine rose then and moved to kneel painfully at his feet, "Because I am your mother and I would die rather than cause you a moment's more distress" For the first time in many weeks, the King smiled at her, an almost pathetic smile that signalled a weariness which had not existed before.

He had started to help her to her feet when one of the King's messengers arrived. The Queen Mother visibly bristled when de la Valette held out his jewelled hand. The rider paused for one moment, glancing uncertainly at Catherine before the King snapped, "Well hurry man! Give him the letter!"

The gesture was not lost on the Queen Mother – she had hidden behind a façade of acceptance. In this case however, it was becoming obvious that this most despised popinjay had ambition, and was already the recipient of her son's complete faith.

"From Dreux, Majesty," de la Valetta said looking straight at Catherine as he handed the document to his master. Suddenly the King let out a scream of oaths, and physically hurled the letter towards his mother. "Read it Madame! Read what the maggot demands – demands of me!"

Catherine took the document and as her eyes ran across the lines, her heart sank. Alençon had, as expected, set himself up as a figure-head of the dis-enchanted anti-Royalists, and would almost certainly join the gathering group of aristocrats of both Huguenot and Catholic faiths who were so strongly opposed to the King and his claim to be an "absolute Prince".

Only several months before, Catherine and Henri had faced a deputation from the Politiques demanding amongst other things, a bill of rights allowing complete freedom of worship without hindrance, a prosecution of all those guilty of planning and executing the massacre of Saint Bartholomew. Both the King and his mother were outraged at the demands, and talks had broken down. As a result, fighting broke out again, and the wars of religion began afresh.

The document from Dreux surprised even Catherine; her youngest son had compiled a concise list of demands, and for a moment she wondered if his idleness had been merely a pretence, had he possibly the makings of a leader? But no, she could not believe Alençon had composed such a list by himself, unless he playing a very dangerous game, the result of which could easily be his downfall.

Many of the demands were trivial and even personal; Alençon clearly intending that there would be casualties if his terms were to be agreed *"The expulsion of all foreigners from the Royal council."*

Catherine sniffed in annoyance. *"A religious pacification until such time as a general church council could be called."* Indeed, many of the demands were certainly bold.

"Well?" demanded the King, "I will have my guard attack his stronghold and bring him back in chains if necessary."

De Vallette's handsome face displayed a barely concealed smirk, as he looked to the Queen Mother. At length Catherine sighed before declaring, "It seems he would ruin us all, I see I shall have to go to Dreux and deal with the wretch myself."

◆

The King's favourites had turned their bile towards Margot, now that Alençon had fled to Dreux. They whispered about her, giggling stupidly like a group of young maidens. They had begun to get bolder in their vindictiveness; sometimes openly insulting her. One evening they had discovered which new gown Margot had planned to wear in honour of a visit by a delegation from the Spanish court. Margot had felt every inch the

Royal that she was arriving at the reception beautifully dressed in a rich crimson gown with diamond beading around the tight sleeves and a low cut neckline. Rather daring of course, but the choice delighted her, and she wore her hair braided with golden thread – a most dazzling sight!

It was, however, causing some amusement rather than the adulation and gasps she was expecting, she passed courtiers who chuckled between themselves and turned away to conceal their mirth. It was upon approaching the King, seated on his velvet throne at the end of the large chamber, that she realised the humiliating truth. There surrounding her brother stood three of his mignons actually dressed in exact copies of the very gown she was wearing. One of them, Livarot had actually dressed his hair in the same style as Margot's.

The King's favourites actually laughed aloud, but for a moment that seemed like long minutes, there was absolute silence apart from the mignons' sniggering. Standing near the King's chair, the Queen Mother's face registered nothing of the anger and disappointment she concealed so well; surely Henri would check this outrage, this flagrant insult to his own sister. She was about to speak to the King quietly when she heard her daughter speak, "Ah, messieurs," she spoke boldly, "You are almost perfect, but not quite as many diamonds on the front bodice or indeed on the cuffs. I really must remember not to overdress so much next time we choose the same gowns! Indeed, I feel flattered that you gentleman who honour your master by often dressing as he does, should now pay the same compliment to myself." And so saying, she curtsied to the astounded King, and swept to one side of the chamber to speak to the Spanish ambassador.

Catherine could not conceal the brief smile that crossed her lips. Clever Margot, she thought. Whatever fury she must certainly be feeling, the insult would have been most keenly felt, but the Queen Mother's brief mirth would be short-lived. This would of course be an insult that Margot would not forget. Battle lines would inevitably be drawn.

♦

The Queen Mother was aware that the blood in her vomit was a bad sign at this stage of the affliction that had brought her to perhaps her final hours. At times she wanted to send the physicians away. Did she really want to recover? Her confessor continued to mutter incantations so close to her ear that she could feel the heat from his breath. What good now monsieur? What pity could be expected for her? She, who had led such a life of drama, sadness and danger. She had sinned so often that she expected no mercy.

Although now enjoying some measure of mobility in her limbs, any movement tired her, and she would only turn her head to cough up the phlegm that built up in her throat. Once or twice she thought she saw her beloved son, the King. Had he come to her? Surely he had come? Whenever the chamber door creaked open, she would strain herself to see if it was he that entered; but sadly it was only ever a servant, her confessor, although her granddaughter had been to see her. At least, she believed it to be her. God's death, she cursed to herself, she was slipping away, she could feel it. When there was so much to do, what would become of France...

The bile rose in her throat again and she turned to raise herself up, but not before she projected the acidic liquid all over the bedclothes, its gory mess splattering across the gold-stitched, slightly worn cover that had been doubled over to keep her from chill. She felt only the indignity of it all. The priest was not quick enough to get out of the way from the forced vomit that burst out. That was at least satisfying! The sight of the man's horrified face as he attempted to wipe himself clean amused her, but she was too weak to even smile. Was that the door again? Who had entered? Was it Alençon? That stupid boy. He had been such thorn in her side, he had caused them all so much unrest, she had anguished for many hours, but, he was here now, although she could barely see him standing by her bed. Why was the image of him so hazy? He was there though surely? Bowing to her, taking her hands in his......

♦

François, Duke d'Alençon embraced his mother warmly and both of them shed tears.

Catherine was startled by her youngest son's appearance. Like his brother, he appeared to have lost weight, and looked desperately tired. Why on earth did none of her sons enjoy the rude health of Navarre or Guise? Why did they seem destined to burn out before middle age?

Long hours were then spent in discussions, grievances were aired, and promises made. Alençon's demands were bold, and yet there was very little with which to bargain. Yet Catherine, whilst urging the King to make as good a peace as could be achieved, added that as a precaution he should prepare for further war. She sat one day with her son and listened again to his insistence that the main victims of the massacre in Paris be publicly rehabilitated. "What you suggest is too dangerous a precedence my son," Catherine said with irritation. "They threatened the life of the King and the security of the realm, that cannot now be seen to be pardonable." Alençon laughed at his mother's outrage, "Yet it is a rational demand, and one that my brother must honour," he said, "The massacre must be declared to have been a great merciless crime"

Catherine looked sharply at him "You stupid boy, do you not realise even now, that if the deaths of Coligny and others not been achieved, you would not be able to have enjoyed the freedom that you have had."

"Freedom?" Alençon shouted in disbelief. "There has been no freedom for me, the gilded cage that is the French court has been more of a prison to me than an oubliette in the Conciergerie! I am the subject of mockery for the sodomites that surround my brother." Catherine gasped at the ferocity of his outburst, and sought to check it, but Alençon had thrown his wine goblet to one side in his frustration, and ran his short fingers through his thinning, wiry hair.

"Tell my brother to honour the demands or I will make so much trouble for him that he will beg me to stop." Catherine eyed him with a mixture of fury and pity. When she spoke, she was again calm and controlled. "I hear you would now be titled merely "Monsieur" yet you would in truth rather your brother dead and you titled King. You are a foolish boy, you who would rally to the forefront of any cause merely to own the leadership of it. Consider however, François, that you may yet make a great match and be King of both England and France, although I pray to God that your brother will sire heirs to the throne. Yet, should he not..." Catherine made no further comment. She felt a stab of disloyalty to her darling, and the thought of him no longer being King distressed her, but it was as well to draw Alençon back from his quite fantastic demands. Could they be tempered by welcoming him back into the family fold?

She watched her son for a few moments, and he sighed as he turned to her. "The conditions of peace remain as they were, maman. I suggest they are put to my brother before it is too late." With that, he bowed to his mother and marched from the room.

Catherine felt a mixture of both sadness and rage. To be thwarted in this way was intolerable, yet she could see that it was either agreement or war. She must send to the King, urging him to accept such outrageous terms. Alençon had other additions to what was already a ruinous set of demands, her expedition was nothing short of failure. She had won some concessions, but they were of no real consequence. She must return to Paris and the King, there was really little else that could be done.

♦

The Queen Mother had been away from court for several weeks and eagerly awaited a tearful reunion with her beloved son. What she got however, was the worst possible shock. The King waited for her in his chamber. He did not greet her as she had hoped, but instead, flanked by d'Valette and d'Arques on either side, he sat and glared at her. Catherine, refusing to be in any way intimidated by the two favourites. "Might I sit, my son?" she asked "Or is there no longer room in this chamber for your poor mother?" The King swallowed awkwardly and motioned to d'Arques, who placed a chair before her. Once settled, she looked to her son with a calm expression.

Henri was brutal, his voice as cold as ice. "It would appear, Madame, that you have not consulted your magicians, your hideous masters of prophecy lately? Had you done so you would not need me to tell you that the other Royal bird has flown our nest – your son-in-law the King of Navarre has this day escaped from the court and as we speak is riding hard for his own Kingdom."

Catherine's horror was palpable; she paled visibly. This was certainly a disaster for her both personally and politically. Her concerns about Navarre had been wrong, she had allowed herself to believe that he was a dullard, who would happily lounge around the court, in the company of many beautiful women, none more so than Charlotte de Suave who had presumably been abandoned. How could she have been so trusting? Having absconded from under her very nose, there was surely no chance that he would return to Paris, unless good fortune followed him and he became King; a prospect that could not be seriously considered.

More than anything, it was the hatred in Henri's eyes that hurt the most; at a time when he was, as Charles had done before him, listening to other advice, it was intolerable that she now had to admit to a considerable error of judgement. She had advised the King to allow Alençon and Navarre a little more liberty, a show of trust and yet this was the result! The two abominable creatures, one either side of the King, must be relishing this moment; a chance to sneer at her humiliation. It saddened her also that her son could not have vented his frustration at her policy in private.

Rarely had Henri been so cruel. "So what am I to do, Madame? Tell me if you please, how I, King of France can now be expected to govern my Kingdom when I have practically opened the gates of Paris and waved my brothers goodbye! Perhaps it is not only them who should consider quitting the court."

Catherine looked at him aghast with horror. What was he saying? Her own beloved, he whom she had cherished above all others, he whom she had lied for, honoured and nurtured, moulded into her own creation, was now at loggerheads with her. He had no further need of her perhaps. She could not bring herself to consider it.

The Queen Mother turned away so that the two mignons at least would not see her tears, but her son mocked her still. "Your false tears will serve you ill, Madame" the King continued ruthlessly."

"I have watched such false emotions so many times, but they will not soften my resolve as they have so many before me!" He cast her a further withering look before he strode from the chamber, followed by his two friends. Catherine sat and wept.

The weeks following Navarre's escape had been spent considering Alençon's conditions for peace, and whilst he railed at his council as well as his mother, Henri knew that there was little choice but to accept the terms and be done with it, as much as it pained him. Restored to some favour, Catherine had urged him to accept, suggesting that Alençon would come to heel eventually – the man could not act the statesman for long, such was his propensity for drama. Once he was back at court, he would distance himself from the fray. He was no leader, even if he believed in his vanity that he was.

Catherine's next aim would be to arrange a marriage between her youngest son and the Queen of England. This was surely to be her greatest hour, a match with the red-haired minx would be a great jewel in the Valois crown. It would also mean that, with the exception of her late daughter Claude, each of Catherine and her late husband's children would have been crowned.

◆

The Peace of Monsieur had at last been signed, but rather than bring some measure of harmony, it served only to force the Catholics into the waiting arms of Guises Catholic League. Many regarded the treaty as merely a further humiliation. With the Huguenots now virtually on parity with the practice of Catholics throughout the country, feelings of resentment within France ran deep, and the Queen Mother was forced to admit that she had not expected the league to be established so quickly.

Of course to Parisians, the Duke of Guise was a hero and had, strangely enough, during a victory on the battlefield at Dormans, received an almost identical scar to one his father had suffered so many years before. Here again was "Le Balafré" – scar face – a brave gallant that would lead the true faith in France.

Catherine had her spies within the Guise household and reports reaching her implied that the Duke was becoming rather bold in his role. This gave her some cause for concern; the enmity between the King and his kinsman was growing, but against all odds, one relationship that was flourishing was one between Henri and his own brother – Alençon. Catherine felt a genuine emotion of pleasure at the sight of the two of them together, more companionable than she would ever have believed possible. Yet, being both cautious and realistic, she knew that all was not as it seemed.

It was true that since the *Paix de Monsieur,* Alençon had, as expected, begun to distance himself from the Huguenots he had been so eager to protect and preserve such a short time before. The peace treaty that the King had so reluctantly signed, had as his mother had prophesised served to draw Alençon back into the heart of his family. Where better to keep an eye on him? Henri, meanwhile, had become more and more frustrated at Guise's name being on everyone's lips. The Duke made certain it was known that he could trace his lineage directly back to the great Charlemagne. This, in Catherine's eyes held an unspoken threat, suggesting that the Guise were on a parity with the ruling house of Valois.

As had been expected, further hostilities broke out, and it was at this time that Alençon most certainly distinguished himself most foully, by demanding the slaughter of several thousand Huguenots at Issoire. By this most cruel act, Alençon had turned his back on those he had so recently defended. Naturally, the association with the Huguenots was now at an end, the King's brother had shown his true colours, and he was welcomed back into the fold of his family.

Troubles threatened from all sides, sporadic fighting was breaking out daily it seemed. Letters and visits from her legion of spies told a sorry tale about the state of France and the resentment and hostility that had grown towards the King – and herself. The enmity of the people did not bother Catherine personally, she had never felt loved in France, and indeed had never sought love from it. To the French she would always be the Italian witch, Madame Serpent, the Italian Jezebel, the Medici Poisoner. What did she care for that? Names could not hurt her, she would do whatever she had to do to keep her sons and the line of Valois on the throne of France.

Yet, in the midst of such troubles, and with a warning that the unrest in the provinces threatened to overspill once again into open rebellion, Catherine felt herself ostracised by the King who chose to closet himself away with his favourites. Nevertheless, she knew he had need of her still. She was his darling maman, and he loved her above any others, he was merely temporarily amused by these gentlemen of his, and whilst their behaviour was sometimes shocking, the King would grow tired of them, and he would need her again. She must be there for him as always.

The fragile peace that had ended yet another civil war was, as expected, ill received by both Huguenot and Catholic alike, and with a wish to strengthen the weak treaties, hear grievances and attempt to promote peace, the Queen Mother gathered a small court, including some of her *escardon* and the Queen of Navarre, and set out on an enterprise around France that she referred to as her "journey of pacification.

♦

"Your most gracious Majesty" Jean de Simier bowed low as he knelt before the Queen of England. The young French courtier had been sent by the Queen Mother as an envoy to convey the best wishes of the French Royal family – and in particular the Duke of Alençon. Negotiations about the possible marriage between the French Prince and the English Virgin Queen had been re-established. Simier had crossed the channel on several occasions to act as a go-between. Here then, he had again to deal with the capricious English Queen. Earlier portraits and gifts had been exchanged, but very little was decided, and it was with a dispirited heart that he again presented himself to the Queen at the magnificent splendour of Hampton Court.

With the English courtiers looking on, he had been loudly announced, and approached the Queen with some trepidation. Elizabeth Tudor was now forty-five years old, and what measure of beauty she had once possessed was beginning to fade. It was already suggested that she was losing her once abundant red hair and was resorting to hair pieces. Her features were now sharper and slightly gaunt; the once smiling lips were, for the most part, merely a thin, determined line. Her eyes had lost some of their early sparkle, and now darted suspiciously around her as though sensing danger. In France, stories about the Tudor Queen were greatly exaggerated, and the envoy was surprised not to find a harridan with no hair or teeth! She could indeed, still beguile with her charm, and nothing delighted her more than flirting. Even as a grown woman, she derived great pleasure from the attention of her male courtiers, knowing that she was teasing them mercilessly.

The Frenchman who now kissed the offered hand of the monarch, was pleasant looking with a kind smooth featured-face, large brown eyes, and dark curled hair. He was richly attired in dark red velvet and silk, and the cap in his hand sported an elaborate feather. His grasp of the English language was good, and whilst the Queen was fluent in French, he was happy to converse in her native tongue, lest there be any misinterpretations by her ministers, several of whom had only a poor head for languages.

"I bring greetings and fondest wishes from my master, and to assure you of his undying respect and goodwill." Simier spoke aloud so that all could hear him. "I am further charged," he continued "to present this miniature portrait to you in the hope that you will keep it with you always." Elizabeth smiled widely. The small framed gift was handed first to one of the ladies in waiting and then on to the Queen.

Elizabeth unwrapped to picture, gasping with delight at the image. "Your master is blessed with looks, pleasant as they are strong and noble. Come, walk with me Simier." She rose from her chair, and the courtiers stood to one side, bowing or curtseying as she passed them. The two of them stood by a large window that looked out to the vast green lawns of Hampton Court. "Your master is well I trust?"

"He enjoys the finest health, your Majesty. He enjoys the outdoor pursuits, hunting, archery which I know to be also your own favourite pastimes." Elizabeth smiled tightly at him, "Unfortunately, as a Queen, I have so little time for such activities. The business of state is over and above all else."

Simier nodded in understanding as she continued. "Your master, you say, is in the best of health, yet I have often heard that the sons of Catherine de Medici are plagued with ill health-both of her eldest, dying before they could enjoy the flush of middle age."

Simier coughed nervously at her abruptness. "It is true, your grace, that God saw fit to claim the Duke's elder brothers far too early, but the Duke enjoys a vigour that they did not, there are no fears that he will follow them to an all too early grave." The Queen looked at him with some disapproval. "We must all be prepared to die at any time, monsieur," she admonished. She looked out across the landscape and sighed. "Ah Simier," she spoke softly, "I would have your master come here to England, that we can get to know one another. My late sister was affianced to King Philip of Spain with only a portrait to admire; when he arrived in England, many at court found him unappealing and a disappointment." Elizabeth seemed lost in her own thoughts for some moments, before she abruptly began to question Alençon's recent involvement in affairs of the Netherlands. "I learn that the fragile reunion between your master and his brother the King has all but broken down."

Simier looked contrite and opened his mouth to attempt an explanation, but the Queen continued. "No sooner has the ink dried on the so called "Peace of Monsieur" than the Duke orders the massacre of several thousand Huguenots at Issoire. How could I then bring your master here, present him as the next King of England, with the blood of those three thousand innocents on his hands? If he would easily turn his back on those he once protected, how can I with good conscience expect my people to trust and love him?"

Inwardly, Simier groaned. He had dreaded the matter of Issoire being brought up. He himself had been surprised to learn that no sooner had Alençon allied again with his brother the King and been welcomed back into the fold, than he had turned on those he had sworn to defend. Once upon the theme, Elizabeth was merciless. "If he were to become my husband, would he then seek the extermination of my own loyal Protestant subjects who displeased him? Would he then round up all my Catholic subjects and urge them to slaughter?" Simier would have at that moment, rather been anywhere but standing with a Queen whose voice had taken on a passionate, sharp tone. "I am further told that your master has many mistresses. Do you think me a fool, Simier? You look at me as though I should have learnt nothing of this, but I know a great deal about your master and his family."

Simier cast his gaze down to the floor; but then Elizabeth seemed to change again. "Return to your master, good Simier, and tell him that I would meet with him, yes – ask him if I am worth the journey across the water, so often does he profess in his letters that he would walk ten thousand miles to be with me." She then removed a ring from one of her fingers, and after kissing it gently, she placed it in Simier's hand. "Give your master this – with my deepest affection." And before the puzzled envoy had chance to speak, she had simply smiled and walk briskly away.

♦

The black coach of the Queen Mother rattled along badly made roads, some almost impassable. Workers had been sent out ahead of her journey to establish at least some measure of surface on which to travel. Catherine's sciatica and rheumatism had begun to plague her in the last few months, and her body railed at her for submitting them to this extra stress. Nevertheless, she bore these privations with patience, and endured them as best she could.

All this, she told herself, was worth the agony if her travels were deemed a success and she was restored to favour with her darling son. She knew she had perhaps underestimated the power and influence that the mignons enjoyed with the King. She had laughed off suggestions that they were gaining in influence with her son, assuring herself that nothing could ever separate that special bond between her darling and herself. While she had been able to destroy d'Epilat, for his treason, and had had an indirect hand in the scuffle that led to the death of Quelus, the power of the remaining favourites remained seriously unchecked. Strange, she thought, that neither the King or Guise concerned themselves much about d'Epilat who had been sent to accompany the Queen Mother from Blois back to the King. Such was the expendability of such men, and there would always be another to attempt the climb to high favour. There was no rumour about why the spy had not returned to court, he was merely forgotten.

Now as her coach, in the middle of the train of wagons that travelled with her, rumbled on, she read the latest correspondence from one of her own trusted spies, and yet she was not in the least surprised at the news.

It seemed that already, the fragile peace between her two sons had collapsed. Further arguments had followed renewed attacks on the mignons by "unknown persons" The King had blamed his brother, berating him in front of the court. Catherine inwardly groaned. What good could ever come from this disunity? Alençon was hot-headed and impulsive; and as a result, he was giving serious consideration to overtures from the Netherlands for him to assist in their fight against the Catholic forces of Spain.

Here was a situation that could so easily get out of control. Alençon, so desperate to create a role for himself in life, now saw the fight in the Netherlands as an opportunity to become the great ruler he had always believed himself to be. Henri, of course had railed at his brother calling him a traitor and threatening to have him imprisoned. Good sense, and with the calming influence of his own ministers, the King had settled to merely warn his brother that whilst he was Alençon's brother, he was first and foremost, his King, and as such he demanded loyalty.

She at once wrote to both sons and implored them to help keep the peace she had set out to maintain. Begging them to present a united France, and not to be induced into false hopes and empty promises. To the King and his ministers, she conveyed her suggestion that in order to occupy Alençon elsewhere, that they press on with plans for a proposed visit by her youngest son to England. Catherine laughed aloud to think of the headache that woman would give her youngest son.

The King of Navarre had recently demanded that his wife be allowed to join him at his own court. Catherine smiled as she recalled his indignity at the couple being kept apart. Margot, she knew, was in no hurry to join her husband in the dull, alien court in the province, indeed she had been heard to say that she herself had planned his escape from the court. Henri had suspected as much anyway, and as a result had severely restricted Margot's freedom. Now, however, Catherine saw the good sense in taking her daughter from the French court.

There was still, she believed, a frisson of passion between Margot and the Duke of Guise, rumours had been heard for years that the two of them still met secretly from time to time. Added to which, Margot's enmity with the mignons was now also at boiling point; they snubbed her publicly at every opportunity, whispering to her brother all the latest court gossip concerning his sister. One of Margot's own ladies in waiting had been all but molested by one of the Royal favourites, and yet when the subject was brought to the King's attention, he had merely laughed, scolding the young man as "a reckless and naughty boy!" Margot had fumed but had been merely ignored by the King and worse still, all the mignons had completely turned their backs on her.

Such was the indignity done to her, that Catherine believed to bring Margot with her made good sense. The young Queen of Navarre had little choice than to obey her mother and brother and accompany the cavalcade, which rumbled on through the south. Here then was uncertainty and danger – Huguenot country.

Never had the divisions in France been so obvious to Catherine than during her travels. She passed fields mainly unkempt and some not even harvested, through towns of silent, suspicious and unfriendly faces. Social and religious strife were evident everywhere. The Royal party was at the mercy of brigands and bandits. Disease still decimated many provinces, with animals left dying in fields, and where, Catherine had been informed, the very birds in the sky would fall to the ground once they flew into an area where the plague was still prevalent.

The vine crops of Guyenne had deteriorated over the years, and were only now recovering enough to encourage a revival of wine making. Elsewhere, the cultivation of crops of barley and wheat was sporadic. The country had become almost exhausted from the incessant civil unrest; they knew nothing of court galas and masque balls, no thought of how the King had spent his day or whether he chose to dress as a woman or a man, whether he favoured diamonds or rubies and pearls with each new outfit. What almost all did possess however was a distrust and hatred of the King's mother.

Often at great personal risk, Catherine would enter a city so silent that her carriage was the only sound she could hear. She had been horrified to see that in the main square of one town she had entered, a mock gibbet had been erected and there, at the end of the noose was a straw image dressed all in black with a makeshift crown on its head, and beside it lay another crowned figure covered in red with his head all but cut off. Her alarm was genuine, and she had the carriage turn around before it was chased out of the town.

Often she would approach a large chateau or mansion only to find that its gates were closed to her and would not be opened. Under such circumstances she would order a camp to be set up where possible, and simply set up the small court as best they could. All this and more, the long suffering Queen Mother endured along with her gout and constant indigestion, bouts of painful rheumatism, and most poignantly without the sight of her darling son.

As she travelled on regardless, she would simply set up a portrait of the King and then summon the local nobility to speak to her, to air their distrust and attempt to resolve their grievances. Despite all her good offices, there were still those who dared not eat and drink with the Queen Mother lest they be slipped the legendary *morceaux Italianise* and never live to return home. All problems would be discussed, and Catherine would attempt to uphold the treaties of the crown and attempt to resolve all wrongs, either through tactful diplomacy or in some cases – intimidation.

Throughout its first few months however, the Queen Mother believed she had some measure of success, and it was with a certain feeling of relief that she was informed the party was nearing the northern edge of Gascony and therefore close to the lands of Navarre. There she could take her ease, of her ailing joints if not her thoughts. Catherine noticed while Margot shared her coach, her daughter was less than pleased that they had arrived at her new home. "See girl," she said "how warmly your new people welcome you?" Margot looked out at the people gathered, many waving to the carriage as it passed by, and her heart sank. How dour they looked, no colour, no bright costumes, just a greyness that made her suddenly sad. She had no expectation of what her new home would be like, but she remembered those who had come to Paris with her late mother-in-law, Jeanne d'Albret, all the women were dull and almost lifeless, very like their mistress as she recalled! Soon they were met by a party of horsemen who welcomed them and prepared to accompany them to where they would meet up with the King of Navarre.

Catherine was slightly aggrieved at the change of arrangements; the meeting was to have taken place in Bordeaux, and indeed, Margot had made a particularly successful entry into that city, but the King did not arrive. The Queen Mother immediately sent to Nerac with messages of concern that the proposed meeting had not taken place. Margot had sighed with resignation, this was too typical of her husband, no doubt idling his time with a new mistress, she complained to her ladies.

Navarre, it appeared was unhappy about the location of their planned meeting place; Bordeaux was too far from Nerac, and indeed too dangerous for one who had only recently gained his liberty. Whilst impatient and angry, Catherine agreed to anywhere her son-in-law should deem 'safe' and would abide by his decision.

Eventually an uninteresting and plain manor house some miles from the town of La Reole was chosen as the meeting place, and it was there that Catherine embraced Navarre. He looked changed from the jovial youth that had vexed her so much during his captivity at the French court. His face was lined with some of the weight of office, and his eyes had lost some of the sparkle they had once had, and Catherine fancied that responsibility had drawn some of the carefree humour from him. In many respects however, he had changed very little. He had never taken to being a gallant when with the French court, and in that respect, he had learnt very little from men around him. His outward appearance disgusted his wife who, although prepared to join her husband as he had requested and indeed, her brother had insisted, could not bring herself to kiss him. His rather vulgar greeting, sweeping her up in his arms and lifting her into the air had shocked all but the Queen Mother.

"The King cannot wait to be alone with you, my child," Catherine had teased Margot. The Queen had huffed, mumbled about her husband being a provincial oaf, and made herself scarce.

Navarre's appearance was certainly more suited to this small, insignificant court than it had been to the cone in Paris. Here in his own Kingdom, his clothes were invariably stained with wine or food, his breath smelled of strong onions and his beard was a wiry and unkempt, already showing flecks of silver. Catherine knew he had always laughed at the absurdness of the court dress, especially the men surrounding Henri.

Navarre's King stayed with the party through much of the journey to Nerac, although he would often take his leave of them and not return for some hours, or even days. The Queen Mother's cavalcade was escorted through many towns and villages, all of which cheered as the party passed by. Margot had, on the success of her entry to Bordeaux, decided to ride on horseback so that she could be seen. Having dressed in the richest colours and costliest of her gowns, she was a spectacle that delighted the crowds, and the hostility about which she had felt nervous had not materialised.

At last, the King eventually met them just outside his city of Nerac for their triumphant arrival. Catherine, happy to be left at the rear of the procession, prided herself that after great pains and hardships, some measure of success had been achieved.

Despite the relief of having Navarre and Margot reunited, in public at least, the Queen Mother had prepared for important talks with her son-in-law and his ministers. She had of course brought her advisors with her, but they knew that it would be she who would oversee the tense negotiations that were to follow.

Each long day, the Queen Mother would try to remedy all ills, attempt to pacify and bring harmony to the fragile negotiations. They had gathered at the first such meeting which had none of the formality to which Catherine was accustomed. The great hall seemed to serve all purposes, even for talks with the King of France's mother.

Catherine had eyed the courtiers that stood in corners or lounged about in groups, laughing and talking, and immediately requested that Navarre dismiss them so that they might converse privately with his ministers and her advisors.

Navarre smiled at her. "This is not Paris, Madame," he said abruptly, "Here in this place, these people are at my court, we have no secrets here. No spies, no holes bored into the ceiling or wall panels, no secret passages." Catherine caught his eye and for once it was she who looked away first. Yet she would not be riled by his impertinence, or submissive if that was the purpose in showing a united force against the wicked Queen Mother. "If that is your wish my son," she raised her hands in a gesture of submission. "You will surely allow your old mother-in-law to sit, the rheumatic pains trouble me greatly and I can longer stand for too long." Navarre signalled at once for a seat to be brought, and with obvious relief, Catherine sank heavily onto it.

"It is time, my son, that your wife settled here with you, and you can clearly see that she is eager to be mistress of your court, and join you as your Queen. It is unnatural that you should be apart any longer. I know that you have been eager to have her come to your Kingdom as God and the church intended. It warms my heart to see the two of you casting glances between you, it has been my fervent wish that –" Navarre had stood before her, and abruptly swung one of his booted legs onto a stool next to her and leaned down. "Supposing I will not have her back?" he said suddenly. Catherine lowered her eyes and smiled thinly, "Ah, my son, you jest of course. I think we both know that you are not in such a strong position. Do not seek to offend your brother and King and my daughter who has been your ever faithful wife…"

Navarre threw his head back and laughed loudly, drawing looks from the assembled courtiers. "By God, Madame, your daughter has bewitched you if that is your honest belief. I hear of nothing else but how the Queen my wife has taken another lover; she seems to tire of them frequently. Do you think that news never gets to these provinces? Let us speak no more in platitudes, there is no suggestion that I would not have my wife here with me, and God grant that we may have many sons to follow after I have gone – whichever crown of mine they wear!"

Catherine was startled at his words; less by his opinion of his wife's virtues, which she could not deny, were certainly questionable, but by the term *"whichever of my crowns."* His impertinence was close to treason, and her temper nearly got the better of her. "Have a care, my son, even the walls of your court have ears. You forget you stand a long way from the throne. The King, will yet be blessed with a healthy son, and yet there is also his brother." Navarre stared at her for a moment; a glint in his eye held her gaze for a few seconds more, but he was then the jovial buffoon again, and called for music, courtesy of a small inferior gathering of four musicians. Catherine felt a depression creeping over her, she had been made uneasy by his words. In those last minutes, she had been transported back to a chamber in a tower at Chaumont may years before – the Ruggieri's mirror!

No, she would not think of it. This was a trap by Navarre to unsettle her, and she would have none of it. Yet, it was disturbing, and even in her bedchamber that night, she had moved restlessly, heaving herself from one side of the bed to the other. She had woken several times in a sweat, frightened, but she was not sure of what.

The following few days were spent in talks and meetings aimed at agreeing to some of the demands the Huguenots made. Whilst determined not to completely capitulate, Catherine won several points when a rather brash Navarre assured her that she could trust that the Huguenots would not disrupt any plans for a lasting peace. Here then Catherine played a trump card; news had reached her only that very morning that would unsettle the King of Navarre and check his arrogance.

"You say, my son, that you can assure the King that your Huguenots would not be the cause of any unrest or uprising whilst talks between us continue. Yet", she licked her dry lips, "your own cousin and kinsman, Condé, plans such disruption." The Queen Mother delighted in the dark uncertain scowl that crossed the face of her son-in-law. How invigorating talks such as these could be when one was able to throw all into chaos. "I am reliably informed – and you know that my sources are impeccable – that your brother in arms has not forgotten his defeat at Picardy and is currently summoning troops to seize La Fere near the Netherlands border. I also learn from this same source that the scoundrel has told any who would listen that he has not completely dismissed the idea of an alliance with the Guise! Forgive me, I thought you at least would have been a party to this outrage" The Queen Mother sat back in her seat as though the news had shocked her, whilst enjoying the reaction her words were having on the King of Navarre, who was ill at ease on hearing this most humiliating information.

Catherine felt a lot more would be achieved now she could counter the attacks from Navarre and his ageing ministers, and although some clauses were impassable, she was nevertheless able to arrive at a successful conclusion, and the terms were thus set out and sent to the King in Paris for his ratification.

With the business end of the visit concluded, Margot had already begun to try and bring some light and laughter to this new court, and had arranged a banquet with music and dancing. The generally straight-laced, masculine court were uneasy at first, but the women seemed to be delighted at the prospect of some gaiety, despite one or two matrons who grumbled at such behaviour. Before long, the assembled ladies and gentlemen had begun to enjoy themselves, much to the delight of their King.

Navarre had seen many such occasions during his enforced stay at the French Royal court, and would have to admit that there was nowhere to rival a masque ball at the Louvre.

The Queen Mother sought in her own way to test the men who surrounded their King. She had brought with her several women from her *flying squadron* and, like a general commanding her armies, she set them loose upon the straight-laced court at Nerac.

One such lady was a recent recruit – Victoria de Ayala, of Spanish birth, a woman of impish rather than classic beauty; a porcelain white face with large hazel eyes and pert, ruby coloured lips. A dazzling smile showed almost perfect white teeth and dimpled cheeks. Catherine had sat and watched the admiring glances that Navarre gave to the young beauty. The Queen Mother could almost laugh aloud at his audacity; only Navarre could welcome his wife to his court as his Queen, and yet spend his time casting lascivious glances at one of the Queen Mother's ladies.

This state of affairs prompted Catherine to send her dwarf to bring Victoria to her. Once at the Queen Mother's side, the lady sat at Catherine's feet on a low stool. The Queen Mother smiled, "You are enjoying yourself, my dear," she said "That is good. This is how you young people should spend your time. It was the same in my youth-the King, my husband, and I would enjoy such occasions as this." As she spoke the words, Catherine was reminded that her husband, Henri Deux had not been a lover of dance, and when he did it was generally accompanied by his detested mistress, Diane de Poitiers. Even after so many years, there was a hatred of that woman that still burned inside her. It mattered little now of course, Diane had died thirteen years ago, and yet, what a strong power that emotion still had.

Catherine was stirred from her reverie by the sound of her daughter's laugh, always quite infectious. There she stood, deep in conversation with two young male courtiers. How she lapped up the attention she always seemed to provoke! Margot and her husband were not very different. She saw Navarre glance at his wife but he merely smiled and returned his gaze to the young woman, still waiting for the Queen Mother to continue. "Forgive me, my child, now I see you have caught the eye of my son-in-law the King – ah, no matter, I am not cross with you, far from it. The King finds you attractive, and I would think you would find little trouble in finding yourself his lover. Now you know of course that I want only the best for you ladies, and in this particular case I would know the King's thoughts. I hope you will find him entertaining. You in return will be guided by my suggested topics. The King, is known to be a passionate man, a competent lover I am told." Catherine laughed aloud, a deep, gutsy laugh, "Ah do not look so shocked my dear; I have lived through too much not to know the way a man's mind works, and I am astute in recognising an infatuation."

The Queen Mother waited for the lady to register shock and delight at the revelation, and her mistress appearing to condone it. The response from Madame de Ayala was less than enthusiastic. "Madame, I thought that Madame de Suave –"

Catherine interrupted, her smile had faded slightly, "Madame de Suave will be asked to step aside, her work with the King of Navarre is done now, he has tired of her I daresay, it is of no matter. You my dear have caught his attention, and I would know all he is thinking. A secret thrown away in the throes of passion, a sleeping draught that will loosen his tongue as he sleeps, dreams can tell us so much, and whatever there is to know – I wish to know it."

Victoria tried again to distance herself from the task she had been set. "But Madame, what if the Queen were to discover? She has always been most kind to me." The girl was starting to panic; she had no qualms about the simple seduction of some court visitor or even a foreign dignitary.

The excitement could be invigorating to someone like her, but the task ahead did not fill her with any excitement at all; she had never felt the slightest attraction for the King of Navarre. He was scruffy and unkempt, and less than scrupulous regarding his personal hygiene, one could smell his breath from some distance, his fingernails were dirty...the list of his unattractive qualities was endless.

Nervously summoning up her courage, she faced the Queen Mother. "Madame, I don't believe I am up to the task you would set me. The King, I'm afraid is not to my liking."

Catherine's dwarf, standing by his mistress's chair could not supress a slight gasp at the young woman's defiance. The Queen Mother had chosen to seat herself away from the main throng of the entertainment, as much to be unobserved while she could see all. No one else was aware therefore when she grasped Victoria's arm, almost pulling her off the small stool, her nails almost digging into the girl's flesh.

Suddenly, the Queen Mother's face was no longer wreathed in smiles, but a hard, cold demeanour; and when she spoke it was an icy, almost vicious tone. "You will do as you are bid, mademoiselle or risk my displeasure, which would be most unfortunate for you. You would do well to learn from Madame de Suave there, or Madame de Limeuil, both have taken lovers they did not wish, but I insisted, as I do now. You will give yourself to the King, play the whore, or anything else that attracts him, but attract him you will, and I am to be informed of every detail of his conversations, his thoughts, his fears, his dreams for the future. Do you understand?"

Victoria was now becoming frightened; the Queen Mother had spoken sharply before for many trivial reasons; but this side of her was alarming. "Madame, I beg you, I cannot –" Catherine tightened her grip on the girl's arm, causing her to wince in pain, almost crying out. This time the Queen Mothers voice was delivered in a cold, harsh, angry hiss. Victoria felt the fine spray of saliva, the warm breath that carried words of ice. "You are my creature, girl, and will do as you are bid, or I shall have you thrown into the deepest cell of the Conciergerie, after I have given you to the army barracks where a battalion of men would use you until you collapse in agony."

Victoria was visibly horrified at the Queen Mother's tirade. She said nothing further, but cast her eyes down to her lap in submission. At once, Catherine's anger had subsided, no-one had noticed the exchange between the two women, and now she loosened her grip on the girl's arm and straightened the silk sleeve. "There," she said. Such a delightful gown, my dear. I declare that you are by far the most beautiful of my *squadron*. Ah, and it would appear that I am not the only one that thinks so. I see the King approaching. Go to him girl, and remember our little chat." Victoria stood up nervously as the King approached and invited her to dance. Catherine motioned her consent, and followed the pair as they joined the other dancers for the Volta. As the music began again, the Queen Mother yawned. She longed for home, for Henri, and her thoughts were never far from her concern for him. Who knew how much longer the talks with Navarre would continue? She rose, with the aid of her cane, her poor rheumatic body screaming its displeasure at the movement, and it was with small steps, she slipped away unnoticed as the court of Nerac danced late into the night.

♦

After some months debating and negotiating a peace treaty, Catherine left her daughter and son-in-law, and began the long return homewards. The continuous journeying over at least fifteen months, had wearied the Queen Mother severely, and her constant rheumatic pain now rebelled against the harshness of her travels and only the desire to embrace the King again had kept her going, testing her indomitable spirit.

Her final few days there had been to impress upon her daughter that this was now her home, and to remember that she was an essential go-between for her brother and her husband. Margot it seemed was beginning to enjoy herself trying to bring some colour and fashion to the otherwise dowdy, masculine court, yet Catherine could not help but think that boredom would soon tempt her daughter into some folly.

The ladies of the Queen Mothers *escardon* had been a great success during the months at Nerac, although they revealed very little other than personal peculiarities, and irrelevant family details. Catherine was nonetheless eager to hear all, indeed even those types of information could be useful. She justified in bringing her squadron, it had been prudent to have brought them with her. Even the insolent Victoria had wisely chosen to do her mistress's bidding and become better acquainted with Navarre; although during her latest report to the Queen Mother; her early appeal already appeared to be waning. It would seem that already the King of Navarre had lavished attention on another. Catherine was incredulous as she questioned Victoria regarding her fall from grace. "What do you mean there is another female vying for the King's favours? Perhaps this is just a scheme to relieve you of the task you were so against undertaking." Victoria recoiled as her mistress leaned closer. "Madame, I swear to you, the King though flattering does no longer seek me out for his attention is on another."

"You fool!" Catherine hissed. "You were to have held his favour, not allowed some court strumpet to turn his head, get out!" Having dismissed the lady, she then called other informants to see what they could tell her. Their reports revealed a darker side to her son-in-law than she had hitherto realised. It appeared that the King had fallen in love with a girl – who was only fourteen years old!

The Queen Mother's initial response to her informant had been horror, yet later in the company of her *escardon,* she had laughed, exclaiming that such perversity amused her, and she would like to have been present when her daughter was told of this young girl from the Montmorency family, a daughter of the Baron of Fosseux. She laughed even louder to hear that the girl had quickly been nicknamed "La Fosseuse" ("the grave digger"), Who would have though that this dull court could have been so amusing?

On finally arriving home, Catherine's joy at the reunion with the King was short-lived. She had returned to find that both of his *premiere* mignons, Valette and d'Arques were now almost exclusively her son's advisors. The remainder of the council were ignored or belittled, and were subjected to malicious insults. It was however, the King's health that primarily concerned his mother.

Henri had now lost what handsome youthfulness he had enjoyed upon becoming King. His figure was skeletal and he appeared gaunt and ill. It was rumoured that his early excesses had robbed him of what virility he had. His suspicious nature had turned its attention on the mignons, who had at one time been so close to him. He had accused them of being spies, laughing at him behind his back and being in the pay of either the King of Spain or the Duke of Guise. As each of these favourites fell from grace, they were not replaced, and his trust now lay in both these formidable young men.

Alençon meanwhile was again causing his mother great anguish. Catherine had dreamt that he would marry the Queen of England, appealing to her youngest son's dream of military glory and more importantly – a crown. A marriage with Elizabeth could bring him the wealth of England as well as the hand of its Queen. Alençon had already been assured of financial help from his intended bride, and had arrived in person to be delivered on all promises.

The farce that had been played out at the English court would have been worthy of one of the comedies of which Catherine was so fond. The English Queen called Alençon "her frog" and had declared that she was happy that they could be wed. The caprices of Elizabeth had, however, caused continuous confusion. Catherine urged her son to remain at the court, and not to be paid off with false promises.

It was with fury, therefore, that Catherine received a letter from the French ambassador that the Duke had been promised a loan of £60,000 by Elizabeth for his campaign in the Netherlands. News now reached France that the Duke of Alençon had made an official entry to Antwerp, and had been officially installed as Duke of Brabant.

♦

At the court of Nerac, the Queen of Navarre fumed at her husband. Margot had begun to tire of the uneventful court. More than that, however, was the humiliation that the King's affair with "La Fosseau" had now resulted in a pregnancy. Margot raged at the King, "How can you have been so stupid to not expect that this would occur?" She paced the floor in her fury, whilst her more sanguine husband attempted to dismiss the implications. "I have other bastards, Margot, this will merely be one more."

He gulped back the wine from his goblet, putting his feet up on the table in front of him. "You have indeed sired many children, I am no fool, of course I know it; but it matters little if the humblest kitchen maid is blessed with your seed, but that a girl no more than a child from an aristocratic family should carry your child should cause you some shame."

Navarre was no fool, he knew that this represented not only a grave error of judgement on his part but also the most acute humiliation of his wife, who had the misfortune of being the sister of the King of France. That this Royal couple were not yet blessed with a child of their own, merely added to his wife's shame.

Of course Margot had taken lovers herself; it was not in her passionate nature to accept a loveless marriage and not seek comfort from elsewhere. Whilst these affairs had been carried out with the utmost discretion, Navarre was well aware of them. He was however, deeply in love with the girl, and despite the uproar and scandal that would be caused, was determined not to give her up. Whilst Margot would caution him about the folly he had created, his own ministers would, he knew, take a very different view. Most of them belonged to his mother's age; stern and outdated. They would mumble to themselves that this would not have been tolerated in "Queen Jeanne's day"

They sat in silence together, this King and Queen. Navarre, wondering how best to deal with a situation he could not control, and his wife realising that she must decide soon whether to endure the humiliation this affair would cause her, or return to her brother's court in Paris. Of course Margot was no stranger to scandal, and Navarre refused to believe that she personally had felt the barb of this affair as acutely as many Queens would have done in her place. It was nevertheless, her position and status that would be offended and slighted. No, Margot would rail and rant at the injustice, but maybe that was merely that she was piqued that little Fosseau had been able to become pregnant when she herself was childless. He had heard the rumours for years that she had given birth several times due to her succession of lovers. He did not believe that to be so; and it was certainly not from want of trying that she had not become pregnant by him. He did not doubt his own virility, there were enough bastards running around to vouch for that. So, maybe the problem was with her alone.

He did however recall the stories about his mother in law, who had tried for the first ten years of her marriage to Margot's father to become pregnant. Her resort to all manner of weird and wonderful remedies, desperate to provide an heir. The sons had eventually come of course, Catherine's position was saved and the sons had grown up to reek misery and bloodshed upon their country.

Margot too was lost in similar thought. She had for some time believed she was barren and would never have a child; she had taken lovers, but had never once had the slightest concern that she might have been pregnant; it was not to be, and how demeaning that the Queen could not bear a child, but that a stupid country girl that Navarre drooled over could.

What was more of a concern to Margot however, were her personal finances. Added to which was an increasing sense of boredom; she had delighted at first to furnish and redecorate the dull court and try and turn it from its austere atmosphere to a place of sophistication and glory.

All this had only partially been realised. Navarre, after complaints from his ministers as well as court officials, had asked his wife to show some restraint in these costly refurbishments. Nerac, he was eager to point out, was not Paris! Moreover, now that her husband had begun to shake off the mantle of a lazy indolent and ineffective monarch, he was considered by her brother and mother to be more dangerous than they had first thought. Henri had even suggested that his sister, being a Valois Princess, afforded Nerac with a large degree of prestige, and that maybe it would serve his interests for Margot to return to her family.

The two of them sat, each with their own thoughts, and for a moment, Margot felt a sense of comfort that she had rarely felt in his company. A rare occasion when he was at least sat still and quiet, not tearing around the court with his ministers in tow, or out hunting with his closest friends.

The long period of silence was then broken suddenly with the arrival of Navarre's secretary; he must attend to his duties he stated and left the chamber; his few moments of solitude ended. His Queen watched him go and felt a sadness for a moment; the two of them had been forced together for political expediency, their wedding remembered for the horrific butchery and loss of so many lives. She had to consider, was her future really here in Nerac? Changes must soon be made.

◆

It was with a great sense of foreboding that the Queen Mother joined the extravagant, costly celebrations to mark the new eminence of the King's most trusted companions. Henceforth, Jean Louis de la Valette was raised to the Dukedom of Epernon, and Anne, Baron d'Arques was similarly ennobled to the Dukedom of Joyeuse. The latter had also recently further cemented his relationship with the King by marrying the sister of the Queen, Marguerite de Vaudemont. All this had given Henri a great deal of personal pleasure, indeed, he had wept openly that he had been overcome with the joy he had brought to the two men he most loved.

As Catherine watched the lavish celebrations from a seat in a discreet corner of the ballroom, her heart sank. Henri had not discussed his intensions with her before he had unwisely sought to bestow such honour on these two ambitious men. He had kept very much to himself in the past few months and she worried about him. He barely took council with her anymore. They seemed to have lost that special understanding they had once enjoyed.

The ballroom was fuller than was usual, adorned with candles on elaborately decorated candelabras, rich velvet hangings were festooned with flowers and jewels that shone almost blindingly. At one end of the large room, tables groaned under the weight of the most elaborate dishes: salmon dressed with peaches and grapes, stuffed pheasants, beef, cheeses, eggs, oysters poached in wine and garlic, all manner of culinary delights. Elaborate cakes and pastries, ices and fruits of all description.

The cost of the ceremony itself had been ruinous enough, with the King insisting that no expense be spared in this celebration of the faithful service these two had rendered their master.

The Queen Mother had insisted that her *escardon* amuse themselves, she debated whether to let loose the now obedient Victoria de Ayala on Epernon himself, but had thought better of it, although it would be extremely useful to know what was spoken in that man's dreams. Never had she felt so frustrated as she did now; the expense of this lavish entertainment would have to be reckoned with, and she knew only too well that the Parisian in the street would blame her, either for condoning it or not being suitably powerful enough to prevent it.

Henri's health continued to be a concern to her; in both mental and physical affect. Henri had become a master of so many moods, on one day he could be morose and none could penetrate the indifferent mood he wallowed in except his mother. Catherine could at least be useful in knowing her son better than anyone else. She had lived with his temper, his sulking and recalcitrance, his petulant temperament. His fragile mind barely kept pace with his deteriorating appearance. Once he had been celebrated in his court for his radiance, his laughter and carefree manner. Now he appeared wan and a little confused.

His sycophantic courtiers proclaimed him their brightest star, but behind his back they mocked the pathetic way he dressed his hair, the thin wisps that remained looking rather silly now that the full head of hair he had once enjoyed had gone. His costumes were looking very dated, and he no longer enjoyed the pleasure of choosing the most sumptuous cloths and colours that had once made his eyes light up. Perhaps however, his most pathetic delight was to arrange a ball and insisting that all the men should dress as ladies and all the ladies likewise should dress as men. Very few of the court had felt it necessary to besmirch further the reputation of their court and subsequently, only a few had dressed accordingly. The King, when he entered would at one time been met with cheers and gasps of wonderment at his appearance, now there was almost total silence. A few diehard courtiers had clapped for a few seconds. The sovereign had stood rooted to the spot, and Catherine had felt her heart lurch at the sorry sight he was, dressed in a gown of richness and jewels, completed with garish make up. Queen Louise herself had quickly caught the mood of the audience and began to clap, casting a beseeching look at her ladies to do likewise, but the half-hearted effort could not disguise the fact that the theme had been a social disaster. Catherine blessed her daughter-in-law, but no one person was bigger or greater than the court itself, and Henri was beginning to lose his judgement of its mood. All those in attendance had tactfully acted as though nothing had happened, but their humiliated King had made an early exit.

Henri had also become even more religiously fanatic as he and his Queen became more and more desperate to have an heir. The King would set out on regular pilgrimages, often on his knees, and public processions were commonplace, sometimes he even felt the need to march naked through the streets of the capital, until public ridicule forced him to desist. More and more now Henri had begun to step back from his responsibilities as the King; he became introvert and suspicious of those around him, save for Joyeuse and Epernon and, occasionally – his mother.

Catherine could only look helplessly on as, despite her advice, no less than seventeen different parties, balls and extravagant masquerades followed Joyeuse's wedding. She would look out at the streets of Paris, the starving citizens would huddle in groups together, occasionally glancing up at the palace windows, the candles burning long into the night. Catherine knew she would be blamed for everything; the people had no respect for their King whom they denounced as a Prince playing at dressing up, and worse. Catherine however, they hated without exception. Those few who believed she was trying hard to maintain peace were vastly outnumbered, and for safety's sake, kept their opinions to themselves.

It was, then, to a much-maligned King and an anxious mother that an announcement was made. A Royal visitor was expected – the Queen of Navarre was returning to Paris.

♦

The boredom of Nerac and her husband's continued fascination with his teenage mistress, convinced Margot that she should return to the French court. Also, recent letters from her mother and brother urged her, for dignity's sake, to return to Paris.

La Fosseau had fallen very ill during her pregnancy, and Margot could read her husband's thoughts as he learnt of her suffering: Margot is Valois but she is also Medici. Would he be able to say that he had no suspicions that his mistress may have been poisoned?

Margot could laugh at such absurdity; of course she could have had the girl smothered, there were many gentlemen at her husband's court that would do anything for her, but what would be the point? The girl would soon be replaced in her husband's affections she was sure. It was not in Navarre's nature to remain faithful.

The Queen of Navarre was settling in to her old rooms when her mother arrived. A quick nod from Margot and the attendants curtseyed to both her and the Queen Mother before leaving as swiftly as they could. Mother and daughter did not embrace, and Catherine seated herself as she appraised Margot. "You are well, daughter? It gives me great joy to see you amongst us again. I had hoped that you would have persuaded your husband to be with you, he is like a son to me as you know." Margot smiled tightly,

"He showed no enthusiasm for the visit, he cited the fact that he had been held here against his will for four years as his reasoning." Catherine was shocked at her daughter's directness, but chose to ignore it. "You have borne the insult of your husband's continued infidelity with dignity."

"The Fosseau is nothing to me," Margot replied "He will tire of her the way he does all of them in the end."

"And yet, Margot, Catherine stated, "you must turn a blind eye to such things, your dignity as a Princess of France demands that you accept this state of affairs and willingly return to your husband. It is well for the time being that you have returned to your brother's court, but in time there must be reconciliation."

Margot seated herself by the window, looking out at the city. "I don't know when I shall go back, if I go at all."

Catherine responded with a shake of her head. "This is not the way to deal with an unfaithful husband daughter, believe me. You will know from the gossips that your late father felt the need to have a mistress, yet he remained married to me. He was ever loath to give me up, because I loved him faithfully and I learned to accept the inevitable."

"The difference, Madame is that I do not love my husband as you did my father. My husband fondles and caresses a teenage virgin, sitting her on his knee like an infant, until inevitably she is with child, no more than a child herself."

Catherine sat back and surveyed her daughter. Margot was no fool. Yes, she may have used the excuse of La Fosseau as a pretext to return to Paris, but she did not think Margot would have surrendered her position so easily, and then a thought occurred to her. She caught her daughter's eye and held the gaze. "I trust you have not come here to spy for your husband?"

Margot laughed falsely. There was no humour in it, but the irony of her mother's words found their target. She had indeed, whilst justifying her need to visit her brothers court, assured Navarre that she could be of some use to him; she could keep him informed of the machinations of the King and the Queen Mother. "I have not come to spy for anyone, but I am shamed by my husband and have no intention of returning to him."

The Queen Mother saw little to be gained by arguing the point further, but before she rose to leave, she looked sternly at her daughter. "Remember, Margot, that you are the daughter of a King as well as the wife of one. There is a great difference between public behaviour and the morality we let the public see." The warning was not lost on Margot, and she was relieved that, with those words, Catherine rose and left.

Once she had gone, Margot puffed out her cheeks. Even as a grown woman, a Queen herself, she could never feel easy in her mother's company. Perhaps she needed to move away from the court. Was it too close to the cut and thrust, the menace and intrigue to be here in the palace under the same roof as the King and her mother?

She would never try and persuade her husband to return to Paris, why indeed would she want him here? No, her mother's passing barb – a subtle reminder of maintaining the dignity of a Queen – was not lost on her. She hadn't, of course, agreed to be dignified.

♦

No sooner had the Queen of Navarre settled once more into life at the French court, than old enmities were rekindled. Margot had never forgiven the mignons of her brother. Whilst their number had certainly decreased, there were still a few of these men buzzing continually around their sovereign, like wasps around wine. There was no possibility of them becoming as important as Epernon and Joyeuse in the King's eyes, Henri was fond of them, and stated that they kept him youthful. Now she saw them again, she was reminded how much she had despised them.

The King raged at his mother that he had been told that, on more than one occasion, Margot had deliberately snubbed Epernon, acting as though she had not seen him whilst passing one another in the palace. At any opportunity she had, Margot would remark about how the court needed more mice for so many cats. Whenever possible one of her great pleasures would be for herself and her ladies to "abduct" one of the mignons who was was attracted to women rather than men, and lure him successfully away from the more effeminate group of the King's followers. This enraged Epernon who, in response to the blatant insults, whispered his outrage to the King, suggesting also that word had it that the Queen of Navarre was eagerly soliciting aid for her brother's enterprise in the Netherlands. Henri was determined to be avenged.

Margot had, after a short time of returning to Paris, quit the Louvre and taken up residence in a large house in the Marais quarter of the city. Here at last, she was able to hold court herself, and her parties were becoming the subject of gossip. Little did she care that her mother disapproved of how she lived. Margot was conducting a very enjoyable affair, and could see no reason why anyone should disapprove. More delightfully, she had actually been able to finally encourage one or two of the King's mignons to attend one of her *soirees,* and their continued absence from Henri's court did not go unnoticed – or unpunished.

A special Royal banquet had been arranged, and the Queen of Navarre was required to attend. Margot sighed as her ladies dressed her for the occasion. She had spent a most enchanting afternoon in the company of her latest lover and was feeling happy and satisfied with her life in Paris. The need to obey the summons from her brother was tiresome, but it was only for one evening and she would try and make the best of it.

The palace was resplendent for the occasion, a reception for the Tuscan ambassador. The court musicians provided a light interlude, and a short ballet was staged to entertain the guests who were delighted at the honour. The Queen Mother with her keen sense of intrigue and danger felt uneasy, although she was not sure why. It was only when the meal was started that her worst fears were realised. The King was, by this time, a little the worse for drink and yet he seemed excited as he raised his voice to be heard above the music that temporarily stopped playing at his signal. "Ah, monsieur ambassador," Henri's voice rang out, "I am honour bound this evening to beg your forgiveness for a distasteful guest that we are forced to invite this evening. You were, I think, introduced to the Queen of Navarre, were you not? She maintains a house of ill repute in the Marais quarter." The whole room had fallen deathly quiet. Catherine was powerless to stop what she now knew was coming. "The Queen, my sister, is nothing but a common strumpet, monsieur, a harlot who entertains her lovers at all times of the day and night. Ah, yes monsieur, lovers. She had so many before her marriage, and has entertained as many since she was wed. You may note, monsieur, that the Queen of Navarre has – I am told, gained a little weight, and we are informed that she carries the child of one of her paramours. Which of them is the father, I doubt if she knows herself."

Margot sat frozen on the spot, she heard one or two mutterings of "shame, shame" as Henri began to list the lovers he believed she had entertained. The King paused to gulp down his goblet of wine, and Catherine immediately rose from her seat to stand next to him, leaning down to speak in her son's ear. "Henri, my son, you must not do this, how can you bring such shame on...?"

"Shame?" cried the King, "The shame is all from that strumpet that calls herself a daughter of France. She sickens me, just the sight of her, Mademoiselle prostituée! Well we will have no more of it!" He stared at his dumbstruck sister. "Get out of Paris, you have degraded our house by your depravity, get out, get out!" The King then pushed everything in front of him away, wine and platters crashed to the floor, a candelabra was knocked to the ground. Epernon was at the King's side helping him to his feet, while he continued to rage at his sister.

Catherine had by this time moved to where her daughter sat and helped her to her feet, and clutching at her arm tried to pull her away. "Go now, she hissed "leave Paris as soon as possible."

Margot had recovered her initial shock, and her eyes blazed as she attempted to shrug off her mother's hold. "How dare he? He has humiliated me...and who is he to talk of morals when he keeps those boys around him constantly?" Margot winced as her mother practically dragged the young Queen out of the hall. "Get away from Paris tonight, the King will show you no mercy, he will chase you out if you do not go willingly. Go back to Nerac and your husband. I fear great harm will come of this."

Margot could hear the King ordering the musicians to take up their instruments and play again, and still in a state of shock, she allowed her attendants to hurry her away to her chambers.

The tocsin of Saint-Germain-l'Auxerrois tolled two o'clock in the morning as a carriage sped out of the Rue Culture Sainte-Cathérine and headed out of Paris.

♦

Catherine considered Margot's hasty departure with grave reservations. It always made her both sad and angry that these offspring of hers could not see that strength was only in unity. How often had she told them just that? It seemed at times they were hell bent on their own destruction – and indeed her own. How many more miles must she travel to broker a peace agreement? How many more emergency meetings must she convene when the King was too indisposed? Her poor darling needed her now more than ever. Perhaps he should heed her more and the two detested Dukes less. She had seen the sly delight on the faces of both Epernon and Joyeuse as Margot had fled from the banquet. Nothing pleased them more than the humiliation of an enemy; and they could not have hoped that Margot would suffer the indignity that she had, their joy was complete.

More shocking news came from Antwerp, and an event that would surely mean the end of Alençon's military career. Word reached the court that the Duke had for some catastrophic reason decided on an assault on not one, but four cities simultaneously. Antwerp, Dunkirk, Bruges and Ostend. The results had been a complete disaster, and one from which Alençon had barely escaped with his life. He had, it appeared, arrogantly insisted on taking Antwerp himself; he posed as an all-conquering hero, persuading the citizens to allow him entry that they may be honoured with a parade. In his vanity and lack of military experience, he had welcomed the inhabitant's decision to open the city gates and allow him entry. No sooner had the gates been shut behind them, than Alençon and his army were under attack. Cut down by the defending garrison, and butchered by the angry mob, the result was annihilation. Catherine's spies reported that although the Duke and a few of his soldiers had escaped the slaughter; at least ten to twelve thousand had been butchered.

The courts of Europe were shocked at such an outcome. The King, who had heeded Epernon's advice and sent no further funds to aid his brother, declared himself "heartbroken" that a brother of his should be responsible for such an appalling tragedy. Catherine, meanwhile, had gone to meet with her youngest son, who after negotiations with both the Spanish and the Dutch, had travelled to Chateau –Thierry where he had fallen ill. Catherine, in spite of having been un-well herself, raised some energy and travelled to her youngest son.

♦

Upon arrival at Chateau-Thierry, the Queen Mother climbed the stairs to her son's chamber and dismissed his servants. His room was stifling; outside the sun shone brightly and a summer breeze was a welcome freshness. His chamber should have been aired. Catherine was a great believer in vigorous exercise in all weather, and as such did not agree with the physicians that shut out the sun with heavy drapes and blinds. He did not appear to notice her pass by the end of the bed and unlatch one of the small windows. For a moment, she breathed in the fresh air deeply before turning to him. The marks of his childhood smallpox seemed more pronounced, his skin appearing scaly and red, his hair stuck to his forehead. Although his fever had broken his physician had assured her before she ventured into the room, he still bore the perspiration, and his breathing was laboured, almost rasping.

As she watched him sleeping, she was suddenly aware of how much she had suffered by his hand. How his jealousy and hatred of her darling Henri had caused so much anguish. He would never listen to her advice, intent on attaining glory for himself, with little appreciation for all that had been done on his behalf. Had she not defended him against Charles's fury? Had she not insisted that her ministers find some way to negotiate a match with England's Queen? God knew she had done all she could, but the stubborn boy had let it be known that he did not consider he had a mother, as she had always so favoured his older brother, the King, over all her other children. Such a monstrous lie!

His vanity, his womanizing, his arrogance; she had worried for him so much, but she could do no more. For a moment she almost stretched out her hand for one of the pillows that he reclined on; surely this was the best way? He could never inherit, and yet –

At that moment Alençon opened his eyes, they were dull and discoloured. He made no sign of pleasure in seeing her, nor was he surprised she had come. "Ah, mother," he croaked, "have you too come to gloat over my misery? Has my brother and his sodomites sent you out again to assure him that I am dying? Tell Henri to go to the devil!" He went to turn away from her, but she pulled him around. "So," she snarled, "This is how you repay everything I have done for you, you stupid, stupid boy! Would to God you had died young, that I might have been spared the hours of hardship on your behalf. That ten thousand brave men might have been spared the folly of a commander incapable of sound judgement."

She paced his chamber as she breathed deeply, trying to calm herself. "All that I have Sacrificed! I wept when the smallpox ravaged you, but I believed that the cruelty that had been visited on me by your illness would be rewarded. All would be well, and you would grow to be your mother's pride and joy as your brother has been."

Alençon had shifted uncomfortably as the discomfort in his chest brought on the fever again. He had lain there for days it seemed; the pains had come and gone, but this attack took his breath away. Catherine continued, "I am only thankful that your dearly departed father is not alive to witness the indignity of seeing his youngest…"

"Mother, help me to sit up," Catherine heard the rasping voice. Looking over, as he sought to get his breath. "For pity's sake, I must sit...help... help me!" She watched as Alençon pathetically struggled to heave himself to a sitting position, but something stayed her, she did not move to his aid, and his rasping became worse the more he struggled. His wide frightened eyes met hers which held them a look of desperate pity. His flailing hand knocked over the jug of water by his bedside, sending its contents all over the wooden floor. Still he struggled, becoming redder as he exerted all the energy he had left. His eyes grew wide and horrified as the realisation set in that he was choking, almost too weak, and she....

Catherine almost moved, but those few seconds seemed an eternity, until, with one last gasp, Alençon slumped to one side. After some moments, she moved cautiously to her son's side; his eyes were wide...but lifeless. She then let out an awful scream, and the servants she had dismissed came running to her call closely followed by the physicians. Reluctantly, the Queen Mother allowed herself to be led from the chamber she declared she could not leave. She glanced back only once-her son's lifeless body was being gently laid back down, yet still those haunted eyes seemed to watch her. She wailed hysterically declaring that this was all too much for a poor woman to bear alone, how could a mother live to see so many of her children buried?

Catherine's ladies begged her to rest, but once she had been left alone in a chamber designated for her use, she picked up the rosary from the small altar that she always travelled with, and after painfully managing to kneel, she began to pray until the waves of emotion overcame her, and she sobbed.

In the chamber of the Duke of Alençon, the physician gave instruction for the body to be laid out, and await further instruction. "This is," he said "no ordinary death, God only knows what will come of it."

♦

PART THREE

♦

"History will see the similarities between the two Jezebels the first was the ruin of Israel the second was the ruin of France"
– Anon (circa 1576)

♦

In the magnificence of his monastic palace in El Escorial, twenty-eight miles from Madrid, King Philip of Spain sank into a seat in his private study and pinching the bridge of his bulbous nose, let out a deep sigh and closed his eyes. He would, he told his attendant priest, take mass again shortly.

His secretary, de Valesco, entered and quietly approached, eventually omitting a light cough when he had not been acknowledged. The King did not open his eyes but spoke with a quiet authority. "I am aware of you Valesco, silence for another moment if you please."

Juan Lopez de Valesco, was short and dark with a full beard unlike the shorter, defined fashion favoured by the rest of the court. His ruddy, healthy complexion contrasted with his master's sallow, unhealthy pallor. Suddenly the King hissed in discomfort, shifting in his chair to a more comfortable position. "Shall I send for your physician, Majesty?" asked the secretary. Philip shook his head wearily, and sighed again in resignation of his painful bowels. "I have no blood left for them to purge me of; sit, sit Valesco."

The secretary drew up a chair and, unfolding the file he carried, produced a number of documents. The King opened his rheumy eyes and glanced at the first missive Valesco held out to him, but did not take it. "From Guise, I imagine?" The secretary nodded. "No sooner is the Duke of Alençon cold in his grave than Monsieur Guise would make a move in France." The King nodded with a slight smile. Correspondence had come thick and fast from the Catholic Duke, eager to press on with raising a fighting force. "He is young, and the young are all eager for change and advancement. The glory must be almighty God's, of course; we do his bidding in all things." The secretary inclined his head in grave understanding.

"The League is growing in France Valesco, and God wishes us to build it greater still. Strange how the youngest son gave his mother so much trouble when he was alive and now further compounds it by dying. We shall never have a greater opportunity to advance our interests in Paris than now. Arrange to have Mendoza brought here; he will carry our condolences to the King and his mother. He will visit Guise and I will send instructions to take with him. The Catholic League will carry out God's work in France."

Valesco licked his dry, thin lips, "There are reports that the King of France will officially recognise the heretic Navarre as his heir."

Philip shook his head, "Never, never shall we let that happen. Guise will be sent further aid. We will formally send funds to him, see it is done Valesco. I will draw up the necessary documents and instructions for Mendoza to take. The Holy League will do the Lord's work in France. Nevertheless, there are dangers, and usually in the form of the Queen Mother. All in France will pledge allegiance to the Holy League, God's will be done."

The secretary quickened to help the King as he got shakily to his feet. "You will hear mass with me, Velasco?" The invitation was not negotiable and Philip cast a steely look at the younger man.

"Your Majesty is most gracious," he bowed and helped his master into the adjoining chamber and the waiting priest.

♦

The ruined Palace of Exilés lay about a hundred kilometres west of Paris. Its once handsome arched entrance had almost completely collapsed. The shell still held its fantastic seven light window, merely a skeleton without glass that had long since fallen to the ground. At one end of the main hall was the sad sight of what was once the west door, clinging on to the last of the rotten fragments that still showed the fine diaper work in the tracery panels. Mere fragments remained of what had once been a fine barrel vaulted ceiling, much of which now hung dangerously loose.

A cool night breeze had enough air to collect some dead leaves, a remnant from the Autumn That had first turned them to a golden hue before blowing them from their branches. A bright moon threw light down across the exposed stairways and crumbling towers that were once commanding, but which were now exposed to the elements and choked by the wiry creeping ivy. A silhouette of a tall figure rose up one of the ragged inner walls.

The Duke of Guise chose a large stone on which to sit while he waited. He was now thirty-four years of age, and all those who had been alive at the same time as his father, were struck by the strong resemblance; not just by his height and bearing, but the same angular face and, most uncannily, the exact same scar below his left eye. A wound from battle he had let it be known. In truth, the scar had been an idea from his mother to endear him to the citizens of Paris, where he was a hero. He had bravely borne the scar caused by a sword during an intense fight to the death, so ran the popular legend, when in reality, he had been held down while his faithful brother had sliced into his flesh just slightly below the cheekbone. He often smiled to recall it. The wound had certainly been a master stroke –in all senses. The men of the court envied his casual self-assurance; never had a battle scar brought forth so much admiration.

An even greater reward was the admiring glances from the ladies of the court. He smiled to recall the tenderness his mistress, Charlotte de Suave, lavished on him when he had arrived at their meeting one night still sporting the bloodied bandages around his face. The Queen of Navarre, Margot, his first love, had also looked horrified, but dignity would not permit her to ask how it must have hurt; he had merely bowed as she passed by. Charlotte was still his mistress, and he marvelled at how faithful he had been to her, if not to his wife. He knew Charlotte was an important member of the Queen Mother's *escardon*.

Yet it had been years since Catherine had given her the task of seducing the young Duke, and she had done so – admirably! Since then she had been given instructions to become close to the King of Navarre as well as the late Duke d'Alençon. However, Charlotte was no fool, but neither was he. Both realised the risk of becoming close to one another, the Queen Mother had not intended that they should be so selfish as to fall in love. Guise trusted Charlotte, and she had not told her mistress anything she had learnt without first discussing it with her lover. Nevertheless, Charlotte played a dangerous game, it was unwise to thwart the plans of Catherine de Medici, and Charlotte's mission was to find out and report back, not become enamoured of the victim!

He was suddenly startled by an owl. He had seen several small mice scurrying around the deserted shell of the building, all manner of creatures called this faded artifice home and the bird had flown over him several times clearly, seeing it's prey and objecting to the visitor. Guise's two male companions stood aside having tethered all three horses to a bush. They shrugged their shoulders, how long should they wait? Guise believed he had heard horses, but could hear nothing else. He was, like his father, unable to patiently stand around and do nothing.

Inactivity was wasteful of one's time; he often thought that was why he loved being a soldier, there was always activity, and like his father, he became alive once on the battlefield. There could be no paperwork for him, he left that to secretaries. He began to idly kick at a crumbling lump of stone, when he was sure he heard a tapping sound and was suddenly startled by a familiar voice behind him. "Well Monsieur, you grow impatient. Did you doubt I would come?"

The Duke swung around on instinct before bowing his head to the Queen Mother of France. Catherine was swathed in a black fur cloak, her large open features pale and heavy, her eyes wide and as black as the skull-cap that covered her head.

"Madame," Guise said, turning and dismissing his men, "I am at your service always."

Catherine had likewise dismissed the two soldiers who had accompanied her. Guise believed them to be Italian, more of the Queen Mother's creatures. The Duke at once removed his cloak and laid it onto a large flat boulder for her to be seated. "Forgive me Madame for the choice of rendezvous. The French court is always a hotbed of gossip, and what we have to discuss must not reach the wrong ears"

Catherine smiled. "The wrong ears being the ones belonging to my son – your King."

Guise could do no more than cast his eyes down to the dirt floor. "The ghosts of this place will not speak, of that we can be sure."

Catherine cast a rueful eye over the surroundings, not without a slight shudder; many knew of her association with the 'dark arts' and the mention of ghosts or spirits piqued her curiosity.

"The reason for this meeting, Madame, is to discuss with you my recent communication with Spain." Catherine made no comment, her plain pale features remaining impassive. Guise continued, "The tragic death of the Duke d'Alençon has opened up a hornet nest. The King has as yet no son and heir, so if such a state remains, Navarre considers himself the heir presumptive."

Catherine smiled softly, "My son, your King has named Navarre so. I pray to God that my dear daughter-in-law, the Queen, will soon bear a child to end the uncertainty. As yet, he has not yet answered my prayers and blessed their happy union with a child, but it may well come to pass."

Guise rose from his seat next to her, scoffing and shaking his head. "Madame, you and I both know that the King will never have a son, or any child while he allows himself the immoral company of those two preening coxcombs and takes his pleasure…"

"Have a care monsieur." Catherine interrupted. "You speak of your King – and rather boldly."

Guise stood, towering over her. He was an imposing man, articulate and certainly given to vanity and it was quite clear that he had grown extremely arrogant. "And yet I would be bolder still!" he retorted. "I would be a fool to think that you have not considered the threat of the Holy League. You know it has the backing of Spain, the Pope and all the Catholics of Europe, and yet now the King openly supports Navarre's cause, advising him to take up arms." Guise ran his hands through his hair, turning away in annoyance and exasperation.

Catherine looked grim. All her instinct told her to slap the arrogant Guise, and demand he show allegiance to his King. The criticism of her darling Henri hurt her deeply. However, she had always been a realist; as time went by there seemed to be less and less chance of the King and Queen producing a son and heir that would put an end to this problem of the succession. "This League is an outrage, my son. Yes, I do think of you as my son. Have I not watched you grow before my eyes in the Royal nursery, watched you take your first steps, and comforted your true mother as she wept at you going to battle by your father's side? Monsieur, the King, I fear, will never forgive this calumny, you are a good Catholic boy, as is he."

Guise shook his head, "Madame we are no longer children, the King would rather see a heretic Bourbon on the throne of France than-"

"Rather than you my son, Catherine interrupted. "You would have this Holy League destroy the fragile country we both love? Ah yes, I am Italian, and yet when I was raised by my late husband to be his Queen, did I not embrace this country, do I not even now wear myself to an early grave by trying to retain any type of peace? Is it not so that you would have Philip of Spain overrun this country, and uphold your tenuous claim to the throne? You would be merely his puppet sovereign, bending to his will, forever beholden to Spanish policy and the will of its pious King. Ah, yes, all can be excused if it is said to be doing the Lord's work. Philip of Spain cares nothing for you, Monsieur, and when it is the will of God to cast you aside, the Lord's work must be done!" Catherine clenched her hands in frustration.

The Queen Mother was aware that the Spanish ambassador, Mendoza, whilst ostensibly bringing Philip of Spain's condolences on the death of Alençon, had far more important negotiations to conduct with the man standing before her. "Will you not go to your King, my son?" she could hear herself almost pleading "Go to him, and speak with him. Those two vipers that are constantly with him, could be called away, or – an accident maybe." Even as she spoke the words she knew that particular route was impossible. If either Epernon or Joyeuse were to meet with any physical harm, or found with a dagger in their throat down a dark Paris alley, Henri would immediately suspect her involvement, whether she had some hand in it or not. How pleasant it would be to sprinkle a *morceau Italianise* into a goblet of wine that both mignons would enjoy for the twenty seconds before their throat was afire.

Guise interrupted her pleasant thoughts. "Madame, your son plays at being the King. He showers the two fops with lands and titles. He will not receive me at court, and when he does it is under sufferance, and then I am waved away with indifference. He now declares all leagues are illegal."

"And you would create more bloodshed simply because the King prefers a new suit to discussing war and religion with you?"

Guise sniffed in annoyance, but Catherine sighed and continued. "My son, I am a poor widow trying to protect her family, and although God has seen fit to take them all from me, save two, I must do all I can to keep them alive when so many would cut them down."

The slight was not lost on the Duke, but no-one could ever say that the Queen Mother did not do all she could for her family's preservation.

"My son," Catherine eventually spoke "The King will never support a Holy League that is paid for by Philip of Spain. There is agreement between us that Navarre should not inherit, but if not he, then who? Your eyes tell me that you already have the answer to that question." His answer did indeed surprise her. "The Cardinal de Bourbon, Navarre's uncle."

Catherine looked for a moment as though she would laugh aloud, she thought that he was jesting, but he looked serious enough. "That vain prelate!" she snapped, suddenly annoyed that Guise had no doubt discussed this question with Mendoza. "The man is more foolish and arrogant than his brother Antoine, Navarre's father. You would split this land in two merely to place that preening idiot on the throne?" Guise could not argue that the choice was a good one, but as a "temporary measure" he would suffice. Mendoza had already begun to flatter and appeal to the Cardinal's vanity.

"So monsieur, while you play the Kingmaker, I am again cast in the role of peacemaker. It is I in my advanced years that will need to find a compromise. Rest assured, that I will thwart the plans of Philip with all the feeble power I have. I will not become a tool of your family as I once was, nor will my son. Meanwhile you would tear this land apart." Guise shook his head. Catherine rose from her seat, leaning on the Duke's arm. "Tell me, monsieur," she said "did Charlotte know of your meeting with Mendoza?"

Guise looked sheepish, 'Forgive her, but I made her swear to tell no-one. She is most loyal to me."

Catherine sniffed in annoyance, "But unfortunately not to me." She waved her hand as though dismissing the matter as unimportant. "Will you not reconsider, my son?" she spoke imploringly, "The League you support will be tantamount to opening the gates of this Kingdom and letting in the hounds of Spain."

Guise raised his chin proudly "The King must recognise the League and all it symbolises. There is to be no compromise about Navarre, and every Catholic will rise with me."

Catherine's face hardened "Then you will be forever cast as traitor to your King." She held his stare for a moment before rapping the end of her walking cane against one of the decaying stones. An attendant and the two guards appeared on cue and leaning on the arm of one of the men, the Queen Mother shuffled out into the fading moonlight.

Some moments later Guise could see the two torches that lit the carriage, and watched them recede into the night. He stood for some moments until he could no longer hear the carriage wheels or the horses, and then the night was still again. He sighed and walked briskly to where his own attendants waited, and after mounting their horses, he too rode off into the forest.

As the sound of the horses grew fainter a haunting stillness settled once again on the ancient ruins until suddenly the waiting owl swooped down to catch its prey.

♦

While the Queen Mother's coach rumbled along on its way back to Paris, she sat and considered the meeting with Guise. She was greatly affected by his words. Her fury at his brazen arrogance was, however, in danger of blinding her to the reality of the situation. Of course, she would not stand back and let Guise and Spain control French affairs. Her horror that the young Duke had even had the audacity to decide who would be heir apparent had not been feigned; she had not known what to say. That empty headed Bourbon prelate was barely worth the consideration she gave him. What alarmed her most, however, was any plans involving Spain. Had Philip not been in the forefront of her thoughts for many years? She had a dread of Spanish troops marching into France, and what would become of her beloved son, or indeed – herself?

Of course she knew that Alençon's death had changed everything. She thought sadly for a moment that the pivotal role he had always sought in life had become a reality with his death. She immediately shook herself from such sad thoughts; she could not bring herself to recall that stuffy room and her son's eyes...no, must not relive that dreadful day and the part she had played in his death, she must look forward. It was essential, however, that she ensure that Henri saw the importance of this new league. She was well aware that Mendoza visited France, not to bring his King's condolences, but to meet and discuss progress with

Guise and his generals, her own spies in his household had informed her of that. Once more, France was teetering on the edge of further violence.

Navarre was making gains in some of the provinces, and these would inevitably be met by Guise's opposing armies that she learnt were gathering strength. Whilst she was well aware that Philip would pour some of Spain's vast wealth into Guise's coffers, what was to be offered in return? Had she been too hasty in drawing a line of enmity between herself and the bold Duke? If she did not talk with him how on earth would she keep abreast of proceedings?

Her spies were legendary for their cunning precision of working and finding out the most explicit details. She was for a moment reminded of Charlotte de Suave, and the thought made her scowl, but that was an issue for another time; at the moment she must give all her attention to the greater matter in hand. As always in times of anguish, she fingered her amulet bracelet with its strange symbols and small skull-heads; its strange qualities calmed her in times of great stress.

It was essential that Henri seize control of this dangerous situation and stood firm, and most importantly, took her advice as he used to. Now was not the time to rely on opinions from the two feather-brained creatures who were making the King of France something of a laughing stock. She may yet have to walk in step with Guise, but first and foremost she must keep her increasingly decadent son under control – if she could.

♦

In the market of Les Halles, an elderly woman shrouded in a simple wool shawl closely inspected the apples and melons on display. Occasionally she would stop and laugh at the street jugglers, clowns and musicians that lined the main thoroughfare making sure to ignore the ever present beggars that held out a scrawny hand or rattled a pewter dish. All around was vibrant and colourful, dyed cloth, flags, ribbons and bonnets in an array of designs. The sellers had set out their wares under the tents, fruits, all manner of vegetables, cheeses, fish. Bread stalls with loaves of varying sizes, pastries and jams, nuts and figs all of them doing a healthy trade in the chilly but bright day. Now and again, soldiers would saunter through the streets and markets, occasionally shoving their way through the throng of citizens.

The old woman would occasionally stop and mingle with the Parisian housewives who gossiped about the present troubles. "They say," one woman spoke to two others "That the King is living out his last days as a recluse. He rarely leaves his chamber. When he does, he is always accompanied by his two friends, they sleep in his bed sometimes to comfort him when he is frightened." One of the women shook her head "What sort of a King is that eh? My old father remembers old King Francis. Now there was a man he often says, useless King but at least a popular one, and his great love of women – scandalous really!

One of the wives noticed the small old woman, her shawl up close to her face, who was checking the ripeness of some greengages. "You must remember him, old mother?" she said. The elderly woman shuffled a bit nearer to the group. "Indeed, yes, he was a great man and a noble King. Is the present King so bad? I hear he is a man who wants to do much good, but is kept in check by the Guise."

"Ah, long may that be so," spoke up one of the other women, who then cast a quick glance around her before leaning towards the others, speaking in a low voice. "Well, my brother has a friend that works there at the palace, and word has it that the King of Navarre will be King of France himself within the year!" There were collective gasps; not least from the hunched old woman standing close to the group.

"Heaven help us!" spoke another "the Bourbons will tear this country to shreds. "What would become of the King then, or that bitch of a mother of his?" The women all shook their heads.

The little old woman again joined the conversation, "Perhaps then it would be better to keep the Valois on the throne." One of the women dismissed the idea, "How could you want that, old mother? Have you not suffered as we all have under that family's rule?" The old woman nodded slowly, "Yes, I have had many sleepless nights with worry." The group again shook their heads in collective concern.

The market was getting busier now, and several times the women had to move until they eventually broke apart, and continued on their way. The little old woman was deep in thought for a moment before she moved on. A bookstall stood to one side of the market place, and she shuffled over to it, stopping to inspect the books of all sizes, some covered in expensive velum and soft leather.

The trader eyed her suspiciously, but was curiously attentive to another man who had also stopped to view the titles. He was however, acting quite suspiciously. The bookseller greeted him, and looked around him, furtively. It seemed everyone was wary of who might be about. The visitor then appeared to take a package, letters perhaps, and hand them to the merchant, who tucked them inside his own tunic. The two men exchanged words, before the visitor turned to leave, and as he did so revealed that underneath his cloak he wore the livery of – the Guise.

The old woman who had by chance witnessed this brief encounter, paused for a moment as if frozen to the spot. The bookseller bustled towards her, waving her away like an annoying fly. She was most certainly not the kind of buyer he wanted to encourage. The old woman moved on, pulling the shawl further over her face before turning away from the market, and making her way through the parish of Saint-Eustache towards the Hôtel de la Reine.

♦

The Queen Mother walked as stealthily as she could towards the apartments of the King. Her ailments did not allow her a significant pace, but nonetheless she moved with purpose. She had arrived at the Louvre from her own town house where she had taken to spending more time as her bodily afflictions wore her down. She battled bravely on through the curse of rheumatism, gout and chronic toothache. Much as she delighted in the residence she had been ambitiously adding to over the past few years, she was never happy to be away from Henri, now even less so as he became so bewitched by his two sycophantic companions.

Her heart leapt with joy as her son rose to meet her, embracing her warmly. Never far away, unfortunately, Epernon and Joyeuse stood arrogantly at one side of the chamber, barely acknowledging her arrival or paying the deference to her that they should. The King led her to a chair in the centre of the room

"Mother!" he spoke with excitement. "You will be amazed when you see them. Now sit here and you must be prepared to be dazzled." Catherine smiled at him, how delighted she always was to witness something that gave him so much joy. After a moment or two Henri nodded at Epernon, who insolently sighed like a recalcitrant child before clapping both his hands together twice.

On that signal, several of the King's attendants filed into the chamber dressed entirely in bright green with large puff-sleeved arms slashed with red velvet, a gold band clutched at the wrist. They wore caps of the same pattern and colour, and likewise on their feet, slippers bearing the King's monogram. The King personally straightened one of the caps, wagging a royal finger at the culprit before tapping the servant on the side of his head and playfully pinching his cheek.

"Well," said the delighted monarch, "Are their new uniforms splendid? I have designed them myself, so exhausting. There will be new attire for members of the state council too, but I have been too drained to even have them made up yet."

Only Catherine's gift of concealing her true emotions prevented her from screaming her frustration. When she spoke, it was warmly, but with an edge of annoyance. "They are perfect, my son. All credit to you my darling, who else could have created such a transformation?"

"Yes they are rather splendid, are they not?" Henri continued to discuss the various merits over each design until all the attendants were dispatched back to their duties. The King was aware that his mother obviously had things to say that did not concern the new livery of his servants. Catherine however, could not resist one jibe at the arrogant favourites.

"My son, you have no costumes for either of your Dukes?" The new tension in the air was suddenly palpable; both Epernon and Joyeuse bristled at the intended slight, both men standing straight and looking at her with unfathomable hatred.

Henri's smile did not drop, he was after all half Medici He continued to stare at his mother, whilst he also made a signal with his hand that both companions knew to be dismissal. The two men then made a point of standing in front of the King and bowing, but ignored Catherine. Both of them had reached the chamber door before the Henri's voice stopped them. "My friends, you will observe the courtesy of my court, and treat the Queen Mother with the manners and honour her status and rank demands."

For a moment there was utter silence, and then both the men walked slowly to the Queen Mother and made a curt bow. She smiled tightly at the bent heads. They then continued bowing before backing out of the room. Catherine was exultant. How she had waited for Henri to insist that she be shown the deference she was due from the two arrogant Dukes. She could not help but permit herself a rare smile of triumph, and a sigh of relief that they had left the chamber.

Her delight was to be short-lived; when she faced her son again, he still wore the smile he had bestowed on her, only now it had become dangerously fixed, without feeling and emotion. "Never again," he now spoke, coldly, "are you to insult either of the Dukes. Your wit was misplaced Madame. You sought to put them down by belittling them, but you have come close to being dismissed from my chamber. Only your advancing years and your occasional good counsel has saved you from a humiliation."

Catherine was aghast at her son's quiet and controlled fury, and for a moment she could say nothing more. Henri finally stood and helped himself to some wine from a crystal decanter. He half-filled his goblet and after drinking down all the contents, he turned to her again. "You arrived to discuss something, what is it?" The Queen Mother closed her eyes briefly, desperately attempting to compose herself.

"My son, we must discuss this Holy League. You need to act, my darling, and decisively so. In Paris I believe Guise works covertly. You will have heard of course that Navarre has openly invited German mercenaries to swell his armies. Meanwhile every day, Philip of Spain pours more and more money into Guise's pockets to further build his underground organization."

The King slumped back down into his chair again and sighed, "God forgive me, but I wish them both dead! Navarre for his stupidity and Guise for his arrogance and hatred toward me. Oh yes, he struts around the court, using any occasion he can to embarrass my two friends. God knows they only want to serve me, but I can banish him from my sight, from France even.

"My son, your hatred of Guise must not blind you to good sense. We can only fight against him if we can see him, we must walk in step with him until we are able to act."

Henri watched her quizzically for a moment. "You admire him, don't you?"

Catherine had not expected such a direct question, but she grasped her son's hand drawing it to her lips and kissing it gently. "I admire only you my darling, she spoke emotionally. "Have I not proved so many times? Have I not worked hard for your good, dealt with every crisis that your office has to bear? I admire only you, my son, that is why I beseech you to listen to me now. Have I not always told you, caress your enemies? Keep those who are most dangerous close by you. The enemy is Navarre. It is he who will be our undoing. Well, one enemy is in his own kingdom, we can do little about him, but Guise is here, now! And watch him we must."

The King rose again, and walked to the window looking out on a cloudy sky that matched his mood. "Well I shall act against both those traitors, Guise and my brother-in-law; I shall declare the formation of any organizations, be it Catholic or Huguenot, to be a crime against France and its King. I take offence that Mendoza seems to act as though I know nothing about his master's treachery. Does he really take me for such a fool? And that old goat the Cardinal of Bourbon, the ideal instrument for Philip and Guise, a gullible nonentity, who will drown in their flattery, little knowing that they laugh at him behind his back."

Catherine opened her mouth to say more, but the chamber door had opened, and without waiting to be summoned, Epernon stood insolently just inside the chamber. Whilst she deplored the reappearance of this most arrogant of men, she knew that she must surely act as she had always done, and what she had insisted Henri do: keep the enemy close.

The Queen Mother rose, leaning on her walking cane "I will leave you now my son, the Duke is here to assist you, and his wise council will be so invaluable. Monsieur," she said pleasantly, "Forgive an old woman's sharp tongue, I had not meant to treat you cruelly." Epernon almost gaped in astonishment, and he bowed deferentially as she walked past him. Henri felt overcome with the emotion of the moment. Outside the chamber, Catherine offered the same words to the other surprised mignon and walked back to her own apartments with a rare smile on her face.

◆

The King's decision to outlaw any type of organizations within the realm of France was met as Catherine had expected it would be, by a swift response. The League poured out all its vitriolic grievances in its *Declaration of Causes.* Both Joyeuse and Epernon were singled out for particular mention, accused of *"slipping into the favour of our sovereign King to seize his authority and usurp his grandeur."*

It criticized the King for dismissing state servants in order to then sell their offices. Most crucially however, it appealed to all towns in France to refuse admittance to Royal garrisons until the King agreed to the its demands.

Over the following months it was apparent that the League was making significant ground, and had gained support in many major towns and cities. Catherine was kept informed of all developments while resting at Blois, following a heavy cold. Her body was letting her down and she cursed herself for it; having always had such robust health, she cursed herself angrily for her weakness.

The time was surely arriving now when each side must negotiate some sort of treaty. Getting her son to discuss the terms he was prepared to accept was almost impossible. The King had decided that he could do no more other than give his mother authority to act as she saw fit. Weary in body as well as in mind, Catherine dragged herself from her sickbed and held informal talks with Guise.

The Treaty of Nemours was duly agreed between between Catherine and the League. The Queen Mother had done all she could, and the results were uncompromising: a ban on the practice of any religion in France other than Roman Catholic was a direct and inflexible condition, as was the revocation of all of the previous edicts of pacification. Tough and inflexible as the treaty was, there was little else that Catherine could do to avert further bloodshed.

The Queen Mother's audience with her son following the signing of the treaty was as brutal as the agreement itself. A weary, sick woman, she still suffered from the effects of a heavy cold and her bones felt as they could no longer hold her up. The King, strongly aided by his two creatures, remonstrated with her at the indignity of the agreement.

"My son," she had said passionately "What more could have been done? Would you really have wanted to destroy your Kingdom further? Compromises had to be made."

Epernon laughed contemptuously, sneering at the exhausted woman sat before the King. "Forgive me,

Madame, if I say that your obvious game of duplicity is exposed, it is clear that you show favour to the House of Lorraine."

"That is not true!" she cried, alarmed that the two favourites were now turning on her, and yet her son said nothing in her defence.

Henri interrupted angrily, throwing a copy of the treaty onto the table in front of her. "Did you give no thought to this? Did you truly comprehend what it says? Let me quote for you." He spread out the treaty in front of her, his face so close to hers that she could smell the heavy scent, feel his hot breath "............*repel all previous edicts of pacification*" Your edicts, Madame." Catherine rallied, suddenly releasing a rage spurred on by an ungrateful son, and triggered by two men that had played a key role in this humiliation. "Why, you have suggested as much yourself before now! I admit that it was necessary to compromise more than we hoped. The cost of it will be high, as much as will be paid for the expensive follies of you and these two knaves!"

The King, aghast with horror at her rare anger towards him, clutched at Joyeuse's hand for support as Catherine rose painfully to her feet. The act was seen as threatening to Epernon, who made a grievous error when his hand flew straight for his sword. Henri gasped again at the action, but was startled further when Catherine, her eyes blazing, drew back her arm, and slapped the Duke so hard across his face that her ring cut into his powdered cheek, and he staggered back from its force. "You would dare to raise your sword to me" she spat the words at him and then turned on her still horrified son and his other companion leaning down to hiss in his ear "It is not the treaty that you deplore, is it, my King? No, it is the victory for Guise that you hate so much, and because you fear him. That these two fools hate him is a good enough reason is it not? Ah, my son, think well before you take on such a man who can summon your citizens like no other can, consider that when you scorn him as a traitor for I have faced too many dangers on your behalf to have all my work destroyed by your folly!"

With that, she pushed Epernon out of the way and threw open the door letting it slam back against the wall, and calling for her attendants. She would be leaving for Blois as soon as possible. The King stared after her for several moments before breaking down in tears.

♦

In the splendour of his audience chamber at the Vatican, Pope Sixtus V received a representative from the Catholic League, the Duke of Nevers. A wily, uncompromising man, the Pope was a formidable pontiff. His predecessor, Gregory XIII, had been an easy man for the Catholics to deal with, such was his determination to destroy the Protestants at all costs. Sixtus, no less keen to see an end to the heretical scourge, was however mindful of who was employed to further that cause.

The Duke had been sent by Guise to request a bull, or brief that fully endorsed the action that the League in France was now taking. Sixtus sat for some moments, his entwined hands with their long, slim fingers resting in his lap. The Duke began to become restless at the continuing silence, as well as still kneeling at the pontiff's feet, his jewelled slippers just visible underneath his rich robes. The Pope finally spoke

"Tell me my son," he said quietly but with a steadfast tone, "This League in your country was no doubt formed to destroy the heresy that still exists there as well as the good conscience of the Catholic church, but it was nevertheless unauthorized by the church here in Rome." Sixtus raised his hands to silence the Duke before he would interrupt. "And yet, Monsieur, when was Monsieur de Guise as well as yourself and others taught to form such parties in defiance and against the will of your King?"

Nevers was taken aback by the words that were delivered slowly and clearly. The Duke could feel the rush of blood to his cheeks, "Most Holy Father," he stammered, "please be assured that all we have done is with the King's blessing, we have interpreted –"

The Pope raised his hand again as he cut in "You have interpreted your King's wishes, how very interesting. No, Monsieur I see you are no different from your commander Guise, who I have had letters from. You dislike correction. This must be God's will, not that of a vengeful family. You come for my advice, maybe what you seek here is merely an echo of your own conscience. Do you believe that your King does not see you as his enemies?" Before Nevers could reply, the pontiff held out one of his long hands to the Duke nodding sagely. "Return to your League monsieur, I will write to your masters, and I will pray that your King and his mother do not seek their deliverance from such evil with Huguenot assistance."

♦

In Spain meanwhile, King Philip considered he was adopting a wise policy regarding the League, and like the Pope, he had no intention of seeing the French crown destroyed by the ambition of the Duke of Guise, despite Spain holding the purse strings. It must be understood that this was for the glory of God, not the glory of Guise. The endeavour must be to cleanse the country of heretics, not merely remove Guise enemies.

Philip was of course most grateful for the conflict in France. He had welcomed anything that drew attention away from his work in the Netherlands. Now that the foolish Alençon had perished, there was less chance of French intervention to thwart his plans.

Arms and money to the League must also be limited, lest Guise seek to run it independently. Spain did not have limitless funds either, and large proportions of money were currently being used for another enterprise, as Philip turned his attention to England.

♦

The Queen of Navarre, meanwhile, had left her husband's court where she had fled after her humiliation by her brother. Her situation was further compounded by her husband's new mistress Diane d'Andouins. Navarre had fallen helplessly in love with the lady, who appeared to know just how to manipulate a character like him; she was certainly a great deal cleverer than his previous mistresses, and more importantly – older. Already la Fosseau was a distant memory.

Navarre, whilst enjoying this infatuation had the added pleasure of being rid of his wife who had behaved wantonly before his court with a succession of lovers.

For the staid, strict court at Nerac this was behaviour unbefitting their Queen. Whilst the King's own lapses of morality could be excused, those of his wife could not.

Margot had, from Nerac, gone to her own estate at the town of Agen, where she took stock of her situation and appealed to her mother for urgent funds. Never far from scandal and intrigue,

Margot had set about raising troops on behalf of the League, thereby declaring who she would support, although she assured her mother that she was merely raising a small army to protect her person, given the animosity with which both her brother and husband felt towards her. This once stunning beauty was now growing stouter, her once curvaceous figure thickening with the advance of years, she was forced to apply more make-up as she naturally began to age. Elaborate wigs and daringly low-cut gowns were now employed as a snare to catch the eye of any handsome gallant that joined her domestic court, and as usual there was licentious and bawdy behaviour. and the inhabitants of this small holding, already offended by the Queen of Navarre's high-handed treatment of them, were scandalised. From there, Margot now headed to Carlat, another of her properties, where she began an affair with a nobleman by the name of Jean de Lart de Galard, Seigneur d'Aubiac.

Catherine received all this news with apprehension, but mostly anger. Had she not done all she could for her wayward daughter? She declared Margot had been sent by God as a punishment for a mother's sins. With tension still existing between herself and her son, Catherine made the independent decision to offer Margot the manor of Iboise near Issoire. Margot's friends who had remained loyal to her, urged her to give the offer consideration, yet she refused. "I would simply be watched every hour and be constantly at my mother's call. No, I have done with my family and the court in Paris."

Finally, Catherine and Henri were reunited when the King visited Blois and declared that he could no longer bear to be without her. The exultant Queen Mother embraced him with tears and remorse for cruel words said. It seemed that neither Joyeuse or Epernon had been able to convince the King to totally cut her out of his life. A dinner in Henri's honour had been arranged by the Queen Mother at Blois, and she herself had personally chosen the King's chamber close to her own. "Lest he should have need of me," she explained. Soon after the banquet and entertainments, Catherine decided to retire to her rooms. Some time later, her dwarf reported to her that the King had himself returned to his chamber.

The Queen Mother dismissed her ladies and attendants, and after locking the chamber door, she slid her hand along part of the wooden panelling until, hearing the click of a mechanism from behind it, and she carefully slid aside a large section. The aperture was barely the height of a doorway, and the stout figure of the Queen Mother had to squeeze uncomfortably into the small space that not so long ago she could have stepped into with ease. After inching her way through the small gap that ran like a tunnel between two walls, she stopped at a familiar place and slid away a small disc that revealed a hole, and she then pressed her face against it until she had a clear view.

King Henri stretched out his legs as his servants removed first his shoes, and then divesting him of the remainder of his clothes. Sat to one side of his chamber, Epernon slouched into a large chair.

"My darling boy," the King spoke to his favourite, "I am concerned that you should wish to go into battle for me, my dear brave friend. I declare that I shall also take to the field, though it is some years since I last did so." The King looked up as the chamber door opened, and Joyeuse entered and immediately dismissed the King's servants. Rather than be angry, Henri appeared to accept this and became suddenly more serious. "Well, my friend, did you find someone for the task?"

Joyeuse smiled and drew up a chair between the other favourite and their master. "I have engaged a servant of mine, Pierre, for the task. He is close to me and has my full confidence. I have disclosed the nature of the deed, knowing that even if he would not carry out the task, he would tell no-one about it."

"Good, good," the King said, his eyes lighting up, "the stage is set then for my sister to be the heroine she imagines herself in her memoirs. I will no longer have our house shamed by that brazen woman."

Epernon now joined the conversation. "How are we to proceed my King?" Henri was thoughtful for a moment. "It must be poison," he declared "They say that Margot allows no swords to be carried in her presence, so something in her food or wine is really the only option. We must, however, keep this strictly between ourselves; once my mother or any other knows of this plan we are undone."

Joyeuse still seemed puzzled. "But, most gracious King, why can you not just have the wanton Queen arrested and locked up?"

Henri smiled and held his hand affectionately against his friend's cheek. "Because my darling creature, she will then be a figurehead for more of my enemies, she will scheme and plot for her old lover Guise. We cannot afford for her to live. She is soaked in scandal, her husband declares that she is "soiled goods" and will not entertain the thought of her returning to Navarre, and who could blame him?"

Epernon suddenly laughed aloud, "I hear that her latest lover d'Aubiac has said he would die for her, perhaps he could die with her."

The three of them laughed aloud before Henri returned to the main subject of their discussion "When will instruct your man to go?" he asked Joyeuse.

"He can be sent before the end of this week. I will ride out to Paris tomorrow and give him full instructions along with a letter for the Queen supposedly from her friend, the Duchesse of Nevers, commending him to her as a reliable servant and one that greatly admires her and has a wish to serve her."

The King grinned slyly and patted his friend on the hand. "That is good, very good indeed. Have Pierre sent as soon as possible and pay him well my friend, for he surely does me a great service with this. Now, Jean," he said affectionately to Epernon, "I would have you read to me, you know how I am soothed by it, and Anne, you will call my servants to prepare my bed, I am suddenly unaccountably tired

From the other side of the panelled wall, the hot and perspiring Queen Mother edged her way out of the passageway and back into her chamber. She replaced the panel so that nothing was disturbed, and sat down to digest this latest potential crisis. So, Henri and his mignons would see her daughter poisoned? And of course, once the cause of death was known, who would be the most likely suspect?

Catherine felt her heart beating fast she felt faint. So here was a devious plan; Margot to be poisoned, thereby ridding her family from the disgrace and embarrassment she caused. Her own mother would be suspected of removing her by her favoured method.

As was usual with Catherine, however, was the need to look ahead. If there was the slightest chance that Navarre, for his own reasons, could be persuaded to take her wanton daughter back....!

The Queen Mother hated herself for thinking it, but it had to be faced that there was little chance of Henri and Louise having children; were Navarre to inherit, as seemed likely, then Margot would be Queen of France! The matter was clear, Margot must not be put in danger; as much as Catherine was heartily fed up and angry for her daughter's wanton and casual behaviour.

That night the Queen Mother spent a restless night, rising before dawn to compose a letter to be taken, with the utmost urgency and secrecy to the Queen of Navarre at Carlat.

Several days after receiving a letter from her mother, Margot received a visitor; a young man claiming to have come with greetings from her friend the Duchesse of Nevers. She was overjoyed, and welcomed the bearer of the letter, Pierre, promising that he would of course be given employment as her friend had suggested. She would instruct her steward find him suitable work.

It was something of a shock to the Queen when she was informed some hours later, that a body had been found at the bottom of the castle walls. The young servant Pierre had broken his neck from what appeared to be a fall from the ramparts. Margot had the small pouch of powder that was been found on the body returned to the most honourable Baron d'Arques Duke d'Joyeuse in Paris with a note merely stating "Unmasked, and unused"

♦

War between the three Henris was now inevitable as all hopes to avert more fighting faded.

In Rome, the Pope finally excommunicated Navarre and his cousin Condé. This led to a response from Navarre and he counter-excommunicating the Pope! Even sending his own formal bull to be pinned to the door of the Vatican Palace.

The French King had formally removed Navarre from the succession. Catherine was watching events calmly trying as was ever her policy, to take a middle ground in such affairs. The treasury was empty and the King, suffering from lack of funds, assured the League he would field armies to take on the Huguenots. So it was with tears that he bid farewell to his two favourites, Joyeuse to the Auvergne and Epernon to Provence. Henri declared he would move to Lyons to be nearer to both men.

Fighting intensified, with Guise scoring resounding victories at Vimory and Auneau and Navarre completely routing the Royal armies at Coutras – a battle that resulted in the death of one of the King's dearest friends, the Duke d'Joyeuse.

Henri was inconsolable when news of the death was brought to him, and he briefly recalled Epernon that the two of them might grieve together. Catherine advised the King that he should maybe keep the ceremony of Joyeuse's funeral as informal and simple as possible in view of the cost of the continuing fighting. Henri was minded to agree with her until Guise demanded an audience with the King. At the meeting, he stressed that he felt as a reward for the victories that had been won, that he receive at least some recompense in the form of some of the offices, properties and honours that had been showered on the late Duke.

The King's petty response was to ensure that the funeral for his favourite was as lavish as any that had been known outside a member of the Royal family, and simply bestowing all of Joyeuse's titles and honours to Epernon. Catherine's heart sank at the situation, yet she must endeavour to carry on as best she could, still fighting for the Valois, fighting for her son's Kingdom as well as his personal safety.

Henri was beginning to feel vulnerable on all sides, and sought to remedy the situation by entrusting his personal safety not only to the traditional Royal guards, but to personal bodyguards that he instructed Epernon to recruit. They must be of exceptional bravery and agree that during their service in the King's lifetime, they were to remain unmarried! This small personal army were to guard the King day and night, and were to be more commonly known as the Forty-Five.

♦

After all efforts to curb the Queen of Navarre's excesses and the embarrassment and shame she was causing her family, the King finally decided, after consideration with Catherine, that the safest course would be to have his sister arrested. Margot was taken to the infamous Château d'Usson. This building had been a favourite place for the former King Louis XI to hold political prisoners.

Its reputation was not lost on Margot, who laughed at the irony that the property did in fact belong to her as Princess of France. Even more petty of her brother, she thought, when told that she was to hand over to the King all her jewellery.

The gentleman employed to accompany the Queen to this new fortress, Canillac was soon to prove a lenient jailer, and visited Lyons to join the League. Having done so, he returned to give his prisoner her liberty.

News had reached France that, after the uncovering of a planned attack against her life. Elizabeth of England had finally signed the death warrant of Mary Stuart, the former Queen of Scotland and France One conspiracy of many, the Babington plot, so named after the leader of the planned enterprise, had been Mary's undoing. The machinations of the affair had been carefully monitored by the famed Secretary of State and spymaster, Sir Francis Walsingham.

Having been held prisoner by her cousin Elizabeth for almost twenty years, Mary had finally met her end at the executioner's block in Fotheringay Castle.

If there could have been any joy in Catherine's life at present, it was to be presented to her in the unexpected form of the Duke d'Epernon. The Royal favourite had presented himself at Blois where the Queen Mother was staying on her way back to the capital. Once told of the highly unexpected request, she retired to her apartments to sleep for a while; travelling tired her more and more, and it seemed sometimes that she had been on the road continually. Still, there was no need to see the hated creature before she had rested. The Duke was made comfortable with food and wine, but it was several hours before, furious Epernon knelt at the feet of the Queen Mother.

Catherine acknowledged him, but made no signal for him to rise; and each time it seemed as though he would stand, Catherine's raised eyebrow was enough to stay him.

"What is it you wish of me, Monsieur?" she asked. Epernon licked his dry lips and glanced around him, he had hoped for a private audience, but Catherine had made no such suggestion. Here then in front of mercifully few courtiers, he tried to carry his voice with as much dignity as he could.

"Madame, I have come on bended knee to ask for your..." he paused, beginning to regret he had ever made such an impulsive decision. Catherine smiled without humour, and cajoled him into continuing.

"Come now Monsieur, you and I serve the King together, we can have no secrets, nor pride when we converse"

The Duke, whose knee was now feeling uncomfortable, cleared his throat. "Madame, I have not bothered the King with this."

Catherine was alert to this now; was there some fresh plot against the King's life? "I am the victim of a plot, an assassination! This is the third such foul deed that has been uncovered in the last few weeks." Catherine fought the impulse to laugh in his face. As though she was interested in someone picking off this most hated of her son's cronies. "Monsieur, we are surely all walking in the shadow of death, and yet why should anyone wish to harm one who is so close to the King?"

The Duke fought the impulse to march out of the castle; he needed friends and, of limited power as she now was, the Queen Mother was still held in high regard by some. "Madame, I know we have not always been of an accord, but I am begging for your help. I know the Duke of Guise to be behind these wicked plots against my life. I am begging you to intercede on my behalf. The Guise hate me, and would see me dead, I am merely the King's friend. I want no part in this war but to serve my King as you do yourself. Speak to the Guise for me, Madame, I beseech you!"

Catherine was enjoying this immensely, it had been some time since she had felt the urge to laugh joyously, but she looked on him with false sympathy in her eyes. "Monsieur, she said softly, "I do not see what I can do, I have little or no influence with either his Majesty of the Duke of Guise. They are no longer boys, you understand, they are grown men. Indeed, as you know the King no longer consults me on important matters, and the Guise must have their own reasons for considering such a move, I must declare however that I am shocked to hear of it."

Epernon grew more restless with each passing minute, yet still he was not bidden to stand. "Believe me, Madame, I would willingly defer to you in all dealings with his Majesty. It is only right that he should take counsel with his mother. My dearly departed comrade Joyeuse had a mind to exclude you from the King's favour. To my eternal shame, I was unable to deter him, such was his strong will."

Catherine looked at the distressed man without compassion. Only her son's friendship with this opportunist made her consider aiding him, but she spoke with solemnity. "Monsieur we must always be prepared to die. Have I not myself been the intended victim of a poisoners draft, an assassins knife? Monsieur, none of us know when the blow will be struck. Why I myself could have laced the wine you were served earlier while waiting for your audience. The poisoner's art is in the disguise of his weapon."

Epernon looked upon the Queen Mother with absolute horror, all colour draining at once from his face. She hated him, none more so. He clutched at his throat waiting for the burning to start, was that a cramp starting in his stomach? The man looked up to see the Queen Mother's amused face; he heard some sniggering from a couple of the courtiers. He thanked God that so few were there to witness his humiliation.

Without waiting to be asked, he rose with as much dignity as he could muster, and leaned threateningly towards her. Several swords could be heard being drawn from their scabbards, but Catherine held up her hand to stay them, Epernon's weapon was his vile tongue. "Should the worst happen to me you will have to look to your conscience Madame. Whilst you seek to amuse yourself at my expense, I will do nothing to aid you in any way with the King. He hates you, you know? He dreads your harping on about duty to France, to the memory of his father. How many times I have dissuaded him from having you banished from the court? How sorry I am that I spoke in your defence."

Catherine was as adept as always at masking the fury and horror that his words had inflicted on her. She matched his malice, she was not someone to scare easily; how many dangers had she faced over her long life? She leaned toward him when she spoke. "Then you have me as an enemy Monsieur, you will not enjoy the experience. Now – leave me."

The Queen Mother sat back, watching the retreating Duke and wondering how much truth there had been in his bitter words. The man was a fool, but he may yet prove to be a dangerous one.

◆

Catherine had been summoned by the King, and as usual these days, she dreaded to think what could have occurred since she had last been with him. There had been barely a day since she had returned after travelling again on Henri's behalf to meet with Navarre. The talks had resulted with the same questions unanswered, the same denials and excuses and the determination to see the war through to the end. What had shocked and horrified her more however, was that Navarre no longer considered her to have enough influence over her son to be able to sit and discuss any possible solutions. Navarre had been heard to say, that to talk with the Queen Mother was to waste one's breath!

Now back in Paris and with Epernon away raising fresh troops, she was enjoying an all too brief spell as her son's closest confidante, but in her state of age and failing health, such duties tired her, even though she still refused to fully give in to her ailments, much as her doctors advised it.

The King paced his apartments, and even though it had been only hours since she had last seen him, she was reminded again how much he had changed in recent months. He rarely ate, and when he could be persuaded to, it was merely fruit or the sweetmeats of which he was still fond. His usual immaculate appearance was beginning to draw amusement from the court.

He would some days appear with rouge on his face, but often overdone giving him the appearance of the jugglers in the troupe of circus players that had entertained him so often in the early days of his reign. His teeth had become brittle and he had lost several of them. He took no measures to cleanse his breath, that had become fetid and unpleasant. His once carefully crafted hair was now so thin that most of the skin on the top of his head was exposed. He chewed at his nails constantly, as a result of which his fingers, once delicate and perfectly manicured, were often bleeding sores.

It was however, his mental state that worried his mother the most; he would rage, much like his late brother Charles, and throw objects about in his temper, he would curse and cry at the indignity done to him, and he now seemed to withdraw further into the Louvre and showed no sign of wanting to venture from it.

Now as soon as she had entered his apartments, he turned on her with fury. "Guise has left the court! he shouted at her "Did you know? Ah, of course you knew! Why did no-one think to tell me?" He threw himself into a seat, pushing away one of his favourite dogs, who yelped in annoyance. "You are with him are you not, mother? You think I do not know, but I do, I do!"

Catherine took a seat next to him and was thankful that only his bodyguards at the chamber door were in attendance. "My son, listen to me, you know those are evil rumours about me spread by my enemies as well as yours. You know that my life is endured only for your comfort and safety. Have I not proven to you in all these years that I work only for your advancement and glory?"

She reached out and held his hand between hers. "Be guided by me will you not?"

Henri stood up and began pacing again. "Yet you would argue that I allow him to raise my capital city against me!"

"My son, these are surely rumours…"

"No Madame, they are more than rumour. Do you think only you have spies in this city? The Guise incites the city to rise against me, their King. He would have an uprising and I taken as his captive!"

"What you have heard is wrong, Henri, I beg of you listen. If you and I were to be…."

The King spluttered an interruption "Me, Madame! Me! I am not concerned with what happens to you! It is me!"

Catherine composed herself as best she could; the pain of his words wounded her, but surely these were not meant. Her son was frightened for himself, and of course, she was an old woman now.

"My darling son," she said somewhat shakily, "you must be careful. Whoever you put your trust in, hear my words, you must not voice such suspicions about Guise here in the capital, it is most unwise."

Henri turned to her with a grim look of satisfaction on his face, "It is of no matter now, I have done with him." Catherine was immediately alert, she almost dared ask what he meant. Noticing her look of panic, he leant towards her "I am interested to see your concern for him, but he has been told not to re-enter the city until he receives my summons to do so."

The Queen Mother could not conceal her anxiety "What have you done, my son?"

"Simple!" replied the King "I have forbidden him to re-enter Paris without my consent."

Catherine shook her head even as he spoke "No, my son, no. There will be anarchy in the streets, to forbid Guise entry into Paris will light the touch-paper that will ignite the capital, have I not warned you that the city is loyal to him?"

"Then I will send my troops into the city, any rebellion will be subdued. I will not have him back in Paris and if he defies me, his King, then he shall suffer the consequences."

◆

On a hill overlooking the capital, a group of horsemen stopped to view the rooftops of the city. A light mist had settled over Paris lending the scene an ethereal appearance, wind and rain had made the journey harder for them, but only another few miles and they would reach their destinationand at least one of the group knew he may never leave it alive.

This proud nobleman sat upright in his saddle, his mouth set in a determined line, his eyes squinting now against the harsh elements. The distinguishing scar below his left eye was irritated by the cold wind, and throbbed.

Here then was his date with destiny, and he recalled the tall noble man whom he had called father, a giant of a man, of whom he had never stopped thinking of as he entered each episode of his life. Would his father have been proud of his son, or would he have thrashed him for his insolence? He was sure that it would be the former.

He recalled also the long summer days spent with the Princes and Princesses at court, the early formative years that had all led to this defining moment. Here was the city he adored, one that he had been proud to rouse to deal with the scourge of Huguenot enemies. The Parisians in their turn had made him their hero; cheered for him, waving flags and banners throwing flowers at his feet. Yes, the Parisians loved him as they could never love the King who had treated them with such contempt.

There was no doubt what he should do now, he knew that this was his destiny and the matter was in God's hands. Suddenly he smiled; the way was clear and the day was upon him.

He turned then to his companions with his handsome grin. "To Paris, my friends!" he shouted before he led the party on towards the capital.

♦

In the seclusion and peace of the Hôtel de la Reine, the Queen Mother tried to still her aching joints as well as chronic toothache, by taking a rest. Her increased weight was making her rheumatism worse, as her physicians continued to tell her, but she was too old to deny herself the pleasures of food.

The Hôtel de la Reine served as her town house now that she had decided to move from the Louvre. How strange that once she would not have even contemplated a move away from the centre of the government. She would have always wanted to be wherever the King was.

She had purchased the site for the Hôtel, in the parish of Saint-Eustache and had all the buildings demolished that she might build a house for her old age, where she had at one time imagined she could retire once Henri was firmly established as King and she could do no more. She had employed the famed architect, Jean Bullant for the project, the jewel of which was to be a Doric column that stood in the central courtyard.

Here then in this grand building, the ageing Queen Mother housed her personal collection of family portraits as well as the rarest antiques and her vast collection of books and manuscripts. Numerous portraits of her sons and daughters were present all over the building, serving as a constant reminder of all she had treasured. And indeed all she had lost. It did her good to lie on her couch with a couple of her ladies busy over their embroidery frames.

Suddenly there was an intrusion on her peace and quiet when her dwarf came running to her in an excited state. "A Guise, a Guise! he cried. "He is here, your Majesty, here in Paris, the Guise is here!!" Catherine caught the little fellow and slapped him hard. "Be still, you little fool! Be still! What nonsense is this that you would disturb me in such a manner?"

The Queen Mother's ladies had now left their sewing and were all trying to get to the open window so they might see for themselves. Catherine had sat up and demanded an end to the hysteria. She looked to her other dwarf, the faithful Krassowski, and nodded. The man knew what was required, and he quickly slipped out of the chamber.

Once he had gone and some order had been restored, Catherine sat to consider this latest catastrophe. She desperately wanted to be told that her servants were mistaken, but her heart sank when the Polish dwarf returned, bowing his head in affirmation that the Duke of Guise had indeed returned to Paris, and judging by the cheers that she could hear as he rode through the streets, he was a welcome sight.

For one of the few occasions in her life, Catherine was completely at a loss as to what action she would take. It was almost unbelievable that Guise would have openly disobeyed his King, and yet who else but Guise would have the nerve and confidence to do it? She had risen from her seat, but felt weak and listless and sat back down again shaking. She turned to Krassowski who had run to her side. "Go to the Louvre, tell the King of this arrival and tell him not to act until I get to him – go!"

The man ran out of the chamber, but there was consternation in the corridor outside as voices were raised in protest, and the captain of Catherine's guards entered the chamber looking flushed and angry.

The Queen Mother noted his anguish, and nodded, "Let the Duke through," she spoke calmly, seemingly in control of her emotions and keen that there should be no bloodshed.

There was silence suddenly, and in marched the Duke of Guise. His crystal clear eyes met her dark hooded ones, and he made a sweeping bow, taking the offered hand and kissing it lightly. He had matured, now she looked at him she was struck by how in this hour of excitement and danger he resembled his father.

There was a man who had driven her to distraction at times; bold, blunt and always determined about what he must do. Now she looked at his son, she realised how proud he would have been of the determined, brave man who faced her. There were however, consequences in acting as he did now.

"Do you realise the risk you have taken riding into Paris when my son, your King, has forbidden it? Are so so far along this route to your glory that you would defy the very estate your own father gave his own life to defend?"

The Duke stood up straight, his chin raised in proud defiance, "My father did not die fighting for the King Madame, he was foully murdered as well you know."

Catherine dismissed the irrelevance with a wave of her hand. "Would that same father be proud of you today, Monsieur? Proud to see you take up arms against your King, causing further distress to a poor woman who has thought of you as her own kin?"

Guise stood, his dominance surprised her, and yet she could not help but admire the courage to have acted as he did.

Whatever she felt personally about the Duke however, he was in defiance of his King's command. She had rarely felt at such a loss for what she could do next. She was exhausted; mentally and physically, and at a time in her life when she could have expected to retire from public life, she was still in the throes of this latest crisis – and she was now heartily sick of it.

However, she knew that the King would act without thinking, he would make demands when he should be silent, he would argue when he should listen, and more importantly, he would act when he should plot. The question was why then had Guise come to her rather than to the King himself.

"Monsieur, you come first to me, a poor woman worn out from her trials and mediation, when you could have gone first to the King." Guise sat down, leaning his elbows on his knees and burying his head in his hands, rubbing his face as though to wake himself.

Catherine interpreted the signs correctly. "With age and power come responsibilities, only now will you understand Monsieur, now you will realise."

"Madame, I come to you because there is still a way that the King and I can save the country we both hold so dear. Your own good works and honest intentions at mediating have led to nothing, there is no other option than this. He must be made to see that change has to come. He will listen to you, I know it."

"You would ask me to mediate between you and my son. How can I stand by his side and tell him to agree to what is nothing more than a coup? Besides which, the King rarely listens to me these days, I simply do not have the influence I once enjoyed. Monsieur, you, Navarre and my son have waged another war on this exhausted land. You hold all the aces in this game, my son. The League you now lead as a figurehead on behalf of Spain, oh Monsieur do not speak to deny it; I am not so old, and such a fool that I do not know it. You are leader of this pack, the Parisians cheer your name, both you and I can hear their shouts still. Think carefully, my son, will they cheer you as the first Spanish soldiers march into the capital?"

Guise could hear the cheers, and in a brief moment, a flash of doubt and fear danced across his face. Had he been wise to come to her first? So many, Spain included, had told him not to trust the Queen Mother. Yet, as he looked at her now, he saw not the evil scheming 'black Queen' or the "maggot from Italy" or the famed Serpent of the Valois. All he saw now was an old woman who was tired, and very much alone, unable to stop a wayward son riding headlong into disaster. Yet, he was certain, there was no-one else. "Madame, come to the King with me now, together we can discuss what must be done to save France from disaster.

Catherine looked at him, earnest, uncertain, maybe even frightened of what he had helped to create. Finally, she rapped her cane against the floor, a call that was answered by her attendants. "Have my captain prepare my carriage, we will go to the Louvre"

♦

The King of France had rarely felt such fear and fury at the same time. He had slept little during the last few days and his appearance startled even his closest servants. His normal fastidious attention to his attire and appearance no longer seemed to matter to him. At least his dearest Epernon had been a constant figure, and the two of them spent almost the whole time together, awaiting fresh developments. The great mechanism that was the government of the realm limped on, but with no real real leader at its helm. The King had given his ministers their usual instructions, had signed what he was given by his secretaries, but all else was at a standstill. The tensions in the palace became palpable as word spread that there had been riders drawing a gathering crowd. Henri had taken little notice until a messenger arrived from the Queen Mother.

Some minutes later, the King dismissed the dwarf and, still seated in his study, he let out the almightiest scream, and buried his head in his hands. Epernon caught the Queen Mother's messenger by his collar as he was running from the room, demanding to know what news had caused such anguish.

At once Epernon was at his master's side; whilst he personally was in fear of his life on a daily basis, the threats had at least stopped, possibly at the instigation of the King's mother. Henri sat without moving for some minutes before he rose and drew Epernon to one side. "We must act swiftly, my dearest," he said quietly, "Take your Swiss guards and a regiment of our own guards and leave the city as soon as you can. I will send further word to you – go now, with all haste!" Epernon kissed the King's hand fiercely, and then swept out of the chamber calling the captain of the guard as he did so.

A solitary tear ran down the face of the beleaguered monarch, and he stared after his friend, whispering softly, "Adieu, my dearest friend, God knows when we shall laugh together again."

There was a sullen and palpable atmosphere as the Queen Mother's black carriage wound its way slowly towards the Louvre, the Duke of Guise walking beside it. The crowds reaching out their hands to touch him, waving and calling his name. Catherine was astonished at the reception he got from all these different citizens, from beggars and vagrants to lawyers and traders, all cheering with delight. Every so often, she would also hear a hiss directed towards her, but she felt safer than she had ever felt in this city that had hated her when, as a young innocent Italian girl, she had entered the capital of her new home. They had not loved her then and all the troubled years since then, they had no love for her now.

Eventually, the carriage drew into the courtyard of the Louvre. At a window high above, a small pale face peeped out with awe and wonderment at the large crowd that had gathered behind his mother's coach. He studied the Duke, now helping her down the steps of the carriage. How like Guise, he thought, drawing the crowd along with him, such bold arrogance. How he detested such theatricals!

He made to turn away, but suddenly noticed his reflection in a large mirror as he did so, and for a moment he paused to study the image that stared back at him. What had happened to destroy the handsome looks of which he had been so proud? The face that looked back at him now was almost a withered old man, gaunt and tired. His once black sparkling eyes were now dull and almost lifeless, his shoulders, previously broad and proud, slumped with the weight of his troubles. What his mignons saw now was not a dashing and spectacular sight, they saw only riches and high office, titles and properties. He wondered how many times they must have left and laughed at the pathetic King who, moments before, they had appeared to worship. His youth was gone, he was frightened, and seeing his mother take the arm of his deadliest enemy, perhaps even she had deserted him. He looked away in disgust.

The Queen Mother and the Duke of Guise mounted the great stairway which was lined on both sides by guards with their swords drawn. Catherine felt a shiver run through her body, her natural instinct for danger heightened her senses. She did not fear the guards, they were not here as a warning to her, but to show Guise that the King was not to be threatened, the menace of the reception was not lost on the Duke.

Henri did not look up as the two entered. Catherine made to greet her son, but he stepped to one side, avoiding her. The King looked straight at Guise with a look of contempt and when he spoke it was with a cold fury. "What are you doing here, cousin? I thought I had made myself clear; you were forbidden to enter the city. Not only do you disobey my express command than you would rouse the populace against their anointed King."

Without a pause, Guise answered, "Your Majesty's command was clearly understood, yet I came at the urgent request of the Queen Mother."

Catherine thought quickly, she had not believed that Guise would draw her into this scheme, but there had to be an accord between these two. "My son," she said "I asked the Duke to come to Paris that we may sit together and talk through all differences and resolve these matters before they are the death of us all. My son, I beseech you, sit now and discourse with the Duke and myself." Henri turned his cold stare on his mother and for a moment said nothing.

"Do I deal with more than one traitor here?" he eventually asked quietly looking straight into his mother's eyes, the bitterness all the more evident by the manner of its delivery.

Catherine was startled by his words, and stared at him in disbelief. The Duke made a step forward, and four soldiers at the door re-drew their weapons. Now it was Catherine's turn to act decisively and take control, "There will be no blood shed here," she said with calm determination. "My son, dismiss your men." Henri tried to stare her down, but she only spoke with more determination and a rising anger "Dismiss them!" After a moment or two, Henri looked beyond her to his captain standing at the chamber threshold. A nod from the King, and the soldiers withdrew, closing the door behind them.

Once alone, Catherine drew her son to the window, quietly speaking to him so that Guise could hear only a string of words. "Look there, my son. This man carries the mob with him, this is no longer a threat that can be overlooked, there is no squabbling over one of your companions, no street brawl for others to delight in. This is a turning point. I myself underestimated the power of the Catholic League to my eternal shame. Now, it has grown beyond our estimate, if we act foolishly now it will be the end of us all."

Henri looked again at the gathering mob of Parisians, they had always been a law unto themselves, capricious and dangerous when roused. He turned, cast his mother a withering look and stalked from the room to his bed chamber. "We will talk further tomorrow, now I am tired" he stated in the Duke's direction as he went. Catherine closed her eyes, pinching the bridge of her nose in her fatigue; when she finally looked around – she was alone.

The following two days were spent in further talks with the Guise and his advisers and the King with his council and the Queen Mother. After the tense reception towards the Duke of the day before, now Henri was almost openly hostile, and Catherine felt a nervousness at the personal guard that he had stationed permanently at all doors of the Royal apartments.

Talks dragged on throughout the day, but to no avail. The League's demands were nothing short of treason, declared the King, the demands were necessary, countered Guise, and far more moderate than he would have liked. A curious occurrence however, caught the Queen Mother's attention. The King left the chamber suddenly, and it was sometime before his return. Neither Guise nor the Henri's counsellors appeared to be interested, but Catherine knew her son; she alone caught the nervousness in his manner when he returned, his look towards her was one of disdain.

It was almost dawn, and back in the Hôtel de la Reine it seemed that no sooner had the Queen Mother taken to her bed than she was being woken by one of her ladies. "What is this outrage? Catherine asked crossly. "Am I to get no peace? On what account am I woken, girl?"

The nervous lady told the Queen Mother that one of her informants had news of great urgency for her. Catherine was at once alert, and quickly dressed to meet a young Parisian man in her service. "Madame, I have news that I felt you should know at once."

Catherine could tell this was not going to be good tidings. "Speak man, I would hear all you can tell me." As she had suspected, the information was disastrous. Panic was gripping the city and rumours abounded that the King was in secret talk with the Huguenots, and that a revenge massacre just like the one of Saint Bartholomew was being organised. There was horror on the face of the Queen Mother, surely this could only be vile rumour, and yet... Both she and the informant heard at the same time, the sound of marching soldiers, and as Catherine looked out on the city, the noise of the troops became closer and closer; her worst fears were confirmed – troops were being deployed around the city.

The Queen Mother sent out word to Henri begging him not to act with haste, and be influenced by Epernon, who was leading the King's forces. Having done that, she prepared to go to the Louvre.

♦

From his headquarters at the Hôtel de Guise, the young Duke was already alerted to the influx of troops, and now he seemed uncertain of what to do next. He had now been told that the citizens had no intention of being caught out like the heretic Huguenots had been sixteen years before. All around the capital barricades were being set up in the streets. Furniture, tumbrils, sandbags, barrels filled with rocks, bottles, crates and anything that could be used as a missile was stored in readiness for protecting themselves, and indeed many had already begun pelting the hapless troops, some with pistols even picked off one or two soldiers. Heavy chains cut off the streets, and citizens armed themselves with anything that might conceivably be used as a weapon.

The young Duke was for once, hesitant. Whilst he had an easy affability with the citizens of Paris, there was growing concern within his own family, that having successfully entered the city and hoisting his banner, he was now unsure of what he should do next. Raising the ire of the Parisians and standing at their helm was one thing, but to hold the King a prisoner in the Louvre was another. Guise's family pressed him to be bolder and not to be drawn into protracted discussions where an astute negotiator like Catherine could easily trip him up, and put words in his mouth. Still, however, Guise hesitated.

Catherine, meanwhile, had made the dangerous journey to the King, the barricades making the journey more uncomfortable. The Queen Mother was aware of the haunting silence that greeted her black sedan-chair that she had needed to use. Due to the barricades, it would have been impossible to use her normal carriage. As she rode along the streets lined with faces of determination and zeal, many times physically encountering very uncomfortable conditions, she fingered the amulet bracelet on her wrist, its soothing qualities energised her flagging health; she must keep strong for Henri's sake. Now was the time for him to show true leadership, and she yearned for the young strutting general he had once been, his victory at Jarnac that she had most clearly foreseen so many years ago. Then he had been bold and confident, and – more importantly – happy to take her advice.

The Duke of Guise, meanwhile, was considering his next move, and assistance came in the form of the Spanish ambassador, Bernardino de Mendoza. The ambassador had swiftly made his visit from his house in Paris, which the League used as their headquarters. Mendoza, a small man with pinched features, dark and swarthy and with one blind eye. What he lacked in some features and stature he more than made up for with a quick brain and sharp intellect that King Philip trusted implicitly. The Spaniard at once set about assuring Guise that whilst the King of Spain would welcome the progress that the League had made in such a short space of time, he was certain, knowing his Spanish master, that

Philip would caution against having the French King made a prisoner in his own capital. "We must tread with care, my friend," said the Spaniard, "securing the affirmation and goodwill of Paris is not to say the rest of the country is with the League. I have my own spies here, and they tell me that it is strongest here in the capital, but elsewhere the King of France still rules."

Guise paced around like a caged lion in the Royal menagerie; he was at his best when he was active. Like his father, he was no diplomat, and ignorant in statecraft and government. "You have a plan Mendoza?" Guise could tell by the slight grin on the face of the ambassador. "You have all the gates out of the city locked and guarded?" he asked slyly.

"Of course, once Epernon had entered with his troops, I had them all secured." The ambassador smiled again. "Then maybe this will work. I need someone brought here from my house." Guise immediately summoned one of his men, who after a word from the ambassador, left immediately.

It was only a short time later that the guard returned accompanied by – Victoria de Ayala. Guise was about to inform the ambassador that he was certain that the lady was a member of the Queen Mother's infamous 'escardon' Mendoza smiled, "Yes, so it would seem."

Guise was dumbstruck for a moment, "You mean she is…?"

Mendoza laughed, gallantly drawing up a seat and inviting the lady to sit. "Victoria is of Spanish birth, Monsieur, it has been of great assistance to have a friend within those who serve the Queen Mother."

Guise took the young woman's small delicate hand and kissed it, permitting his lips to linger longer than they needed to. How annoying that he had often seen the girl and wanted to know her more intimately, but had dismissed the possibility once he had learned that she was part of the Queen Mother's 'flying squadron'.

Mendoza coughed diplomatically, and Guise at once stepped away, allowing a smile to play on his lips. Victoria's large hazel eyes looked downwards. Mendoza and Victoria spoke for some time in their mother tongue, with Guise afterwards being advised what must now be done. One of Duke's captains entered the chamber to report that the Queen Mother's sedan would soon arrive. Mendoza rose swiftly. "We must not be here when Catherine arrives, let us leave from the back door, come Victoria." The two of them left by a back route as the Queen Mother arrived at the front.

Later that day, the King met the messenger from his mother. Could he trust one from his mother's 'escardon'? It seemed he had little choice. He allowed Victoria de Alaya to enter, and listened carefully to the message his mother had sent. It sounded incredible, and Henri was at first unwilling to believe that the League had made such a blunder.

"The gate of the Porte Neuve is unsecured?" exclaimed an incredulous King. It was scarcely possible, and yet who else but his mother could have ensured that the gate was unguarded? For the first time in days, the King felt almost jubilation. His eyes, sullen and soulless but a short time before, were now sharp, and they flicked between Victoria and Epernon who seemed as surprised as his master.

"The Queen Mother begs you make haste, your Majesty, she says that at some point the gate will be checked, and the opportunity lost." Henri looked to Epernon and smiled.

♦

The Tuileries gardens were an excellent place to stroll. The Queen Mother had spent a great deal of time and planning to make a spectacular area to walk for both relaxation and exercise.

Catherine had commissioned the garden construction to resemble the Italian fashion, divided into six individual plots. Its exquisite lawns and dazzling flowerbeds were a delight to look at, a grotto and a number of fountains as well as the practical kitchen gardens and vineyards. A small cluster of trees complemented the look of tranquillity, although the gardens had been used for stately court functions.

Here then, the King of France walked, slowly and in deep in conversation with Epernon and a few other close companions. Their stroll took them as far as the stables, where horses had been made ready. Caution was needed now, they must ensure they were unobserved, and that there were none of Guise's soldiers lying in wait for them to leave the safety of the palace. All checks confirmed that somehow his mother had discovered this most remarkable oversight, and with the wind in his hair, and riding like the devil was on his tail, the King and his companions galloped out of the capital.

♦

"Monsieur", the Queen Mother stated, "the King is most vexed by the demands of the League. "You claim you are loyal to the crown, but you would destroy it. There will be no question that the men my son has in recent years kept too close, must of course be banished. The extravagances must stop...."

The meeting was interrupted by a message for the Duke, who walked to a corner of the room to read the note that had been delivered.

Catherine was startled by a loud curse from the Guise, who marched over to the Queen Mother. "Forgive me, Madame," he said brusquely "But I am betrayed. You have sought to dally with me here, just long enough for your son to make good an escape."

Guise paced the room, but Catherine's face was one of horror "But I never..." she stopped as she realised that she had been abandoned by her son. He, who she had fought so hard for had left his own mother to the wolves. "You must believe me Monsieur that I knew nothing of this." Guise looked down at the fearsome Catherine de Medici, and saw a woman now at a loss as to what to do.

"The troops will withdraw," Guise commanded, "and only then will I order that the barricades be destroyed." He handed Catherine one of the documents the messenger had given him. "It seems from this letter that was left for you, Madame. You are appointed by your son to negotiate in his absence. Your power, it would appear is restored."

The Queen Mother allowed the implications of her son's escape to sink in before she assured Guise that she was completely unaware of his plans. "Monsieur," she stated, "would I, an old woman sick in body as well as in spirit, risk the dangers of the very streets of Paris attempting to be an arbiter between the two of you when I could merely have stayed in my sickbed and let this carry on without any intervention?"

Guise put on a good show of outrage, but of course he knew exactly what had transpired and the role he had played in it; Catherine, as yet, may not. The Queen Mother however, had not played this game of intrigue, plot and cunning all these years without being certain of events, and the role that others played in them. Something of her old vigour was returning; in the space of a mere few minutes, she was feeling rejuvenated, in mind if not in body. Henri had left the stage of this drama for the time being; yet he had entrusted the complex negotiations to his mother. Her sadness that he had run and left her behind was understandable, even with this dreadful state of affairs, he needed her more than ever. In his desperation he had called on the one person he could trust to save him; *'and my darling son, I will make it all better – or die trying!'* Once again he needed her, when all others had deserted him, his mother was constant.

With some of her energy, strangely restored by this latest setback, she now turned on the Duke. "Many will ask of course monsieur, why the King was allowed to escape. Believe me, I wish with all my heart that he had remained in the capital. Yet questions will be asked will they not?" Guise frowned at her as she continued," Will your Spanish masters – do not attempt to tell me this has nothing to do with Philip – will they not be curious as to why one gate was left completely unguarded....?"

She stopped momentarily as the realisation became clear to her now, and she smiled in satisfaction that even in her ailing state, she had deduced for herself exactly what had happened. "Of course!" she chuckled as the

Duke turned away to the window that looked out at the barricades, and the citizens still gathering. "You had the gate left unguarded. At the last hour you panicked. What could you do with a King that you had effectively caught in your net? You forgot one vital rule my son, he who stirs the hive must bear the bees. Was this a revolution only half-planned? I daresay, the Spanish ambassador had a hand in this did he not? Well it is of no consequence now it is done."

Guise sighed and flopped into a chair, exhausted by the current stream of events, and the subtle art of intrigue; and he marvelled at the old woman sat near him; how many years she had played at this most complicated of games, always she had fought with her agile mind. Intrigue was in her blood as it had been from the day she had arrived in France. One could never completely trust Catherine de Medici, but you could certainly not fail to admire her strength of purpose.

As far as Catherine herself was concerned, sheer power of will was almost the only thing keeping her going, so sick was she; her limbs ached, her stomach made her nauseous, and at this moment she would have welcomed her bed more than a million écus. There was however, work to be done, and in her son's absence, she must do what she could to stem the tide of the League's advance.

"You realise of course, Monsieur," she broke the uneasy silence, "that you have put my son in a room with many exits. You are puzzled? Then let me explain. Up until now, the King has joined you in trying to supress the King of Navarre, the 'War of the three Henris as I understand it is called in jest, and yet it was exactly that, a battle of egos perhaps. Now of course, you have the King in a corner; do you expect that he will simply give you the keys to the Kingdom? Of course not, he will fight – fairly or otherwise! He is now at liberty to join with Navarre; remember there was an accord between them until recently. Or he could negotiate with the Politiques. Remember, my son, Paris may well be yours, but Paris is not the whole of France."

Guise pondered on her words, he had been told as much by Mendoza. He was aware that he had disappointed many in his camp by not declaring an outright war on the King, but some vestige of honour to one's King staid his hand.

News was arriving for Guise almost continually, Parlament was in contact with the King at Chartres, and its president, Achille de Harlay, was unflinching in his condemnation of Guise: "It is a great pity to see the lackey drive out the master. As for myself, my soul belongs to God, my heart to the King and my body is in the hands of scoundrels. Do what you please!"

♦

In his chamber at Chartres, the King had risen at about midday, as had become his habit and now paced the room holding one of his small dogs in one hand and a letter from the Parlament in the other. The letter was not dissimilar to one his mother had also sent – both urging him to reason.

Devoid of all his finery, jewels and perfumed hair and body, Henri was a normal enough man, and although he chose to disguise it, could when the mood suited him to be an extremely intelligent individual.

How, he wondered, had it all come to this? He was going to be such a fine King, he wanted to do so much with his life; he had yearned to be King, to be master of his own destiny, and had vowed that, as adept at state-craft as she was, he would rule without the dominating figure of his mother behind his throne. His time as King had taught him much about how vulnerable he was. How he had pitied his brother, not only when Charles was King, but since he had died. He had never really understood until the most recent years how big a weight being the King was to carry on one's shoulders. He had broken free from his mother who treated him like a boy, and seemed to look at him with disappointment what-ever he did. So, he had surrounded himself with other pleasure-seeking men like himself. Yet, he was no fool; he realised, as he knew his mother and maybe the entire court did, that these comrades were merely hanging by the Royal coat-tails. They would follow him as long as they still stood to gain, and while he was still in a posi-tion to endow them with riches and titles.

So now, most of his friends were gone. Some had travelled with him, and some had made their excuses and left. Well, they were unimportant now. His mother had so often said that the past was an inconvenience that should be forgotten once its lessons had been learned. The now was all that mattered.

Well, he had learned some lessons, maybe now was the time to be on the offensive. He had run far enough. His first objective would be to effectively pull the ground from underneath his rival's feet. He put to the back of his mind his ultimate plan concerning Guise – events would guide his hand. He stood immediately, dropping his lap-dog onto the bed beside him. He called for his valet to bring him writing paper and ink, and before he had even begun to think of what suit he would wear that day, he detailed his proposals to the League.

♦

The document of new proposals from the King at Chartres met with some success. With overtures of deeply-felt sincerity, he was, he said, prepared to over-look the revolt by the Parisians, and was eager to re-establish the government before the state suffered any more. However, he did stipulate that the city be returned to its former state and once again show allegiance to their King. As a secondary compromise, he was pre-pared to revoke many of the former edicts that he knew had caused great friction.

Catherine received Guise at her apartments in the Louvre. Her health was no better, and yet once more against the advice of her physicians, she had insisted on working from early morning until late in the evening such was the commitment to her son's cause.

Both Guise and the Queen Mother studied the document from the King. During a break in their talks, she had taken time to be with her daughter-in-law, Queen Louise. The King had all but deserted his wife, and she had been sickened by the worry of the danger her husband placed himself in.

In Louise, Catherine saw much of herself; an adoring wife, helplessly in love with a man who hardly acknowl-edged her existence. A wife who will do anything that is asked of her, simply to gain attention. Louise, an attrac-tive young woman still, had lost weight. Her once pert figure had become almost gaunt, her famed luxurious hair now lank and lifeless. She spent a great deal of her time praying and watching for the King, hoping any moment that he may throw open the door and she would run to him. Alas, there seemed very little likelihood of that, and she found the reality a bitter pill to swallow.

Catherine left her daughter-in-law in no doubt that she did not believe her son's concessions went far enough. "What more can he possibly do Madame?" Louise asked spiritedly.

"Ah, my child, you do not know the cruel world of these men as I do, have I not fought against them almost from the time I arrived here? There is always more, when one is pricked, one can be cut, one can be stabbed, one can be drawn and quartered. There is always more." A bitterness had changed Catherine's tone, and she sought to readdress the concern over her son's conditions. "You will see my dear," she stated, "the League will almost certainly demand the dismissal of the Duke d'Epernon. Ah! I think even one as kind as you child will gladly see him hounded out of the Kingdom, do not deny it to me my dear, I watched while my husband spent time with another? You must allow yourself at least one moment of guilty pleasure, and I shall stand with you as we watch that knave quit this realm."

Louise smiled, her good and temperate nature could not feel a delight in anyone's misfortune, but surely she could make an exception. "What else, Madame will they want?"

Catherine sighed as the many concessions began to pile up in her mind. "There must be a role for the Duke, and most certainly they will demand Guise is made Lieutenant-Generale. Also, I fear they will expect a renewal of the war against the Huguenots. Ah, you sigh my dear, yes there is much to consider, there are many old scores to be settled and Paris will not so easily forget past slights."

♦

Finally, after much debate, new conditions and haggling, the King finally accepted the terms and demands of the League and Parlament published the Act of Union in Paris. Within the terms agreed, the League gained recognition, but with the proviso that they sever all their foreign alliances. Furthermore, Navarre was to be completely barred from the succession, and the Cardinal of Bourbon would be declared heir to the throne. Catherine proudly looked on as her son embraced the Duke of Guise, the new Lieutenant-General of France. The King kissed his cousin on both cheeks.

Only Catherine caught the very slight twitch in her son's eye. Later, at a banquet held to celebrate the recent Act, Henri asked his cousin to whom they should drink a toast. "That is for your Majesty to decide," came Guise's answer. "Well then, let us drink to our good friends the Huguenots!" Laughter rang out from all the assembly until the King spoke over their revelry "And to our good friends the Barricaders of Paris."

The new toast was greeted with almost complete silence, and then as though by command all those gathered hurried to talk as though nothing untoward had happened. Catherine, as usual watched all this from behind her son's throne. Henri was playing a dangerous and unpredictable game. The evening was further blighted by Catherine collapsing in a fever. The past few weeks had drained her of all her energy, and her physicians insisted that she rest. For one of the few times in her life, the Queen Mother was happy to agree with their recommendation. The pains in her chest had been getting worse, and she was often struck rigid by them. Never had she worked so hard as she had lately, or at least it seemed so, but she also cursed her ailing body just when all her strength was needed.

A tonic to boost the Queen Mother's mood came in the form of astonishing and extraordinary news from England. The King of Spain had at last unleashed his armada against the "heretical English." Indeed, Catherine had herself given permission for the ships to hug the French coast until a propitious time to attack. No-one could possibly have foreseen the complete and utter defeat that the Spanish King's fleet would suffer. A combination of courageous English commanders and the most appalling weather had resulted in the death of over twenty thousand soldiers and sailors. Only sixty-seven of the one hundred and thirty ships that had set sail with, "God in their hearts" as one commander had put it. Atrocious weather, and gallant English sailors had sent most of the armada and its sailors to the bottom of the sea.

Catherine could not have been more delighted. She had spent so long fearing an invasion from her former son-in-law that it was hard to believe that his defeat had been so emphatic. Finally, the mighty Spain had been served with disaster, and as the weeks passed, haunting remnants of the once glorious armada were still being washed up along the coasts of France and England.

The defeat naturally had an adverse effect on the political situation in France. There was for the King a sense of relief that the shadow of the mighty Spain was lifted. His greatest delight was the concern that it would naturally cause the League. Guise himself wondered about Spain's continued commitment to their cause, both in terms of extra troops if ever needed and more importantly – financial support. Henri felt he could now safely ignore the entreaties from the League to return to the capital as had previously been agreed. Instead, the King declared formally, the Estates-General was to be convened at Blois.

The King of Navarre was enjoying an intimate supper with the voluptuous Corrisande, she who had certainly become the most celebrated of his numerous mistresses, and he was clearly still enchanted by her. They lay on cushions in front of a roaring fire; Corrisande's pale complexion was flushed from the heat, one of the shoulders from her dark red velvet gown had been eased down her arm by the amorous King, his large, coarse hands rough against the smooth texture of her soft skin. He whispered to her, nibbling her ear. It was as he was drawing her towards him for a passionate kiss, that a messenger arrived with urgent news. The King sighed putting his hand out for the parchment.

"Perhaps it is from your wife your Majesty," Corrisande teased, as she drew herself to a sitting position and, drinking from her goblet of wine, continued to stare at him with her bewitching gaze. Navarre raised an eyebrow and his mouth twitched in amusement, as he broke the seal.

"Ha! I need only be told that dear Margot has been strangled along with her mother and I..." he suddenly broke off as he scanned the words. In all but a second, his amorous engagement was forgotten and before his mistress's very eyes, he became red-faced and roared in fury, crumpling the letter in his fist and hurling it towards the fireplace, "Sainte mere de Dieu!" He roared for his ministers, and marched from the room, cursing loudly as he went.

The nimble Corrisande quickly reached for the document that the King had hurled towards the blazing fire. Only the corner had been singed, which she blew on to extinguish before reading quickly lest the King return. The news was not good.

♦

"Ha! So the King, my brother, has declared further war with the Huguenot's after signing a peace with the League, and my oaf of a husband has been completely excluded from the succession." The Queen of Navarre laughed. Word had reached her from an informant who worked for the Royal council, and she could not have hoped for better news. In her stronghold at Usson, Margot indulged in all her favourite pastimes, she spent freely, enjoyed lavish entertainments and took a succession of lovers. She had declared herself loyal to the League, and anything that infuriated her estranged husband was welcome news to her. So, it did not look as though she would ever enjoy being Queen of France, but no matter, why have the responsibility of a crown, when she could enjoy the life she was currently having?

"How much happier I am living a quiet life in Usson!" she joked, laughing again. She must be kept up to date with news she declared, especially the sort that gave her such pleasure.

♦

Catherine travelled with her son to Blois, and again took to her bed; the pains in her chest were more frequent now, and the stress of dealing with her unpredictable son weighed heavily on her. Since their arrival, she had seen very little of him, and when he had visited her chamber and found the Duke of Guise voicing his concerns for her health, he had been sarcastic and suspicious. His reason for visiting her was, he said, a courtesy to inform her that he had this same day dismissed all but a few of his council and replaced them with individuals he could trust.

The Queen Mother forced herself to sit up as she stared at her son with shock, "Why, my son, would you do such a thing? These men that I…"

"Exactly, Madame!" he replied viciously "that you chose! Let me tell you my estimation of these men, shall I?" He walked slowly around the chamber, Guise's eyes followed him as he did so, his contempt barely concealed. "Cheverny has lined his own pockets handsomely over the years. I am asked to believe that Belliévre is a good Catholic when all the court knows he has Huguenot sympathies. Villeroy is –"

"My son," Catherine managed to interrupt, her voice crackling with emotion as well as the burning throat that made even swallowing difficult. "These men have served you faithfully ever since you claimed your crown, why some even served your late brother." The Queen Mother broke into a spasm of coughing. The servant that had tactfully left when the King had arrived now re-entered, helping to administer some soothing liquid for her mistress. Henri looked at his mother with utter distaste, standing back from the bed lest he be in any way infected.

Guise faced the King, "Sire, you say you have dispensed with your council, but was this not an issue that should have been discussed with myself, and your mother? The League should have been informed." The Duke looked crossly at the King but continued, "You say these men are dismissed, and yet who would you appoint in their stead?"

Henri smiled slyly, "Goodness monsieur, I knew there were others I should have spoken to, ah well, no matter it is done now! And yes – my dear cousin, the men have been replaced with some I have personally chosen." Catherine had fallen back on her pillows after drinking the fiery liquid, but she made to get out of her bed.

"My son, I will rise now, you will need me now to –"

"Ah no, Maman, do not hasten from your bed, I have no need of you. Like the gentlemen I dismissed this day, you are no longer needed in my council. You have grown old, and I believe your mind wanders, and your judgement is thought questionable. Rest now, I will send the Queen to visit you, she does worry so!" And with that he walked out of the chamber.

Guise was dismissed, and Catherine lay back, tears streaming down her face, but he was her darling, he loved her, he needed her. They had always worked together. It was true that she had been side lined from current affairs lately, but, as with the discussions with the League, she had spoken for the King, it had been she that had argued, lied, and played for time, all for his glory. She refused to believe that this was truly what he wanted. She cursed her failing body once again. Now more than ever, she needed to have the physical strength to be amongst the courtiers, the other players in this most dangerous of games.

Her maternal instinct nagged at her to rise from her bed, to seek out her son and talk with him, plead with him into taking he back in to his confidence again. Her body, unfortunately, would not support her further, and she was too weak to manage it. She would need all her strength for the opening of the Estates-General and she was determined that she would be there.

♦

The magnificent hall at Blois had been decorated with all splendour and colour. The King had directed that there was to be no expense spared in creating a spectacular event by which to make this most important speech of his reign.

Catherine had surprised everyone by attending; leaning heavily on her cane, she was pale and looked exhausted, her large eyes now ringed with grey, her skin sagged, her mouth merely a thin line in her gaunt features. She tottered unsteadily toward her chair next to her son. The Duke of Guise sat at the King's feet. The crowd at the assembly was primarily made up of League supporters.

The hall hushed as the King opened the assembly. He rose to expectant eyes; every hair in place, dressed in his finest suit, a doublet of claret red, with gold trim and bright yellow satin. Even to the enemies within the assembly, he looked every inch a King in his splendour. His voice rang out with a clear confidence.

The speech paid tribute to the Queen Mother, and Catherine's heart leapt as he talked of her sound advice throughout his own and the late King's reign, had she not sacrificed her own strength and health in working so tirelessly? She should, he declared not just be known as the mother of the King but of the Kingdom itself." Hope soon faded however, as he went on to say that her past service had been of immeasurable importance to the realm, and that she had done all she physically could do in her many years of service.

The speech continued, but Catherine was barely aware of most of it; she sat as though in a daze about how cruelly her son had publicly dismissed her from even the fringes of power. Never had she felt so alone, so useless. There was little else left for her if Henri had no need of her. Of all the many blows she had experienced in her lifetime, this was surely the most painful to bear.

She was vaguely aware of some dissention in the hall, and her wandering attention drew her back to her son's speech.

"Some great nobles of my Kingdom have formed leagues and associations, but, as evidence of my habitual kindness I am prepared in this regard to forget these past wrongs." The assembly suddenly grew animated, and a buzz of voices could be heard. The tension within the hall was palpable.

Catherine's instinct had been to speak in her son's ear, advising him to choose his words carefully. The Duke of Guise certainly moved awkwardly in his chair. It would be said later that the King had in one speech destroyed the two people who could have kept him on his throne. After the day's ceremony ended, Catherine took to her bed.

The Queen Mother's lung infection had returned with a vengeance, and she was finding it difficult to breathe. Her doctors could do little, they said; and whilst they would never have said as much to her themselves, old age would out eventually, none could be spared the passing of years. The King did not visit her for over a fortnight.

♦

A bright moon shone through the window in the bedchamber of the Duke of Guise. He leant against the cold mullions and sighed. He had been unable to sleep; restless thoughts about the path he had set out on, his uneasy relationship with the King, even a care for the health of the Queen Mother. He smiled to himself, how could that concern have ever plagued him? He had not trusted her before the infamous "day of the barricades" and then he had been amazed at her fortitude, her failing vigour, and her sheer bravery. That was certainly another reason to hate her son. For Henri, Guise felt nothing but contempt.

He was startled at a soft hand on his naked shoulder, Charlotte de Suave had woken to find him gone from the bed where they had lain in each others arms. "Henri," she spoke softly, "You are troubled? Can you not sleep?" Guise drew up his shoulder to kiss her fingers. "I am troubled, yes. This is a moment in my life I had never expected to witness, friends tell me that I am virtually King of France, that I can command the whole of the country if I choose to; that I can overthrow the King and make France great again. It is a heavy burden, my love. So, no I cannot sleep." He turned to a nearby table and poured himself some water. "I have had much advice today, almost all of it warning me to leave Blois and return to Paris, that my life is in imminent danger from the King and his band of cut-throats, the "Forty-Five" My brothers, my priest, all of them begging me to make haste for Paris where I am safe."

Charlotte had heard the rumours also, but knew her lover well enough to know that he would never run away "Do you not feel the anger and danger here as they all do?" she asked.

Guise smiled looking out over the town, a mass of rooftops, smoke drifting out from some of the chimneys "There is always danger, he said "Every day is a danger, at any time in my life I could have been killed as my father was, assassinated by some unknown coward, willing to cut my throat for a heavy purse. Henri could have had me killed at any time, he always has those he can ask. Catherine could have many times served me a good claret, laced with poison. Yet, I am here still, and all I know is that this is my destiny, to save this country from destruction by a madman."

He swallowed the remainder of his water and turned to the woman who so often shared his bed. "Even you, my sweet Charlotte, even you could have obeyed the Queen Mother's command and stabbed me while I slept." He turned to put the goblet down on the table, and when he turned around again he noticed a tear run down Charlotte's cheek. He took her chin in his hand and kissed her lips gently. "Forgive me, I did not seek to upset you."

Charlotte's eyes still welled up with tears that threatened to break forth, "Never," she said sadly, "never would I have hurt you. Whatever she had threatened for disobedience I would have endured rather than betray you or do you harm." He kissed her with passion, and they stood for some time at the window, before he lifted her up in his strong arms and carried her back to his bed.

♦

The personal relationship between Guise and the King was near to breaking point, and was not helped by news from one of the King's trusted informants that a plot to murder both Henri and his mother had been discovered. The King was aghast with horror, and ensured that he was constantly surrounded by his personal guard. His food must be tasted in case there was an attempt to poison him. All precautions that could be taken were, and whilst Guise continued to dismiss any suggestion of a physical threat from the King, Henri began to wonder – who should strike first?

The two men hid their growing animosity from all but their closest advisers and attendants, and together visited Catherine still ailing in bed, although breathing easier. Both men had delighted her by embracing and exchanging a kiss of peace. Catherine was being administered some medicine when the King, his hand on Guise's shoulder, turned him away from Catherine's bed. "Brother, I am minded to have the council meet tomorrow very early, I should like you to be in attendance." Guise happily agreed, and it was with a lightness of heart that he spoke with the Queen Mother before joining the King and departing.

Something had made Catherine ill at ease, and despite the kiss between the two men warming her heart and giving her much pleasure; when they had left the chamber and she was alone, she could not shake off this uncomfortable sense of unease. All she could hear was her own voice telling Henri, "Caress only your enemies." Ever suspicious as she was, the uneasiness disturbed her, and when she eventually slept it was a sleep of horrors, nightmares and demons until she awoke, drenched in sweat.

Cavriani, her doctor attended to her, had all her bed clothes changed and suggested a further remedy to aid her relaxation. Even as she drank the thick syrup, she knew she should be alert, why did she have this feeling of dread? It was the last thing she remembered as she soon relaxed into a deep sleep.

♦

At the same time that the Queen Mother was fighting against her sleeping draught, the Duke of Guise was sitting down to dinner, surrounded by his close family. He felt more satisfied than he had for days, a new chapter in his relationship with the King had surely begun, and whilst there was no element of trust between the two men, that would maybe come in time. He did not have to love his King, only work with him. and face the future with optimism. He lifted his napkin, under which was a small piece of paper. Unfolding it he saw it was a simple note bearing the warning that there was a plan by the King to have him killed in the morning.

Guise, flush with his recent success with the King and with his management of the League, simply muttered that "he would not dare" and enjoyed the remainder of the evening. Later that night on his way for an arranged tryst with Charlotte de Suave, he picked up another small note half posted under his mistress's door. He picked it up and read it *"Beware, the King*

means to kill you in the morning." Again, he scoffed at
the very thought, even going so far as to use a quill in
Charlotte's chamber and himself write on the reverse of
the note – *"he wouldn't dare"* and then throwing it to
the floor outside the chamber door.

♦

It was barely dawn when the Duke of Guise opened his
eyes, he had slept well and was feeling refreshed. He
had to attend the council meeting, and was eager to
arrive before the others for private talks with the King.
Outside the rain had started teeming down, and the air
was cold and damp.

He gently kissed Charlotte's neck as he disentang-
led his arms from around her. She moaned softly, and
he carefully got out of bed. After pulling on his
breeches and a loose shirt, he walked to his own suite
and called his valet to help him dress, he must look his
best.

♦

The King of France was also awake early; he had
instructed his valet to rouse him at four o'clock, and
was now being dressed. Outside in the ante chamber, six
of his personal bodyguards stood ready and waiting for
their final instructions. An attendant entered, handing
the King a piece of parchment found in the corridor
outside the apartments of Madame de Suave. The King
read the note and smiled.

The council were all seated, some talking between
themselves, Guise was deep in conversation with his

brother the Cardinal. An attendant entered to tell Guise that the King wished to talk to him privately before the session began.

Guise left his brother and approached the short corridor that led to the King's private study. A heavy velvet drape sectioned off the inner apartment and it was as Guise went to lift it that he saw the first blade sweep down at him, he turned quickly to find other guards had cut off his escape, he had walked right into a trap. Desperately, he felt for his sword, but there was no time. Soon, several daggers had attacked him, his neck his shoulder, and finally his eyes widened at the last thrust as it pierced his heart. He managed to stagger a further few steps, tearing at the velvet drapes as he fell at the feet of the King. The body twitched slightly for a moment or two and both horrified eyes stared at the King as the life from them drained away.

Out in the council chamber, the Duke's brother, the Cardinal de Guise had heard the commotion and shouted out that his brother was being attacked. He was silenced under pain of death, and placed under immediate arrest.

There was silence in the King's study as the assassins and their King looked down on the bloody body of the Duke of Guise. Henri turned his head to one side then the other "How remarkably tall! Do you know, I never realised how tall he was." Then he stepped disdainfully over the corpse and into the council chamber.

♦

The Queen Mother could hear voices, muffled and indistinguishable, but voices – a shout!

What noise was this? She was watching a scene from the doorway of her son's chamber, his study. Soldiers pushed her aside as they concealed themselves in the recesses of the small corridor that led from the council chamber to the study.

Then, suddenly he was there, discussing something in great detail with another, the Cardinal was it? Yes, he was guiding Henri to the study...but why the guards? Where was Guise? She peered around the heavy velvet drape, and there was the Duke and he was drawing his dagger from its sheath. At once she sensed danger, there were guards everywhere, what was happening? "Stop! She had cried to her son, "Stop my son, they mean to kill you...!"

It seemed as though everything was moving slowly, she reached out her hand and grasped Henri by the arm, but a guard pulled her away, she shouted again, only a slight turn of his head...he went to speak, someone stabbed at him with a dagger. She screamed and all around there were guards with knives slashing at the King, his brilliant white tunic was turning a deep scarlet red, yet he stumbled on and there was Guise, he smiled at the King before pushing his own blade right through Henri's heart, she could not speak, she tried to scream......

"Madame, Madame," a voice was calling, she came to and realised she must have been screaming, she was drenched from perspiration again, her heart beat furiously, and she feared she would faint. Her fearful face looked up at Cavriani. "My son, the King, where is the King?"

"You have had a bad dream, the King will be here soon, I am sure of it" The physician looked sadly at the pathetic figure, such a force in her lifetime, but here and now simply a dying old woman. Gone was the great orator, the canny dissimulator. Whoever would have believed that the woman who had dominated the political scene in Europe for so long was now soiling her bed, and vomiting blood, hardly able to breathe. She seemed so meek and helpless, this most wicked of women. How many murders would history lay at her door the doctor wondered? How would she be judged? She was guilty of much, he was certain, but could she have been otherwise?

An unpopular figure since her arrival in France, she had meekly submitted to her husband's mistress, suffering all indignities with a calm acceptance that all marvelled at. When her husband had died, she had finally been released from the humiliation borne so bravely. Who would have thought as her son François mounted the throne, that she would virtually rule France through his brothers?

A murderess and schemer there was no doubt. The people of France hoped she would rot in hell. He had heard that the citizens of Paris had said they would not let her corpse enter Paris or they would let the dogs chew on it, or they would throw her cadaver into the Seine. So much hatred, so many reasons to hate.

Cavriani was startled from his thoughts; Catherine was again calling for the King. He assured her that later her son would surely come, and also told her for certain that the King was alive and well. "Madame, you have but dreamt such a tragedy, we would know by now if aught had happened to the King. On the contrary, one of the servants saw him only an hour since and he was in the best of spirits."

"Good, that is good," the Queen Mother seemed satisfied by that news, yet each time the door opened she looked expectantly for her son, only to face disappointment.

Finally, several hours later, the King marched into the Queen Mother's chamber. The doctor and attendants left by a side door. Catherine had taken another turn for the worse, and her breathing was again becoming laboured. The King, by contrast looked better than he had in weeks, and Catherine smiled weakly to see him so.

"Well mother," he said brightly, "how are you feeling?"

"I am as well as I can be, but better for having sight of you, I had the most awful dream...." The King cut her off with a wave of his hand. "Well I am feeling wonderfully well, and do you know why? Then I will tell you, I have had the Duke of Guise killed, he is dead and will be spoken of no more. He sought to be King, but there is only one King and I am he. He sought my death, yet it is I who stand before you very much alive. My guards cut him down like a dog! His brother the Cardinal is under arrest – there, the task is done."

The Queen Mother could scarcely believe what she was hearing, and she looked at her son with a look of complete horror. "What have you done, you fool?" she hissed "How can you have done such a thing, do you not realise what this will mean? There will be uproar in the city, oh my foolish, foolish son!"

The King had expected praise from his mother that he had dealt decisively with such a dangerous situation, he felt sure she would praise his action, and that he had at last taken a firm control.

"I see you are disappointed with this news. Perhaps you have been hoping that I should have waited for him to kill me!" Catherine began to cry bitterly, but Henri was merciless as he continued. "You must have hoped to hear that it had been me and not the Duke who now lies on the floor of my study?" Catherine sobbed wildly, moving her head from side to side as the King raised his voice over her moans, "Forgive me Madame for choosing to destroy my deadliest enemy before he destroyed me" He leant down closer and closer to his mother's face, but she could only cry out, "I pray to God, that no ill will come of this, but you have most surely ripped this Kingdom apart, now you must sew it together again." And so saying she again broke down in floods of tears. The King, with the potential joy of his visit extinguished, gave his mother one final sneering look, and then marched from the chamber.

♦

The Queen Mother lay breathing noisily, she had given up on her life now, the will to survive no longer burned inside her, and she was now certain that as her pains increased, and her breathing was so difficult that surely she would not rise from her bed again. God's death, why did she take so long to die she thought, but no, perhaps her wicked life did not deserve the luxury of a swift end. She continued to finger her amulet bracelet, as she sought some peace, but now she could only think of the years she had lived through.

From her firstborn François to Charles, to Henri, the journey had sometimes seemed so brief. As for Henri, she was powerless now to help him in the dangerous days that lay ahead. She could just about turn her head towards the window; the good doctor Cavriani sat at the desk talking with her lady in waiting. The rain continued to pour outside, and as she watched the thunderous sky, she could see images – yes images from her lifetime, there were people there now, looking at her through the small panes of the window. Charles, her son Charles and who was with him? Antoine de Bourbon... and yes, there was that wanton Charlotte de Suave and the Cardinal of Lorraine. Ha! Such a handsome couple! Margot and Coligny and Jeanne d'Albret. The panes of the window seemed to fill with so many faces.

Such ghosts conjured up from the past, some who had gone to God already. The memories had haunted her in these her final hours, and they epitomised her failure, there was nothing further to do but give herself up to either God or the devil, it would be they who would decide which.

Doctor Cavriani had glanced over from his desk just in time to see the Queen Mother's talisman bracelet fall from her hand onto the floor. He rose at once and went across to the bed. Then with her confessor, he knelt at its side and began to weep quietly; his patient had left this life as she had entered it: alone, unloved and unnoticed. The news must be sent to the King at once.

Catherine de Medici was dead.

♦

CATERINA MARIA ROMULA de MEDICIS died at one-thirty in the morning on January 5th 1589 of peripneumonia, which in turn brought on an apoplexy.

An autopsy carried out by order of the King revealed otherwise healthy organs, and it was generally agreed that had she not suffered the inflammation of her lungs, she would almost certainly have lived on for some years. Only hours after her death, the King had his mother's talisman bracelet smashed to pieces.

Her body was refused entry into Paris, where the League threatened to drag it through the streets and throw it into the Seine. Due to an inept embalming, the corpse had begun to smell, and Henri therefore considered it better to commit it to a hastily dug grave at the Saint-Saveur at the dead of night. Catherine's remains were left in this "temporary" grave for a further twenty-one years until Henri II's illegitimate daughter had it moved to the Valois rotunda at Saint-Denis.

Her last will contained bequests to her granddaughter Christine (daughter of Claude); Henri's wife Queen Louise was to receive Catherine's favourite retreat, Chenonceau. Charles of Valois, the natural son of Charles IX was to inherit her properties in the maternal line. All else was left to the King. There was no mention of Margot.

A diarist wrote, at the time of her death, *"At Blois where she had been worshipped as the Juno of the court, no sooner had she drawn her last breath than she was made of no more account than a dead goat"*

♦

The fate of others:

Henri III

The King survived his mother by only seven months. After Catherine's death he joined forces with Navarre and it was at Saint-Cloud where a Dominican friar named Jaques Clement sought an audience with the King saying he had come from Paris with "information of great moment" for the monarch's ear only.

For whatever reason, the friar was not searched before his audience, and therefore the knife with which he then stabbed Henri with was not discovered. Clement was set upon by the King's bodyguards, himself stabbed and thrown from the window. The wound to Henri's abdomen was fatal, and he died on the the 2nd August 1589 from perforated intestines and internal bleeding.

Marguerite de Valois (Margot)

The last of Catherine de Medici's children had remained in the Auvergne, and from there she negotiated a clever deal when her estranged husband requested a divorce. All her debts (which were substantial!) were to be paid, and she must still thereafter be addressed as 'Your Majesty' and 'Queen Margot.'

She eventually returned to Paris in 1605 and became a good friend to her ex-husband and his wife, Marie de Medici. Margot grew fat and continued to take lovers enjoying the remainder of her life surrounded by musicians, writers and her many friends. She died in Paris in 1615.

Henri of Navarre

Navarre eventually bowed to the inevitable change of religion declaring, "Paris is indeed worth a mass" and became Henri IV, the first of the Bourbon dynasty. He, like his other two contemporaries, Henri de Valois and Henri de Guise, was the third of that name to be murdered by knife when he was stabbed to death by a Catholic zealot François Ravaillac in May 1610.

Louise of Lorraine (wife of Henri III)

Upon the death of her husband, Louise fell into serious depression and never recovered from the tragic death of the King. She died in Moulins in 1601. In 1817 her remains were reinterred next to her husbands at the Saint-Denis Basilica.

Elisabeth of Austria (Wife of Charles IX)

After the death of her husband Elizabeth returned to her native Austria. Here she received a proposal of marriage from Philip of Spain, which she refused stating "The Queens of France do not remarry." –Mary, Queen of Scots being an obvious exception. Her only child with Charles, a daughter Marie Elisabeth died aged five and a half in 1578. She spent the remainder of her life in a convent she had founded and died there of pleurisy in 1592.

Marie Touchet

Charles IXs only mistress bore him an illegitimate son, Charles de Valois. After the King's death she retired from court although receiving a pension. (Henri III had kept a promise to his brother and raised the boy Charles faithfully Marie later married Charles Balzac d'Entragues giving birth to a daughter in 1579 (the daughter was a later mistress of Henri IV) Marie died in Paris in 1638.

Charlotte de Suave

The most celebrated of Catherine de Medici's *escardon volant*. Charlotte married for the second time in 1584 to François de La Tremoille, giving birth to a son two years later. She died aged 65 in 1617.

Duke d'Epernon – Jean Louis de la Valette

Epernon, who had deserted Henri by the time of the King's murder of Guise in 1589, was still prominent enough to play a minor part in government affairs after the Kings death. He was an outspoken critic of Henri IV and played a part in that King's assassination, the killer Ravailac had lodged with Epernon's mistress Charlotte du Tillet in Paris. Following a public altercation with Henri de Sourdis, Archbishop of Bordeaux, Epernon was disgraced and exiled. He died aged 88 in January 1642.

The fate of Gaspard de Coligny's body

At the start of the Massacre of St Bartholomew, following his decapitation, Coligny's torso, or what was left of it, was taken by two servants of the Duke de Montmorency, and smuggled out of Paris. Today it lies at Châtillon. Whether his head was ever presented to Catherine and then sent on to Rome for the Pope is unknown.

And finally………
A word to anyone with a passion for decaying historical buildings, there is no such place as the ruin of the Palace d'Exciles….sorry!

♦

References

The Later Years of Catherine de Medici – Edith Sichel
Catherine de Medici and the Lost Revolution – Ralph Roeder
Catherine de Medici – Jean Heritier
Catherine de Medici – Leonie Frieda
Catherine de Medicis – Paul Van Dyke (2 vols)
Biography of a family: Catherine de Medici and her children
  – Milton Waldman
The Massacre of Saint Bartholomew – Sylvia Lennie England
St Bartholomew's Night – Phiippe Erlanger
Madame Catherine – Irene Mahoney
Society in Crisis: France in the Sixteenth Century
  – J.H.M.Salmon

♦

Lightning Source UK Ltd.
Milton Keynes UK
UKOW03f1406050117
291435UK00002B/12/P